W9-BWP-811

Japan's Managerial System
Tradition and Innovation

Japan's Managerial System

M. Y. YOSHINO

Contents

arrive at valid objective qualitative generalizations. A factor compensating for this limitation is that the author has been able to verify the validity of his findings and generalizations with a number of experts on Japanese management. It is hoped that the results justify the methods employed.

2. The second major limitation is that of coverage. The managerial system of a highly industrialized nation such as Japan is an extremely complex and evasive subject for exploration. To keep our study within the confines of a manageable scope, and to enable the researcher to examine each area with some depth, only selected areas have been investigated. We should also recognize that the very dynamism of Japanese management has made it extremely difficult to incorporate every significant recent development relevant to the study. Also, to stay within the manageable scope, we have confined ourselves to the examination of the managerial system only of large corporations. The managerial practices and problems of small- to medium-size firms, though an extremely interesting subject for exploration, have been excluded from this study.

bequeathed to modern Japan a prime moving force for her modernization. The heritage of the Tokugawa era had a profound effect on the evolution of modern Japan, not excepting her managerial system. The second reason is the frequently noticed tendency on the part of Western observers to categorically characterize those aspects of Japanese managerial practices that appear unfamiliar and peculiar to them as "feudal" or "traditional," without clearly understanding the real nature of the traditional society. This oversimplified stereotype characterization has resulted in many misconceptions and distortions. It is hoped that our analysis of the Tokugawa society, given in the initial chapter of this study, will provide the reader with a proper perspective from which to view the roots of modern Japan's managerial system.

Chapter 2 covers the background of the past century of industrial modernization; attempts were made to contrast developments prior to and after World War II. Chapters 3 and 4 deal with the ideologies of the Japanese business leadership. Chapter 3 concerns itself with entrepreneurial ideologies in the early phase of Japan's industrialization, and the development of the paternalistic ideology in the modern industrial setting. Chapter 4 seeks to analyze the background and ideologies of professional managers in the post-World War II period.

Chapter 5 discusses the organization of Japanese industries and analyzes intercorporate relationships. Chapter 6 analyzes the competitive behavior of large Japanese firms in the postwar era and examines the efforts to reorganize Japan's industrial structure along more efficient lines in the face of growing international competition. These topics provided the author with an excellent opportunity to examine the intricate and complex interactions between government and big business interests in Japan.

Chapters 7, 8, and 9 deal with managerial processes: Chapter 7 with organization, Chapter 8 with personnel practices, and Chapter 9 with the decision-making process. Throughout these three chapters, emphasis is placed on the analysis of the way large Japanese firms are modernizing traditional managerial practices to meet the changing environment, and what problems have been encountered in this process.

We should point out the two major limitations of this study:

1. It is qualitative. The nature of this study is such that its findings do not lend themselves to a statistical analysis. Recognizing this limitation, efforts were made throughout this investigation to

ment of traditional managerial practices is necessary. Accordingly, they are now intensifying efforts to modernize their managerial practices to meet the demands of the changing environment.

2. The second objective of this study was to analyze how these efforts to modernize managerial practices were being carried out by leading Japanese firms, and what problems they have encountered in this process. It is believed that the Japanese case is particularly illuminating in the study of adaptive processes by management because of both the character and the magnitude of change that the Japanese environment has undergone in recent years.

The data for this research have been drawn from both primary and secondary sources. Published and unpublished data on Japanese management and Japanese society in general, most of which were in the Japanese language, were thoroughly searched. The primary data were gathered through personal interviews in 1965 and 1966 with approximately 150 executives of 20 leading corporations in the following industries: petroleum, iron-steel, petrochemical, electronic, synthetic fibre, and electrical equipment and machinery. Respondents were chosen with great care to assure that they represented various functional areas, different levels in the organizational hierarchy, and diverse points of view. While the author used a carefully constructed and tested interview guide in the field research, the range of questions usually discussed during the interviews was more encompassing than that included in the formal interview guide. The flexibility of the oral interview method made it possible to concentrate in each case on points of view and practices that were most relevant to the study.

Also interviewed were a score of nonmanagerial groups of experts on Japanese management, including professors, consultants, journalists, government officials, and officers of major business organizations and trade associations. The total number of interviews exceeded 200, excluding informal conversations with executives and nonmanagerial groups of experts knowledgeable about Japanese management. Many of these informal conversations proved to be quite valuable in gaining insight into Japanese management.

The book is organized as follows: The first chapter is devoted to the discussion of the Tokugawa period — the traditional era from which modern Japan emerged. We discuss the Tokugawa era rather extensively for two reasons. One reason, of course, is the importance of the Tokugawa period to modern Japan, inasmuch as this era be effective in the future, since Japanese society has been undergoing a basic change in recent years. This change was brought about by two dramatic developments. One is the defeat in World War II and the subsequent economic, political, and social reform measures introduced by the Occupation. These Occupation reforms discredited the fundamental values of the prewar Japanese society. A key significance of the Occupation's reform measures was that they *abruptly* removed the barriers to and stimulated the undercurrents of change that had their beginning — though a slow one — in Japan in the pre-World War II era. This happened despite the intense efforts by the elite to minimize social change and preserve the traditions they deemed useful for the country's industrialization. The second dramatic development, also occurring in the postwar decades, was Japan's achievement of a highly advanced level of economic growth and her taking on, for the first time, the salient characteristics of a highly industrialized society.

It is still debated whether or not Japan has already reached the fifth stage of economic growth, that is, the highly developed mass-consumption society, as suggested by W. W. Rostow.[1] But it is impossible to deny that the very accelerated process of postwar economic growth has brought significant changes in the character of Japanese society. The Occupation's reform measures and the spurt of postwar economic growth have decidedly interacted to shape a society basically different from that existing before World War II.

In view of these momentous developments, there is growing evidence that the traditional managerial ideologies and practices are losing their viability. There is irony in the fact that the very success that the Japanese economy has achieved, to which Japanese management has contributed so importantly, has reduced the effectiveness of precisely the same managerial policies and practices that helped bring about this success. "Many merits which once contributed to the speedy growth of the economy," writes Ichiro Nakayama, the prominent Japanese economist, "are now being looked upon as ailments or defects."[2]

Reflecting this point of view, there is a growing awareness among the more progressive Japanese managerial elite that a basic reassess-

[1] W. W. Rostow, *The Stages of Economic Growth: A Non-Communist Manifesto* (Cambridge, England: Cambridge University Press, 1960), p. 88.

[2] Ichiro Nakayama, *Industrialization of Japan* (Honolulu: East-West Center Press, 1964), p. 67.

Preface

The research upon which this book is based addressed itself to an analysis of the managerial system in contemporary Japan. The study sought two closely related objectives:

1. We set out to analyze Japan's industrial and managerial system in terms of her socioeconomic and political environment. Even a very cursory examination reveals that not only does Japan's managerial system differ from its counterparts in other highly industrialized nations, but in many of its aspects, it runs *counter* to what are considered sound principles of management in the Western world, particularly in the United States. Nevertheless, the system has been highly effective and efficient because it has been congruent with the Japanese corporate environment. The results certainly speak for themselves.

Japan's corporate environment, however, has not been static. Since the effectiveness of a managerial system depends on the degree to which it is compatible with the environment in which it operates, to maintain its effectiveness the system must constantly innovate and adapt itself to meet the new demands made on it by the changing environment.

The strategy that the Japanese elite, including management, consistently followed in Japan's burgeoning industrialization until the end of World War II was an ingenious blend of Japan's traditional values and Western technology. The elite advanced Japan's industrialization in a highly controlled atmosphere, aided by the preservation of a selected set of traditions. This strategy was, as attested by the results, highly successful.

Inquiry into the contemporary Japanese situation, however, suggests that it is highly questionable whether the above strategy will able in the preparation of the final draft for publication. I am particularly grateful to the following individuals: Dr. John Fayerweather of New York University, Dr. David Granick of the University of Wisconsin, Dr. Solomon B. Levine of the University of Illinois, Dr. Raymond Vernon of Harvard University, Dr. Barry M. Richman of the University of California, Los Angeles, and Dr. Richard D. Robinson of the Massachusetts Institute of Technology.

I would also like to acknowledge the generous financial support provided by the Division of Research of the Graduate School of Business Administration, University of California, Los Angeles, and the Bureau of Business and Economic Research, UCLA.

Throughout this study, I was fortunate to have the competent and conscientious assistance of a number of individuals. I am particularly grateful to Miss Ann Dunn, my able research assistant and typist, who has provided invaluable assistance willingly and patiently at every stage of this study. I am grateful to Mrs. Miriam Morton for her competent editing of the manuscript; to Miss Patricia Hay of the Bureau of Business and Economic Research, who provided a variety of services in the preparation of the manuscript; and to Miss Andy Potter, who did yeoman service in typing the final manuscript.

Finally, I would like to acknowledge my gratitude to my wife. Words cannot adequately express my appreciation for her assistance. Suffice it to say that without her unflagging faith and encouragement this book would never have been written.

While many people contributed to this book, the responsibility for the final product rests solely with the author.

Spring 1968
West Los Angeles M.Y.Y.

Acknowledgments

The inception of this book goes back to 1962, when Professor Leonard Marks, Jr., of Stanford University and I embarked on a joint research project on Japanese management. The undertaking had to be suspended, however, when Professor Marks left Stanford University to serve as Assistant Secretary of the Department of the Air Force. Since that time, I have pursued my research interest in Japanese management independently, and this book is the result. Although this study represents independent effort on my part, I am very grateful to Dr. Marks, now vice-president of the Times-Mirror Corporation, for his encouragement to undertake this study, his continued interest in the project, and above all for the warm friendship he has extended to me and my family.

This study would have been impossible without the cooperation of numerous Japanese executives, government officials, officials of trade associations, and professors, who generously contributed their time and expertise and freely shared their experiences with me. I sincerely regret that our original agreement that they would remain anonymous prevents individual acknowledgment from being made, but I do wish to make a general statement of my appreciation for the full cooperation of the respondents. Through this study, I have gained a profound respect for Japanese managers.

While the great majority of my respondents must remain anonymous, I would like to express my gratitude to the following individuals in Japan for the valuable assistance they have given in the course of this study: Professor Susumu Takamiya, Mr. Yasuo Takeyama, Mr. Yukio Uchida, and Mr. Yoshihisa Ohashi.

A number of individuals have graciously read the manuscript and provided constructive criticism and new insights that were invalu-

To my parents

Copyright © 1968 by The Massachusetts Institute of Technology

Set in Linotype Caledonia and printed by The Heffernan Press Inc. Bound in the United States of America by The Colonial Press Inc.

All rights reserved. No part of this book may be reproduced or utilized in any form or by any means, electronic or mechanical, including photocopying, recording, or by any information storage and retrieval system, without permission in writing from the publisher.

Library of Congress catalog card number: 68–30754

Tradition and Innovation

THE MIT PRESS Massachusetts Institute of Technology
Cambridge, Massachusetts, and London, England

1

The Tokugawa Heritage

The modernization of Japan dates back to 1868, the year of the Meiji Restoration. Like most dates that define historical periods, this one, too, suggests a sharp break in the flow of historical development that did not in fact occur. As dramatic as the Meiji Restoration was, there had been a strong latent impulse and capacity in the pre-Meiji period that made Japan respond vigorously to the fresh stimuli and opportunities offered under the new dynamic leadership.

The immediate traditional society from which modern Japan emerged is historically identified as the *Tokugawa* era. Until quite recently, this period was characterized as backward, stagnant, and feudal, and Japan's emergence from it at the time of the Meiji Restoration was considered a miraculous break from the past.

With increasing understanding of the process of Japan's industrialization, however, it has become more clearly evident that the Tokugawa era played a very significant preparatory role in Japan's subsequent modernization. In fact, the seeds for many of the startling changes that occurred after 1868 were sown during the seemingly stagnant, feudal Tokugawa era. A brief but apt description of the importance of this period has been made by Robert Scalapino:

> It was the role of this era to transmit to modern Japan many essentially "feudal" characteristics, while at the same time giving rise, in its middle and latter stages, to the great upheavals that made possible the rapid modernization from the Meiji era onward.[1]

Indeed, the Tokugawa era bequeathed to modern Japan capacities

[1] Robert A. Scalapino, *Democracy and the Party Movement in Prewar Japan: The Failure of the First Attempt* (Berkeley: University of California Press, 1962), pp. 3–4.

both for dynamic change and for discipline and order in its sustained drive toward modernization. In addition, a particularly important link was forged between the Tokugawa period and modern Japan by the Meiji leadership when it persistently and almost systematically turned to traditional ideology and values in meeting the challenges and problems of the new era. This conscious effort by the political elite to apply selected elements of the feudal heritage to the solution of new problems is often regarded as a key factor in Japan's achieving, in a rather brief period of time, a very rapid and relatively smooth transition from a backward agrarian nation to a leading industrial world power.

Consequently, an examination of the character of the Tokugawa society from which modern Japan emerged is essential in understanding almost any aspect of the major economic, political, or social developments in modern Japan.[2] Japan's modern industrial system, the ideologies of the business elite, and managerial practices that evolved during the past century are no exception.

A close examination of the contemporary Japanese managerial system reveals clear imprints of the values and ideology inherited from the traditional past. While there is overriding evidence to this effect, one should guard against overemphasizing traditional influence in shaping the contemporary Japanese managerial system. Confronted with Japan's unique or peculiar managerial practices, students of Japanese management have often found it difficult to resist the temptation of categorically attributing them to the feudal tradition. This tendency has resulted in some serious distortions and misinterpretations. To provide a proper perspective for viewing modern Japanese industrial and managerial systems in the context of Japanese tradition, a solid understanding of the Tokugawa era is indispensable. This chapter is therefore devoted to the analysis of those features of the Tokugawa society that are pertinent to the subject of this book.

It should be clearly understood at the outset that the analysis of the traditional society that follows seeks to provide only a perspective for the subsequent discussion of Japan's industrial and managerial system, and is not an effort to isolate that elusive phenomenon, "traditional Japan." Due to its specific purpose, the treatment is inevitably selective.

[2] For a penetrating historical analysis of the impact of the pre-Tokugawa era on Japan's industrialization, see Everett Hagen, *On Theory of Social Change* (Homewood, Ill.: Dorsey Press, 1962), pp. 310–352.

The Tokugawa Feudal System

Tokugawa feudalism dates from the beginning of the seventeenth century, when Tokugawa Ieyasu conquered all rivals and established the last in a series of Shogunates, or hereditary military dictatorships.

When Tokugawa Ieyasu came to power, his major concern was the perpetuation of the family hegemony. He sought to create a stable society hospitable to the regime by vigorously pursuing two essential goals: the centralization of political power and "an undeviating perpetuation of the status quo."[3] The effectiveness of his policy is proved by the fact that the Tokugawa regime lasted nearly two and a half centuries without being seriously challenged. Moreover, the family attained a greater concentration of its political power throughout the nation than had ever been achieved by any of the previous ruling clans.

Tokugawa feudalism was known as central feudalism in that the regime ruled the nation through nearly three hundred regional lords who, in turn, commanded their own retainers and commoners. The Tokugawa regime firmly controlled these feudal fiefdoms through a skillful doling out of rewards and punishments and a clever application of rigid, detailed, and elaborate devices for control.

Of all the ingenious devices employed by the Shogunate, perhaps none was more important than its attempt to freeze the society into a legally immutable class structure by classifying the entire populace into the rigid hereditary hierarchy of statuses. Below the imperial household and court nobles, four classes were established in the following status order: warriors, farmers, artisans, merchants.

To the most privileged class — the samurai — went all the benefits of education, military training, social status, honor, and, of course, political power. A wide gulf separated the samurai from the other three classes. Indeed, those below the samurai class were commoners, or the ruled. The commoners were, in turn, ranked according to the traditional views as to their productivity. Interestingly and significantly, merchants, as a class, were ranked at the very bottom because they were considered to be unproductive. The Shogunate introduced further rigidities into the social caste system by widening the gaps between the various classes and by demarcating numerous levels within each class.

[3] Scalapino, *Democracy and the Party Movement,* p. 4.

Thus, within each social group, the individual knew exactly where he stood in relation to others. His status in society was clearly determined by his occupation, age, sex, marital status, wealth, position in the family, and so on. Furthermore, virtually every aspect of his life was regulated on the basis of a rigid class stratification, including the kind and color of cloth he could wear, the type and size of house he could live in, and the manner in which he could express himself. Further, each class and even subclass was limited by a different set of elaborate regulations defining its political status and responsibilities. Even religious affiliation was scrutinized. Thus, the Shogunate took great pains to organize the entire society into discrete units by which each member was to be socially identified and his behavior controlled. "This late feudalism," writes Herbert Norman, "represents one of the most conscious attempts in history to freeze society in a rigid hierarchial mold."[4]

In the early seventeenth century — on the eve of great technological advancement in Europe — the Shogunate banned all forms of contact with the outside world to further assure the maintenance of the status quo. This national policy of exclusion was rigorously enforced. The Japanese retained commercial ties only with the Chinese and the Dutch, and even they were most strictly regulated. Thus, for more than two centuries, Japan deliberately isolated herself from the rapidly changing world.

Values of the Tokugawa Society

In establishing and maintaining its rigid society, the Tokugawa Shogunate had found an effective ideology in Confucianism. Much earlier, in China, Confucianism had become closely linked with political power, strongly supporting the authority of China's ruling elite. Confucianism first took root in Japan in the seventh century and soon became a potent force. During the ensuing centuries it penetrated deeply into the consciousness, thought patterns, and customs of the Japanese. Its influence began to wane subsequently, and Buddhism became the dominant religion.

The Tokugawa family resurrected Confucianism, made it the official philosophy, and used it as the ideological framework for an elaborate and rigidly controlled social system. The precepts of

[4] E. Herbert Norman, *Japan's Emergence as a Modern State: Political and Economic Problems of the Meiji Period* (New York: Institute of Pacific Relations, 1940), p. 12.

Confucianism were extremely numerous and varied. Its essential teachings were, however, "this-world-oriented," and unconcerned with heaven and hell. Nor did it teach universal morality or the ethic of good and evil. It placed its main emphasis on the strict regulation of society and the conformity to the prescribed behavior by members of different social classes and subclasses.

According to Confucianism, the basic elements of a "good" society were benevolence, propriety, wisdom, and obedience. These standards were not, however, to be applied universally but only variously, within the specific framework of established social relationships. Confucianism stressed five key dyadic relationships and prescribed appropriate interaction for each: affection between father and son; respect and loyalty between master and servant; harmony between husband and wife; precedence between older and younger brothers; and trust between friends. (It should be noted that four of these five basic relationships were hierarchical.) In essence, therefore, Confucian philosophy concerned itself mainly with the correct observance of social relationships within a hierarchically oriented society. Thus, it is readily understandable why the Tokugawa regime showed so much enthusiasm for the Confucian philosophy.

By emphasizing the most strict outer conformity to what Reischauer calls "the almost ritualistic embodiment of the virtues in specific patterns of conduct," Confucianism provided the overly emotional Japanese with "the external controls they required to form a well-regulated, peaceful society."[5]

Further, Confucianism gave the *Bushido*, that is, the traditional military code of ethics, a new interpretation, consistent with the peaceful Tokugawa society. The samurai code of ethics that thus emerged during the Tokugawa period was a blending of Confucian morality and the indigenous feudal code of military honor. The new version of Bushido held up the samurai class as the embodiment and protector of morality.

The two central teachings of the Bushido stressed absolute loyalty to one's lord and unswerving filial piety. Such overriding importance was placed on loyalty and filial piety that, unlike other obligations, one could never hope to repay in full the benevolence received from one's lord or from one's parents.

Bushido also extolled learning and scholarship. Even prior to the

[5] Edwin O. Reischauer, *The United States and Japan* (3rd ed.; Cambridge, Mass.: Harvard University Press, 1965), p. 135.

Tokugawa era there had already been a strong inclination among the military class to place almost equal value on learning and on a warrior's military skills. The peace and stability achieved in the Tokugawa period advanced learning to a status symbol of the samurai class. The Confucian emphasis on self-cultivation also gave a great impetus to learning.

In traditional Japanese society, Bushido was tremendously important, not only because it served as the official code of ethics for the samurai class, but also because it became the ethic of the entire Tokugawa society. One therefore agrees with Sansom when he notes that the term Bushido, meaning "the way of the warrior," was a misnomer.[6] Farmers, artisans, and merchants used Bushido as a model in structuring master-servant or teacher-apprentice relationships.

We consequently find in Tokugawa Japan a very rigid and hierarchically organized society with strong emphasis on authoritarian control on the one hand and obedience on the other, giving rise, as is to be expected, to a series of complex and highly regulated patterns of interpersonal relationships. The emphasis placed on particularistic relationships gave rise to the important concept of *on*, or benevolence. Those who occupied superior positions in the hierarchy were expected to bestow benevolence on their inferiors, as in the case of master and servant, teacher and student, or master and apprentice. It must be noted that benevolence was to be extended not necessarily as the expression of genuine kindness or sympathy, but as the formal justification of superior status.[7] Superiors, by having conferred benevolence, became almost permanently important to their inferiors. The latter were then placed under obligation to reciprocate the benevolence. In fact, the superiors demanded repayment of the benevolence they extended. The inferior who failed to reciprocate to the satisfaction of the superior was viewed with disdain by the latter as "one who does not know *on*." Often, the particular manner of repayment was not clearly prescribed and was dictated by the whims of the superior, putting the recipient of benevolence in a rather trying situation.[8] Through

[6] G. B. Sansom, *Japan: A Short Cultural History* (New York: D. Appleton-Century, Inc., 1943), p. 500.

[7] Masataka Sugi, "The Concept of *Ninjo*," in John W. Bennett and Iwao Ishino, *Paternalism in the Japanese Economy: Anthropological Studies of Oyabun-Kobun Patterns* (Minneapolis: University of Minnesota Press, 1963), p. 268.

[8] John Whitney Hall and Richard K. Beardsley, *Twelve Doors to Japan* (New York: McGraw-Hill Book Company, 1965), p. 94.

the network of elaborate hierarchical relationships, virtually everyone was put in a position of receiving benevolence from someone superior and thus constantly carrying the burden of repayment.

Another set of obligations between specific individuals was given the name of *giri*.[9] The implications of *giri* were very closely related to the concept of *on* and its benevolence-repayment pattern. In fact, *giri* has been used by some as a blanket term describing all obligations involving specific individuals in concrete situations. According to this view, *on* and the repayment of *on* is a special form of the more generalized *giri* category.[10] Others, however, have distinguished *on* from *giri* on the basis that *on* exists only between two hierarchically related individuals, whereas in *giri* situations the relationship may not necessarily be hierarchical.[11] Benedict observes that in contrast to obligations to one's lord and parent, which are beyond repayment, *giri* refers to those obligations that are repayable with mathematical equivalence to the favor received, and within specified time limits.[12]

But even the most rigidly controlled society cannot function by means of a formal or officially prescribed code of conduct alone. (In fact, the very rigidity increases the need for values providing emotional escape.) The Tokugawa society was no exception; *on* and *giri* failed to curb the development of spontaneous and informal relationships.[13] Even the samurai class needed what Sugi refers to as "informal affiliative patterns of behavior."[14] The commoners, who lacked the extreme self-discipline of the samurai, needed emotional release from restrictive norms even to a greater extent. The need for informality gave rise to the concept of *ninjo,* or human feelings, which we shall now examine.[15] In the highly regulated society of Tokugawa, as we have seen, obedience to authority and fulfillment of one's obligations received utmost emphasis. Duty came first, and one was to suppress all personal feelings and emotions that might hinder its fulfillment. Indeed, any manifestations of personal feelings in conflict with the fulfillment of one's prescribed duties were

[9] For detailed discussion of *giri,* see Ruth Benedict, *The Chrysanthemum and the Sword: Patterns of Japanese Culture* (Boston: Houghton Mifflin Co., 1946), pp. 133–176.

[10] Hall and Beardsley, *Twelve Doors to Japan,* pp. 94–95.

[11] *Ibid.,* p. 95.

[12] Benedict, *The Chrysanthemum and the Sword,* p. 116.

[13] R. P. Dore, *City Life in Japan: A Study of a Tokyo Ward* (Berkeley: University of California Press, 1958), pp. 262–268.

[14] Sugi, "The Concept of *Ninjo,*" p. 267.

[15] Our discussion of *ninjo* draws heavily from the work of Sugi, "The Concept of *Ninjo,*" pp. 267–272.

viewed as selfishness and even cowardice. Nevertheless, under the system, one did inevitably experience emotional pains, frustrations, and personal anguish of various sorts, which, in spite of great self-discipline, sometimes became almost unbearable.

While one could not openly admit to these private feeelings, it was permissible for another person to note that one was indeed suffering from personal anxieties and agonies. Such an observer was expected not only to understand the sufferer's suppressed anxieties and frustrations, but to extend his sympathy. The function of the observer was expressed in the term *ninjo*, and its meaning became almost equivalent to humanism or human nature. Thus, as Sugi notes, *ninjo*, in some respects, differed little from sympathy and kindness as understood in the West; but its essential difference lay in the fact that *ninjo* was an understanding response to another's *hidden* feelings of deprivation and despair. *Ninjo*, important as it was in the drama of private feelings, was nevertheless to be subordinated to *giri*, or formal obligations and duties. One was to fulfill his obligations at all costs, and *ninjo* was not to interfere in any way. In no sense, therefore, was *ninjo* to release the sufferer from fulfilling his obligations; without negating the inevitability of his obligations, the observer was to try, by means of the extended sympathy and understanding, to assist him in the fulfillment of his duties.[16]

Since *ninjo* was generated between two individuals in a private and close social relationship, the particular manner in which *ninjo* was to be expressed varied almost infinitely according to each separate case; there was, therefore, no formula for *ninjo* behavior.

These highly particularistic rules of conduct, so strictly imposed by the Tokugawa hierarchical system, were voluntarily complied with to an amazing degree. Only on relatively few occasions did the Tokugawa Shogunate find it necessary to resort to overt force to exact compliance. How, then, can one explain the power of social conformity in traditional Japan? What motivated the Japanese to willing and voluntary obedience to so meticulous and rigid a code of conduct and ethics? This nearly universal compliance was particularly remarkable in view of the fact that traditional Japanese society lacked a universal code of ethics or categorical religious precepts.[17] Neither did it advance any clear concept of sin. Unlike Christianity, none of the three religions practiced in traditional

[16] *Ibid.*
[17] Reischauer, *The United States and Japan*, p. 142.

Japan offered either conscience or unequivocal ethical precepts as guides for daily conduct.[18]

Obviously, the traditional Japanese society must have had a substitute for a universal code of ethics or religious sanctions. The concept of shame was the substitute. Shame enforced the very particularistic ethical code and prompted one to rigid adherence to specific rules of conduct.

In traditional Japan, the concepts of "good" or "bad" were not determined by an absolute standard of virtue, but largely by the approval or disapproval of the society.[19] What the individual regarded as "society" varied, of course, according to his status, occupation, age, and so forth. For example, to a Japanese peasant, it was his village; to the high-ranking samurai, it was all his compeers in his fief. Shame usually had two related aspects: personal shame — the disapproval of the society heaped upon oneself; and "we-group" shame — dishonor to one's collectivity and the accompanying fear of rejection by the group. The latter was particularly powerful because of the great importance attached to collectivity in traditional Japan. This leads us to the consideration of another key aspect of the traditional Japanese society.

Traditional Japan has often been characterized as a collectivity-oriented society. In fact, the individual hardly existed in it as a distinct entity. In every aspect of life, he was tightly bound to a group and had virtually no individual freedom.[20] Indeed, the basic political, economic, and social unit in traditional Japan was the collectivity rather than the individual. The norms and standards of the collectivity served as the basis for thought as well as for action for every member of the group. The most important criterion for judging actions and behavior was whether they were right and best for the group.

The stress on the collectivity had manifested itself long before the Tokugawa era. It is attributed to the fact that Japanese society developed from small, localized farming communities.[21] The Japanese gave up their nomadic life early in their history and settled down to cultivate rice fields, thus establishing permanent settlements. In such communities, families tended to perpetuate them-

[18] *Ibid.*

[19] *Ibid.*, pp. 142–143.

[20] Yoshiharu S. Matsumoto, *Contemporary Japan: The Individual and the Group* (Philadelphia: American Philosophical Society, 1960), p. 7.

[21] Reischauer, *The United States and Japan*, p. 126.

selves for generations, even to the point at which the entire settlement took on the characteristics of one large family.[22] Moreover, this specific form of economic life required cooperative relationships, and the family, in fact, constituted the very basic unit. In such a society, individuals soon came to be closely interrelated with one another, forming an "exclusive social nexus."[23] Out of this developed a considerable degree of interdependence not only among individuals within a family but also among families within a given settlement. One's welfare and prosperity were most closely tied to those of the group. The individual was identified with a collectivity to such an extent that whatever one did was almost immediately and totally reflected on the collectivity.

Thus, a collectivity had great power to sanction or reject the conduct and behavior of each individual member. Fear of being ostracized from the group exerted a very compelling pressure, even on its most rebellious member, to conform to the group norm. Thus, one cherished his membership in the group, which served as the frame of reference for his thoughts and actions.

The collectivity orientation, which had already been strong, became even more pronounced during the Tokugawa era. Many of the measures taken by the Tokugawa regime for the purpose of social control simultaneously tended to strengthen the collectivity orientation. The Tokugawa authority, as Sansom notes, preferred to deal with groups.[24]

The strictest regulations imposed on geographic and social mobility made one's attachment to a particular collectivity indeed an enduring one. Most frequently, the attachment to and relationship with a particular group lasted for life.

Typically, members of each collectivity acquired a strong sense of solidarity and identification with the group, but, concomitantly, this "we-group" identification developed deep-seated suspicion — if not intense hostility — toward those outside their own particular group, whether they belonged to a neighborhood group, a village, or a guild.

It is evident from the above discussion that in Tokugawa Japan a person was not fully an individual, being allowed few private emotions and virtually no opportunities for making a personal

[22] Hajime Nakamura, *Ways of Thinking of Eastern Peoples: India, China, Tibet, Japan* (Honolulu: East-West Center Press, 1964), p. 413.

[23] *Ibid.*, pp. 413–414.

[24] Sansom, *Japan: A Short Cultural History*, p. 509.

choice between alternatives.[25] All key decisions were made for him either by the group or by its head. His lot was to conform.

An important point to be noted about the collectivity orientation in traditional Japanese society is its tendency to attach enormous importance to the formal leader as a representative of the group. Because of the importance attached to the head of the collectivity, it is not difficult to understand that a person's devotion to his collectivity was symbolized by his loyalty to the leader.[26] It must be noted also that this loyalty was offered to a particular rank of the leadership rather than to the particular occupant of that position. Of course, there was often a strong personal attachment to the leader as a person, but this was not an absolute requirement. Moreover, the role of the group leader was one of representation and was not necessarily an executive one. The latter function could be delegated to someone else in the organization.[27]

The great importance ascribed to collectivity made maintenance of internal harmony equally important.[28] Significantly, Bellah argues that intragroup harmony was sought not for its own sake but for the sake of goal-attainment,[29] noting pre-eminence given to goal-attainment in the traditional Japanese value system. Disunity, contentiousness, and overbearing ambition of one or more members would tend to spoil the chances of attaining the goals of an entire collectivity. But Bellah does note that the integrative values frequently overshadow the goal-attainment values,[30] whereby maintenance of harmony becomes the main concern of the leader as well as of the entire collectivity.

Implicit in the collectivity orientation and the abiding loyalty to its leader was the feeling on the part of each member of the group that, as long as he conformed to the group norms, was loyal to its head, and was content with his status in the hierarchy, he would enjoy the maximum security that the group was capable of bestowing.

[25] Dore, *City Life in Japan*, p. 376.

[26] Robert N. Bellah, *Tokugawa Religion: The Values of Pre-Industrial Japan* (Glencoe, Ill.: The Free Press, 1957), p. 13.

[27] *Ibid.*

[28] It should be noted that the emphasis on harmony goes back to Japan's early history. For example, Prince Shotoku's moral injunction issued in the seventh century began with the following statement: "Harmony is precious, obedience is to be most honored." The translation of the entire First Article is found in Nakamura, *Ways of Thinking*, p. 660, note 42.

[29] Bellah, *Tokugawa Religion*, p. 15.

[30] *Ibid.*, pp. 15–16.

Since the family was the most important and basic collective unit in traditional Japanese society, a careful examination of it is indispensable to the understanding of the character of that society. The importance to the Japanese of the family may be traced back almost to the dawn of Japanese history. Later, under Chinese influence, it took on added significance. The family name and lineage had clearly become important to the Japanese long before the inception of the Tokugawa era.[31]

Sometime in the historic past, the concept of *ie*, or "House," emerged as an inseparable aspect of the family. In fact, the concept of House became so firmly institutionalized that it eventually gained predominance over the family per se, and the welfare and goals of the family as a biological and social unit became subordinated to those of the *ie* collectivity. Sansom makes the following observation on the character of the *ie* system:

> The distinguishing feature of the Japanese family system is the importance of the House as contrasted with an indeterminate group of blood relations loosely described as a family. . . . To be more precise, the House is composed of the head of the House and of members who are subject to his authority. Those members may include not only his kindred by relationship of blood, but also persons, male and female, who are not his blood relations and who enter the House with his consent. The House is in fact a name group and not a blood group.[32]

Thus, the family emerged as a collective organization much broader in its significance and composition than a purely biological unit. Marriages and adoptions were viewed as relationships between *ie* rather than between individuals; the concept of *ie* embodied more than a single house, for it included a network of related households.

During the Tokugawa period, the concept of *ie* became firmly established. Through the Confucian influence and the popularization of Bushido, parental authority and filial duty, which had been indispensable parts of the *ie* system, received added emphasis. To strengthen the *ie* system, samurai ethics were widely propagated as the model for structuring various relationships within the *ie* collectivity. Each family member was prescribed a status in the familial hierarchy and was related to the other members through a

[31] Matsumoto, *Contemporary Japan*, p. 11.

[32] G. B. Sansom, *The Western World and Japan* (New York: Alfred A. Knopf, Inc., 1951), p. 448.

code of specific moral obligations and proper conduct. Takeyoshi Kawashima, a noted authority on the Japanese familial structure, has the following to say on the character of the familial system based on the Confucian-samurai ideology:

> In this [samurai] family system, the relationship between parent and child, and between husband and wife, is a relationship of one-sided dominance and submission of the one side having only powers, and the other side merely duties. It is not a reciprocal relationship in which both sides have "rights" and "duties" toward each other.[33]

An extremely importance aspect of the Japanese familial system is that the *ie* served as the model for structuring all types of secondary groups.[34] The *ie* provided the basic structure and terminology for almost every form of secondary group, including the largest and most extensive — the nation state. On this theme Bennett notes:

> The important point is not that Japan is one large family, but rather that definitions, names, and other aspects of roles found in the family are capable of use as *models* for many other types of positions and relationships. As models, they do not necessarily mean that attitudes of love, devotion, hate, etc., associated with the family must likewise carry over to non-familial relationships.[35]

The basic framework for group activity or organization was the House, and when nonrelated individuals were to function together, they were organized into an artificial or simulated kinship group.[36] This very important aspect of the traditional society had far-reaching implications for Japan's modern managerial system.

The Tokugawa Economic System

The Tokugawa economy was based mainly on agriculture, especially rice production. The major economic burden of supporting the large, unproductive privileged class fell on the peasants. This was the primary reason for awarding peasants the status exceeded only by the status of the samurai class. Despite their relatively high

[33] "A Summary and Analysis of Takeyoshi Kawashima's *Familial Structure of Japanese Society*," in John W. Bennett and Iwao Ishino, *Paternalism in the Japanese Economy*, p. 264.

[34] Matsumoto, *Contemporary Japan*, p. 11.

[35] Iwao Ishino, "The *Oyabun-Kobun:* A Japanese Ritual Kinship Institution," *American Anthropology*, 55 (December 1953), 706.

[36] Matsumoto, *Contemporary Japan*, p. 12.

formal status, the farmers, as a class, were abused and exploited by the samurai as well as by the rising merchant class.

As one would expect, the Tokugawa political ideology with respect to economic activities was highly influenced by Confucian thought. The Confucian philosophy advocated the unity of economy and polity.[37] Its ideology recognized that economic welfare was important, if not essential, to political stability. According to Confucian doctrine, the populace would become ungovernable unless assured of at least a minimum livelihood.[38] It must be noted here that economic activities were important only insofar as they contributed to the overriding political objective.

A sustained period of peace and stability in the Tokugawa society encouraged the growth of commercial activities. Great urban commercial centers emerged, and the merchant class, though its social status remained low, began to attain expanding power.

For the first century or so, the Tokugawa regime paid virtually no attention to the rising trend of commercialization. The merchant class slowly evolved the most elaborate and ingenious commercial system and financial institutions. The system they created had a highly monopolistic bent.[39] Moreover, the merchants developed a class solidarity of their own by devising the most meticulous ethical code and rules of conduct for themselves.

With the growing importance of commercial activities, some of the most prosperous began to exercise important influences over the feudal authorities, influences incongruous with their low social status. Thus, growing commercialization began to undermine the very class basis of the Tokugawa feudal system, with both the peasant and samurai classes becoming highly dependent on the merchant class for their material welfare. When the Tokugawa regime became aware — at least partially — of the implications of these developments to the maintenance of its power, two distinct views emerged. One school of thought sought to eliminate commercialism by urging the samurai class to return to the soil and to frugality and self-sufficiency. This was essentially a cry to return to a purely agrarian economy, the basic premise of the Tokugawa system.[40] The second view was more pragmatic. It recognized the inevitability of commercialization and it maintained that the only

[37] Bellah, *Tokugawa Religion*, p. 108.

[38] *Ibid.*

[39] For details, see Charles D. Sheldon, *The Rise of the Merchant Class in Tokugawa Japan, 1600–1868: An Introductory Survey* (Locust Valley, N.Y.: J. J. Augustin Incorporated, 1958), pp. 3–130.

[40] Scalapino, *Democracy and the Party Movement*, p. 26.

way for the samurai class to remain supreme was to permit active participation in commercial activities rather than to resist the trend.[41]

This view advocated a commercialism strongly controlled by state policy and designed to foster the interest of the state. Confucianism was wholly on the side of this approach. As noted earlier, Confucianism had always recognized the importance of economic activities, though only insofar as they contributed to social order and welfare. Moreover, its emphasis on the ethical state and its repudiation of private gains, antisocial action, and individualism gave a strong ideological support to the regulatory rights of government over commercial activities.[42]

The futility of the first view, clamoring for a return to agrarianism, soon became apparent, and the second ideology became widely accepted. Its acceptance was aided by the need for added revenue for impoverished fiefs. The control by both the central Shogunate regime and the fief governments over commercial activities gradually increased and even led to the formation of Shogunate- and fief-sponsored semimonopolies over certain types of commercial activities.

Thus, control over economic activities began to grow and became strengthened with time. By the end of the Tokugawa era, the control had become quite stringent, though it was not always effectively enforced. As noted by Crawcour, control shifted in its emphasis from occupations and consumption to markets, prices, and production.[43] Some degree of control was exercised by the political authorities in almost every aspect of economic life. In fact, according to Crawcour, the regulations over economic activities had become so strict toward the end of the era that the Meiji government could afford a degree of liberalization of these regulations when it came to power.[44]

It is also extremely significant that by the time of the Restoration, the channels of economic control had become clearly established, which made the Japanese economy far more responsive than most to official guidance and control after the Restoration.[45]

We must now turn to another extremely important development

[41] *Ibid.*, note.
[42] *Ibid.*
[43] E. Sydney Crawcour, "The Tokugawa Heritage," in William W. Lockwood (ed.), *The State and Economic Enterprise in Japan* (Princeton: Princeton University Press, 1965), p. 42.
[44] *Ibid.*, p. 44.
[45] *Ibid.*

that had taken place in the economic sphere toward the end of the Tokugawa era. We noted earlier that the Shogunate banned all direct contact with Europe, except for a very limited trade with the Dutch at the port of Nagasaki. Despite this isolation — or perhaps because of it — the Japanese throughout the Tokugawa era manifested a great deal of interest in what was known as Dutch learning. Toward the end of the era, despite almost insurmountable restrictions, Dutch learning had flourished. It had become the key means by which samurai intellectuals gained knowledge of Western technology. In the face of growing foreign threats, the leadership of the Tokugawa regime and that of some progressive fiefs was quick to grasp the military potentialities of modern technology. The first ones to appreciate this were the progressive and influential fiefs on the island of Kyushu, which were later to provide an important part of the Restoration leadership. These fiefs had not only had the closest contact with the West through Nagasaki, but they were, at the same time, most vulnerable to foreign threats.

These progressive fiefs started, though on a modest scale, some strategic industries related to national defense, including iron smelting and casting, shipbuilding, and armaments manufacturing.[46] The industrial activities undertaken by these fiefs were not limited to strategic ones, though the main reason for initiating nonstrategic industries was to increase revenues for financing the strategic industries. Many fiefs had long participated in commercial activities to supplement their revenues. Consequently, the transition from commercial to industrial activities appeared to be quite natural for them.

Thus, the pre-Meiji developments anticipated several key features of Meiji industrial policy, which, in turn, advanced the industrialization of modern Japan.[47] First, industrialization was initiated for the sake of national defense. Second, the initial phase of Japan's industrialization was promoted and managed by the governments of either the Shogunate itself or the fiefs. Third, in initiating industrial activities, the feudal leadership relied heavily on Western technology and foreign advisors. Finally, the feudal leadership emphasized training programs for the Japanese to replace foreign advisors as soon as feasible.

[46] For details, see Thomas C. Smith, *Political Change and Industrial Development in Japan: Government Enterprise, 1868–1880* (Stanford, Calif.: Stanford University Press, 1955), pp. 1–12.

[47] *Ibid.*, p. 11.

The first steps toward industrialization, perhaps the most difficult ones, had thus already been taken prior to the Restoration. When the Meiji government took over, Japan already possessed several iron foundries, numerous — though scattered — furnaces for smelting iron ore, a mechanized spinning mill, an important coal mine, facilities for shipbuilding and repair, and a modest merchant marine. The new regime also inherited a group of men who had gained through these ventures invaluable managerial and technical experience.

The Decay of Feudalism

Even the most extensive measures undertaken by the Tokugawa government to hold the society in status quo failed to arrest the tide of dynamic developments. Although these developments began almost imperceptibly, they gradually gained momentum.

The marked rigidity of the Tokugawa society often gives the impression that the entire period was static and stagnant. Nothing was further from the truth. As we have noted, the growing commercialization played a key role in gradually eroding the feudal power structure. The once immutable and rigid social class structure slowly gave way because of inept policies and the lack of basic understanding of the workings of commercial economy. The Shogunate was in almost constant financial difficulty from about the mid-eighteenth century, and the great majority of feudal fiefs were in no better condition.

The real power in the feudal society gradually shifted to the prosperous merchant class. In the face of growing commercialization, and for a number of other reasons, feudal lords became increasingly impoverished. They ineptly sought additional revenue by extracting higher taxes from the farmers, thus undermining the very base of the feudal system. The growing tax burden on farmers resulted in impoverishment, discontent, and misery, leading, in turn, to declining productivity, to instability, and even to some serious riotings and uprisings. The samurai were equally impoverished. Commercial development, rising prices, and a new taste for luxuries — acquired in the peaceful and stable society — combined with inept financial management in most fiefs, had forced the samurai into debt. By the end of the Tokugawa era, the entire samurai class was in a very desperate financial condition.

The general economic discontent gave impetus to a quasi-religious, quasi-political movement that had been smoldering since early in the Tokugawa era; it led to a surge of interest in the Japanese tradition and Shintoism. It must be noted that even from early in the Tokugawa era, a feeling of uneasiness and resentment had existed among some samurai intellectuals about the total acceptance of the Confucian philosophy. Deep-seated feelings of pride and veneration of the past and its Imperial rule had endured despite the rather persistent and systematic effort by the Shogunate to inculcate the whole society with the most rigid Confucian philosophy. These feelings gained momentum as it became increasingly apparent that the Confucian doctrines were inadequate to meet growing economic and social problems.

Out of these ideological developments emerged an intense nationalism. Proponents of this view were quick to point out the inappropriateness of applying Chinese philosophy to Japan and urged turning to Japanese tradition for solution of Japanese problems. Inextricably related to this intellectual renaissance was the rediscovery of national tradition and renewed interest in Shintoism. The pride in the uniqueness of Japan as the "divine nation" reemerged, and the glorification of the Emperor received much emphasis. The renewed interest in the past glories of Japan and in Shintoism had a profound political significance: this quasi-political, quasi-religious philosophy was to set the whole tone of the Meiji Restoration and to stir the intense nationalistic sentiment of the Meiji era.

A series of crises, financial and otherwise, that had faced the Tokugawa regime, as well as various fief governments, led to still another important development. Crises demanded leadership that was not always supplied by the traditional hereditary system. Various means were devised to circumvent the hereditary appointments to key positions in order to vitalize the system with men of talent from lower ranks.[48] As a result, toward the end of the Tokugawa era, effective leadership in a number of influential fiefs had passed into the hands of able young samurai of lower status.

Thus, by the middle of the nineteenth century, Tokugawa feudalism was so weakened that it was almost on the verge of total collapse. These developments coincided with the arrival to Japanese shores of foreign gunboats and traders, which precipitated the entire chain of events leading to the eventual downfall of the Shogunate in 1868.

[48] For details, see Thomas C. Smith, "'Merit' as Ideology in the Tokugawa Period," in R. P. Dore (ed.), *Aspects of Social Change in Modern Japan* (Princeton: Princeton University Press, 1967), pp. 71–111.

2

The Century of Modernization

Having examined some of the salient characteristics of the Tokugawa society, we shall now turn our attention to key environmental developments of the past century. This, of course, is the period during which Japan aggressively pursued and successfully realized her very ambitious programs of modernization and industrialization. The record of her accomplishments, by almost any standard, has been remarkable. After having achieved prominence as a great industrial and military power, Japan suffered a total and stunning defeat in 1945. Within less than two decades, however, she again emerged as a key industrial nation of the world. Her remarkable postwar recovery, seemingly miraculous, earned for her the admiration and envy of both developed and developing countries.

In examining the key environmental developments of the past century, we shall use World War II as the dividing line. The period preceding this tragic war we shall refer to as the prewar period, and that following the war, as the postwar period. This division lends itself well to the examination of the striking contrasts between the two periods in almost every aspect of Japanese society.

The Prewar Period — 1868–1945

Fascinating detailed accounts of the Meiji Restoration can be found elsewhere and they need no elaboration here. We should briefly note, however, those aspects of the Restoration that are particularly relevant to the central topic of our investigation: the managerial system of Japan.

First, we should be clear as to the basic and unique character of the Restoration movement: Restoration meant the removal of the political power vested with the Shogunate and the return to direct rule by the Emperor; it was the restoration of Imperial rule and the turning back to the traditional Japanese political system. This movement was not revolution in the popular sense of the term. The extensiveness of basic reforms introduced by the Restoration leadership tends to cloud this very fundamental fact.

Second, we should note that the entire movement was carried out by a relatively small number of young, able samurai of lower rank who were drawn from several influential fiefs. Some of these original leaders of the Restoration later became powerful members of the ruling oligarchy. Thus, the Meiji Restoration was not a popular revolution, with the masses rising against the ruling elite; remarkable and thorough as it was, the Restoration was imposed by the members of the ruling elite.

Early Industrialization

National defense against foreign powers and military protection against threatening dissenting elements within the country were an immediate and most serious concern of the Meiji leaders. Consequently, the new regime placed a high priority on building a dependable military force. The country's brief but dramatic encounters with Western technology were sufficient to convince the new leadership that the building of a modern military force required the development of strategic modern industries.[1] Thus, right from the inception, industrialization was viewed as inextricably related to the attainment of a dominant national goal.

Because of the urgency with which the strategic industries had to be developed, and the delaying weakness and timidity of private capital, the government took the initiative in starting them. (This procedure was consistent with the Tokugawa tradition.) Thus, the government became the major promoter, owner, and administrator of modern industries during the very critical early Meiji years. It did not only take over the enterprises initiated by some progressive fiefs before the fall of Tokugawa, but it also pioneered in developing railroads, communication facilities, mining, shipbuilding, and military arsenals.

[1] E. Herbert Norman, *Japan's Emergence as a Modern State: Political and Economic Problems of the Meiji Period* (New York: Institute of Pacific Relations, 1940), p. 118.

Simultaneously, the Restoration leaders pressed for social and political reforms. In furthering this modernization program, the Japanese leaders eagerly turned to the West for advanced technology, as well as for frameworks of social and political reform.

All this was, indeed, a sudden about-face from the intense hostility and contemptuous attitude toward the West prevalent in the immediate past. Initially, the Meiji leaders almost blindly accepted advanced Western technology as well as social and economic institutions. But they soon became highly discriminating and selective in borrowing Western methods and ideas, and developed a capacity to fit them to the conditions and needs of Japanese society. Moreover, they jealously guarded the economic and political independence of the nation in the face of constant foreign threats. The prevailing spirit was aptly expressed in a popular slogan of the era, "*Wakon Yosai*" — "Japanese spirit and Western technology."

The first important turning point in the process of Japan's economic development after the Restoration came in 1880, when the government decided, for a variety of reasons, to sell all but a few of the government enterprises to a handful of favored wealthy families. Most of these families had maintained a rather close relationship with the new political elite, even, in many cases, in the pre-Restoration era. Some amassed their fortunes at the time of the great upheaval and during its immediate aftermath. The sale of government enterprises with their modern equipment at a nominal price and the transfer of their trained personnel gave these families a lasting advantage. Many of them later developed into huge financial and industrial combines, commonly known as *Zaibatsu*.

While subsequent economic development was realized largely through private initiative, the government retained a powerful hold on the course of this development through official control and through a network of informal influence and pressure. In return for an extensive and varied patronage, the government expected big business interests to serve as an effective instrument of its mercantilistic policy. It must further be noted that the government was the dominant partner in this alliance. Big business interests in Japan, because of their heavy dependence on the government, accepted the supremacy of the political and military leadership and supported the perpetuation of the oligarchy throughout the prewar period.

The first major push for industrialization came in the period between the last decade of the nineteenth century and the first of this century. The growth of large-scale modern industries gained momentum on the foundation laid earlier. While statistics of this period must be viewed with some caution, the crude estimate of the magnitude of industrial growth achieved during this period can be seen from some of the data they offer.

The national income, according to Yuzo Yamada's estimate, more than tripled between 1890 and 1912, the last year of the reign of the Meiji Emperor.[2] Moreover, while in 1890 the output of secondary industry constituted only about 16 percent of the national income, by 1912 over a fourth of the total national income was derived from this sector.[3] Table 1 presents the growth pattern of

TABLE 1

INDICES OF INDUSTRIAL PRODUCTION FOR SELECTED YEARS, 1880–1925* (1921–1925 = 100)

	Manufacturing					
Year	*General*	*Textiles*	*Machinery and Tools*	*Chemicals*	*Gas and Electricity*	*Metals*
1880	1.51	1.10	2.38	—	0.21	1.30
1885	1.51	1.60	2.36	—	0.19	0.79
1890	3.74	5.86	4.67	1.24	0.34	1.29
1895	6.57	14.30	7.70	3.14	0.52	0.84
1900	11.30	20.40	12.53	7.72	1.81	1.34
1905	21.79	27.75	27.78	17.03	4.10	15.22
1910	31.88	36.95	32.46	26.81	14.52	31.48
1915	48.64	57.90	39.93	48.34	38.18	59.55
1920	80.52	77.58	94.33	76.87	68.86	80.55
1925	110.77	115.70	99.21	110.72	131.00	124.38

* Estimated by Nagoya Higher Commercial College.
Source: Adapted from *Hundred-Year Statistics of the Japanese Economy* (Tokyo: The Bank of Japan, 1967), p. 94.

Japan's manufacturing industries for selected years between 1880 and 1925. During the same period, the number of incorporated business establishments increased from 4,296 to 13,887, showing nearly a threefold increase, and the paid-in capital increased over fourteen times.[4]

[2] *Hundred-Year Statistics of the Japanese Economy* (Tokyo: The Bank of Japan, 1966), p. 28.
[3] *Ibid.*
[4] *Ibid.*, p. 324.

Though less dramatic in magnitude than in the case of large industries, the growth of the traditional sector was no less significant. The small family workshop continued to demonstrate its competitive strength as the technical unit of production. Even the very small establishments — those with fewer than five employees — showed marked power of survival and growth.

The Meiji Ideology

Initially, at least, there was a rather intensive debate within the Meiji leadership as to the nature of the political ideology to guide new Japan. Some leaders were strongly attracted to Western liberalism, while others were intensely committed to highly authoritarian political ideology. It was not until the late 1870's that the authoritarian oligarchy firmly established itself.[5]

The authoritarian Meiji elite used a variety of ingenious means to consolidate their power, to achieve national integration, and to build a society responsive to their leadership. They found their basic ideological support in the Imperial institution. They rallied around the Emperor and sought to build a national unity around the Imperial myth. Shintoism, in which the Emperor occupied the central place, was restored as the state religion. Emphasis on the divine origin of the Emperor and on the uniqueness of Japan as the divine nation helped to develop a high degree of national consciousness and strong nationalistic sentiments. Shintoism enabled the leadership to succeed in transforming the strong sense of loyalty to one's lord, already dominant in the feudal society, into a sense of loyalty to the Emperor and to the nation. This dedication and loyalty to the Emperor became an absolute duty and took precedence over *giri* and *ninjo* in ordinary human relations.

The apparent backwardness of Japan compared with Western nations posed a tremendous challenge to the nationalistic Japanese. "Catching up with the West" was used as a rallying point to elicit a spirit of sacrifice and devotion. The Meiji oligarchy was highly mercantilistic in its political ideology. It sought to expand the na-

[5] For a detailed analysis of this issue, see Robert A. Scalapino, *Democracy and the Party Movement in Prewar Japan: The Failure of the First Attempt* (Berkeley: University of California Press, 1962), pp. 40–145. It is highly significant to observe that a sizable portion of the "liberals" emphasized liberalism mainly as a means of building a strong state. They stressed the benefits that liberalism would confer on the state rather than on the individual. Apparently, the vital importance of individualism in the liberal cause was never fully appreciated (see page 41 of Scalapino's book).

tional power as the end of state policy, while keeping an authoritarian control over the society. This was no coincidence in view of the personal background of the Meiji leaders and the tradition of fief mercantilism already forming in the late Tokugawa era. Its philosophy of mercantilism was articulated in a popular slogan, "*Fukoku Kyohei*," or "a rich country, a strong army." This became the dominant national goal, and no effort was spared in achieving it.

This is not to say that the Meiji oligarchy was monolithic. It was, in fact, divided into several major dissident factions whose conflicts were intense. Nevertheless, these factions were united in a basic desire to perpetuate a society that would allow the oligarchy a continued dominance. By their very background and disposition, Meiji leaders were highly authoritarian and autocratic. They were the products of Confucian ideology and authoritarian feudal tradition. Though amazingly enlightened in some respects, they were basically very conservative, especially in their political ideology.

To solidify their power and to perpetuate a social order favorably disposed to their leadership, they deliberately sought to retain many of the traditional values nurtured during the Tokugawa era. The guiding spirit in this attempt was the fusion of highly authoritarian samurai ethics with intensely nationalistic sentiments.

The Meiji leadership exerted much effort in building a nationwide system of education, which served as an effective means for indoctrination with the authoritarian ideology. Thus, as Herbert Passin notes, " . . . the inculcation of loyalty and an official version of national morality became central to the mission and methods of the school system."[6]

One set of feudal values that received special attention as a means for social control had to do with the traditional family. Takeyoshi Kawashima, a noted authority on the Japanese familial system, observes that the traditional familial system of the samurai class and its accompanying values were held by the ruling oligarchy as the ideal for the entire society.[7] This traditional family system constituted the very basis of the national polity. The entire nation was viewed as one vast family, with the Emperor as the father to all. Obedience, self-sacrifice, and harmony within this collectivity

[6] Herbert Passin, "Japan," in James S. Coleman (ed.), *Education and Political Development* (Princeton: Princeton University Press, 1965), p. 307.

[7] For details, see Takeyoshi Kawashima, *Ideology Toshite no Kazokuseido* [*The Family System as an Ideology*] (Tokyo: Iwanami Shoten, 1964), pp. 1–125.

received much emphasis.[8] Moreover, the traditional familial system of the samurai type was formally established as a key legal institution in the civil code of 1898.[9] For the ensuing half-century, the *ie* collectivity, rather than individuals, constituted the basic legal entity in the civil code. The family now was not only morally but also legally bound to develop obedient and docile subjects.[10]

Along with the familial system, the collectivity values and various forms of the traditional particularistic obligatory relationships between individuals were also emphasized. As Doi notes, the heavy emphasis placed on loyalty to the Emperor further hindered the development of individualism by subjecting every individual to the Emperor by a spiritual bond and not allowing him to establish his independent self apart from this bond.[11] The traditional values were given a new meaning in the context of modern industrial Japanese society. The elite persistently inculcated the masses with a view that individualism and individual freedom were contrary to the virtues and traditions of Japan.

The agricultural sector, still predominant, played an important role in perpetuating the traditional values. The Meiji oligarchy carefully sought not to disturb the existing power structure at the village level nor the traditional collectivity orientation and highly particularistic values among peasants.[12] The inclination toward these traditional values in the agrarian sector was further reinforced as peasants, confronted with threats of industrialization, sought refuge in the more familiar conservative values.

The village power structure, dominated by a small number of landlords, was effectively integrated into the national policy. The tight-knit, conservative, collectivity-oriented, and authoritarian control at the village level gave strong support to the preservation of traditional values.[13]

[8] *Ibid.*

[9] Yozo Watanabe, "The Family and the Law: The Individualistic Premise and Modern Japanese Family Law," in Arthur Taylor von Mehren (ed.), *Law in Japan: The Legal Order in a Changing Society* (Cambridge, Mass.: Harvard University Press, 1963), p. 364.

[10] R. P. Dore, *City Life in Japan: A Study of a Tokyo Ward* (Berkeley: University of California Press, 1958), p. 379.

[11] Takeo Doi, "*Giri-Ninjō:* An Interpretation," in R. P. Dore (ed.), *Aspects of Social Change in Modern Japan* (Princeton: Princeton University Press, 1967), p. 332.

[12] Scalapino, *Democracy and the Party Movement*, p. 307.

[13] Masao Maruyama, *Nihon no Shisō* [*Japanese Ideology*] (Tokyo: Iwanami Shoten, 1961), p. 46.

Thus, in spite of extensive social, economic, and political reforms, many of the characteristics of the traditional society remained. True, they were now recast in an environment that presented some semblance to a modern society; nevertheless, the basic orientation was remarkably traditional.

Brief Encounter with Liberalism

By the end of the second decade of this century, Japan had achieved a full transition from an agrarian to an industry-based economy. Spurred by World War I, Japan in this period witnessed the advancement of technically-oriented industries. The economic progress achieved during this war can be seen in Table 1.

But at the same time, Japan began to suffer from the typical ills of industrial revolution, and she began to be plagued with considerable social unrest. The traditional, highly authoritarian solidarity began to crumble, particularly in the large urban industrial centers. A new industrial proletariat was rapidly emerging, giving rise to class cleavages and class consciousness. Labor disputes became quite common.

The decade of the 1920's witnessed a considerable loosening of authoritarianism and a surge of liberal thought. In view of the fact that Western liberalism made a significant imprint on Japan during the earlier Meiji era, the rise of liberal thought in the 1920's was not as sharp a break as it might appear on the surface. The ruling oligarchy, no longer representing the original Meiji leaders, made important concessions to the rising tide of liberal movements; the most important of these concessions was the granting of universal manhood suffrage in 1925.

Forces were constantly at work, however, to check these liberal movements. For example, there were strong voices among conservative educators and bureaucrats exhorting the people to return to an authoritarian and "orderly" society, characterized by strong mutual solidarity.[14] Legal measures were passed to limit the rights of free speech and free political actions, and to stamp out "dangerous" thoughts.

Meanwhile, some significant changes took place in the political

[14] R. P. Dore, "Education: Japan," Part A, in Robert E. Ward and Dankwart A. Rustow (eds.), *Political Modernization in Japan and Turkey* (Princeton: Princeton University Press, 1964), p. 194. In this essay, Dore presents a concise yet penetrating analysis of historical developments of education in modern Japan.

scene as well. The power of political parties grew substantially. The growth of the strength of political parties failed, however, to stimulate an emergence of democracy. Rather, the major parties followed the oligarchic and autocratic tradition.[15] However, the oligarchy had, by this time, become somewhat widened and more pluralistic, including in its ranks career politicians, business and agrarian leaders, and civil and military bureaucrats. With rapid industrialization, big business gained considerable political influence and served as the unifying force for party-bureaucratic alliance.[16] Diverse Zaibatsu interests became closely tied to political parties. The alliance between the political and the business elite became very close, and was often reinforced by marriage and adoption. In fact, big business interests now began to act more as the politician's patron than as his ally. The Zaibatsu interests were cast, though not always voluntarily, in the role of corruptive influences in the political scene.

The Period of Crisis

Meanwhile, the Japanese economy was seriously troubled by the inflationary maladjustments in the aftermath of World War I, which plagued the country for at least a decade. Agricultural productivity ceased to grow at the former rate, and industry was no longer able to absorb the growing labor force. Then the worldwide depression hit Japan most severely. The faction-ridden, often corrupt political leadership that was so closely tied to the Zaibatsu interests lacked both the ability and the will to cope with the economic and social problems of the time. Capitalizing on the frustrations and discontent brought on by these developments, the ultranationalistic and reactionary elements began to gain strength.

The reactionaries found close ideological allies among equally conservative military officers committed to imperialistic expansion — products of extremely narrow and highly regimented military training. The early 1930's saw the reversal of the democratic trend of the 1920's and a surge of vociferous militarism and fanatical nationalism. The military, backed by various aggressive reactionary groups, were now in control of the ruling oligarchy. They quickly

[15] For details, see Scalapino, *Democracy and the Party Movement*, pp. 200–245.

[16] Robert A. Scalapino, "The Inability of Japanese Capitalism to Make a Democracy a Success," in George O. Totten (ed.), *Democracy in Prewar Japan: Groundwork or Facade* (Boston: D. C. Heath and Company, 1965), p. 70.

repudiated the existing political leadership and were well on the way to converting Japan into a totalitarian police state. Also in ascendance within the oligarchy were a number of quasi-fascist bureaucrats who were, ironically, labeled as "progressive" bureaucrats.

This new oligarchy began to organize the country's resources to advance its imperialistic objectives. Initially, the relationship between the military leadership and the Zaibatsu interests was a rather precarious one. The military looked upon big business and capitalism with suspicion and even with open hostility. The feeling was reciprocated by executives of the major Zaibatsu interests. The relationship between these two power centers was unsatisfactory enough for the military to encourage the formation of a number of new Zaibatsu groups, known as Shinko Zaibatsu, to serve as their tool. Shinko Zaibatsu specialized largely in the manufacture of armaments. They also played a strategic role in the economic development and exploitation of Manchuria, which had recently come under Japanese control. Despite their initial differences, the military and the old Zaibatsu interests eventually realized that cooperation would be mutually beneficial. "The coalition of the military with the Zaibatsu interests," observes Reischauer, "was perhaps nothing more than a marriage of convenience but it was nevertheless a successful working arrangement."[17]

In the 1930's, the Japanese industries made another major advance. During this decade, the output of all industries combined doubled. Furthermore, some significant structural changes took place in Japanese industry, as can be seen from the following data.[18] The output of both nonferrous metals and machinery more than doubled; the output of chemical and petroleum industries more than tripled; the production of ferrous metals also tripled. Under the stimulus of war outlays in the 1930's, the engineering industries came into their own, and the value of the output in the engineering and chemical industries began, for the first time, to surpass that of the textile industries in their contributions to Japan's gross national product.[19]

As Japan entered the so-called quasi-war economy, in the mid-

[17] Edwin Reischauer, "The Rise and Fall of Democratic Institutions," in George O. Totten (ed.), *Democracy in Prewar Japan*, p. 8.

[18] *Hundred-Year Statistics* (Bank of Japan), p. 92.

[19] G. C. Allen, *Japan's Economic Expansion* (London: Oxford University Press, 1965), p. 5.

1930's, the government began to assume control over certain key strategic industries, and this control increased steadily for the next decade. The existing concentration of economic power in a handful of Zaibatsu facilitated the transition to a state-controlled economy. Zaibatsu now virtually became economic branches of the state.[20] By the late 1930's, Japan was taking steps toward what Reischauer calls "a curious sort of state socialism, born of Zaibatsu capitalism and sired by militaristic authoritarianism."[21] By 1940, a number of strategically important industries had been brought under a centralized administration, and national policy companies were established under official guidance.[22]

Thus, the new oligarchy, consisting of military and civil bureaucrats and big Zaibatsu interests, took Japan down the tragic road leading to World War II.

Postwar Japan

Years of Occupation

On August 15, 1945, Japan surrendered unconditionally to the Allied Forces, marking an end of an era and ushering in a new one. Much has happened during the last two decades. As Herbert Passin aptly puts it, the two decades are less than a generation in the usual reckoning, but in terms of what has happened during this brief time, they are perhaps the equivalent of three to four generations.[23]

At the end of the war, Japan's economy was in ruins. She lost over 1,850,000 lives, over a third of whom died in Japan proper as a result of air raids.[24] Forty percent of Japan's aggregate urban area was destroyed, and some 2,252,000 buildings were destroyed. The amount of physical destruction is estimated to have been equivalent to about twice the national income of the fiscal year 1948–1949.[25] Industrial production in 1946 sank to less than a third of the 1930 total, and to a mere seventh of the 1941 level.[26]

[20] Reischauer, "Rise and Fall," p. 14.
[21] *Ibid.*
[22] Allen, *Japan's Economic Expansion*, p. 14.
[23] Herbert Passin, "Introduction," in The American Assembly, Columbia University, *The United States and Japan* (Englewood Cliffs, N. J.: Prentice-Hall, Inc., 1966), p. 1.
[24] Edwin O. Reischauer, *The United States and Japan* (3rd ed.; Cambridge, Mass.: Harvard University Press, 1965), p. 207.
[25] Allen, *Japan's Economic Expansion*, p. 15.
[26] Reischauer, *The United States and Japan*, p. 209.

Immediately after the surrender, the Allied Forces moved into the war-torn country plagued with great economic and social confusion. This was no ordinary occupation committed only to a narrow range of military objectives. The Occupation viewed its mission in a much broader perspective. It sought two major objectives — demilitarization and democratization of Japan — in that order of priority. In essence, the Occupation attempted to change the basic character of Japanese society. It is also important to note that, unlike the case of West Germany, the Allied Occupation in Japan was almost exclusively an American operation. This, of course, was eminently important in determining what was to follow.

Occupation reforms touched almost every aspect of postwar Japanese life, involving not only disarming the Japanese military, but stripping the nation of her ability to wage war, which meant, of course, destroying her industrial capacity. One of the most dramatic reforms in the economic sphere was the dissolution of the Zaibatsu, which was carried out in a series of steps over a period of several years. The dissolution of the Zaibatsu was followed by the passage of the Anti-Monopoly Act, designed to preserve a competitive economic structure.

The Occupation implemented a wholesale purge of wartime leaders, including a large number of senior executives of major corporations. The Occupation also moved quickly to initiate reforms in labor-management relations. Under the open encouragement and guidance of the Occupation, and reinforced by serious economic distress, spectacular progress was achieved in the union movement. As many as seven million workers — more than half of the nonagricultural labor force — were unionized by 1949.[27]

The Occupation also sought to broaden the democratic base of postwar Japan by undertaking an extensive land reform program. The reforms resulted in a wide distribution of land ownership, which heretofore had been concentrated in a small number of landlords. It is estimated that in a period of four years, nearly two million farmers came to own the land they cultivated.[28]

Another major reform took place in the area of education. Here,

[27] For details, see Solomon B. Levine, *Industrial Relations in Postwar Japan* (Urbana, Ill.: University of Illinois Press, 1958); Alice Cook, *Japanese Trade Unionism* (New York: New York State School of Industrial Relations, Cornell University, 1965); and Iwao F. Ayukawa, *A History of Labor in Modern Japan* (Honolulu: East-West Center Press, 1966), pp. 232–301.

[28] John M. Maki, *Government and Politics in Japan: The Road to Democracy* (New York: Frederick A. Praeger, Inc., 1961), p. 134.

two significant changes were introduced: The period of compulsory education was lengthened from six to nine years; and education was no longer to serve as an instrument of the state, promoting traditional moral values and political ideology — it was now designed to stress democratic values, including the duties and rights of citizens in a democratic society.

The Occupation directed the Japanese government to draft a new constitution, which was enacted in 1947. Of all the sweeping changes introduced in the Constitution of 1947, the concept of the sovereignty of the people was undoubtedly the most important one. For the first time in the history of Japan, sovereignty now rested with the people. The Emperor, who had earlier denounced his divinity, was formally stripped of his sovereignty, becoming only the ceremonial symbol of the state. Moreover, the new constitution, unlike its predecessor, unequivocally guaranteed the fundamental rights of each citizen.

The basic concepts of the Constitution of 1947 were soon incorporated into various secondary legal codes. Both commercial and civil codes were drastically revised. The revision of the former sought to introduce frameworks for corporate democracy, while that of the latter repudiated the traditional family concept and completely obliterated the concept of *ie,* which had dominated the Meiji civil code. Thus, the Occupation reforms indeed transformed nearly every aspect of Japanese life and had a profound impact on the course of events to follow.

Beginning in the middle of 1947, the intensification of the cold war forced a fundamental change in American policy toward Japan. By January 1948, the basic objective of that policy shifted from promoting demilitarization and experimental democratic reforms to promoting economic recovery and creating a strong Japan as an ally in the cold war. This change of emphasis significantly affected various reform measures that were still being implemented. The militant labor movement, which grew with the blessings of the Occupation, now met with sharp official opposition. Concurrently, deconcentration of economic power proceeded with a more restrained enthusiasm. And to implement the new policy of economic recovery, a nine-point economic stabilization program was adopted in the same year, calling for a balanced budget, credit restrictions, and the expansion of production and trade. The rampant inflation was brought under control in 1949, and Japan began to head for recovery.

The Phenomenal Economic Growth

When the Korean war broke out in 1950, Japan became an important United Nations supply base. The impact of this war in providing the initial impetus to Japan's postwar recovery cannot be overemphasized. It is estimated that during the Korean conflict, the United Nations forces spent nearly four billion dollars in Japan on strategic supplies for the war effort.[29] These payments enabled Japan to build up large dollar reserves; a major portion of them was subsequently channeled toward reequipping Japanese industries. Simultaneously, generous United States aid, amounting to a total of two billion dollars, poured into the national economy. By 1952, when Japan regained her independence, her industrial output had reached the prewar level. By 1956, Japan had completed her economic recovery, with her gross national product reaching a level substantially higher than in the mid-1930's.

Japan's phenomenal growth during the next several years is a familiar story and needs no detailed elaboration here.[30] Here, we shall only attempt to point out its magnitude. The GNP grew at the rate of 10 percent or more annually, recording nearly a threefold increase in real terms between 1956 and 1966. During the same period, personal consumption increased by two and a half times. The volume of output by all industries grew by five times between 1951 and 1965.

During the decade ending in 1966, the output of nondurable consumer goods more than doubled and that of capital goods increased six times.[31] The output of consumer durable goods increased as much as seven times.[32] During the decade ending in 1965, the total value of output by light industries tripled and that of combined heavy and chemical industries grew by three and a half times.[33] Also during this period, the number of factories with 30 or

[29] Allen, *Japan's Economic Expansion*, p. 19.

[30] For a detailed analysis of Japan's postwar economic growth, see William W. Lockwood, "Japan's 'New Capitalism,'" in William W. Lockwood (ed.), *The State and Economic Enterprise in Japan: Essays in the Political Economy of Growth* (Princeton: Princeton University Press, 1965), pp. 447–522; and G. C. Allen, *Japan's Economic Expansion*, pp. 15–262.

[31] *Economic Statistics of Japan, 1966* (Tokyo: The Bank of Japan, 1967), p. 212.

[32] *Hundred-Year Statistics* (Bank of Japan), p. 93.

[33] *Kogyō Tōkei Sokuhō: Showa 40 nen* [*The Preliminary Report on Factory Statistics, 1965*] (Tokyo: Ministry of International Trade and Industry, 1966), p. 14.

more employees grew from 30,868 to 52,449.[34] The number of workers employed by these factories increased from 3.7 million to over 6.6 million.[35]

Looking at various product categories, the output of ferrous and nonferrous metals recorded a threefold increase during the same ten-year period. The output of chemical and petroleum products quadrupled, and that of machinery increased by nearly five times. The phenomenal record of the postwar industrial growth is presented in Table 2.

Particularly extraordinary was the growth achieved between 1955 and 1963, the so-called high-growth or boom years. During this period, the average annual growth rate in real terms exceeded 10 percent and industrial output tripled.[36] Capital investment also increased at a remarkable rate. At the height of the growth period (1959–1961), gross fixed assets formation was as high as 32.5 percent of the GNP as contrasted to 16.3 percent, 16.5 percent, and 23.8 percent for the United States, Great Britain, and West Germany, respectively, for the same period.[37] The growth of total capital investment by all incorporated business establishments was more than fivefold during the eight-year period.[38] The gross fixed assets for the electric apparatus industry quadrupled, and that for the chemical industry grew by three and a half times.[39]

During the last decade or so, Japanese industry has undergone a significant structural change. In terms of value of output, heavy industry accounted for nearly 63 percent of total factory production in 1965, as contrasted to 51.2 percent in 1955.[40] This structural change has been reflected in the composition of Japan's exports. In 1966, heavy and chemical goods accounted for over 63 percent of the total exports.

Japanese industries, anxious to fill the technological gap resulting from many years of virtual isolation from the rest of the world, energetically sought to import technology from the advanced nations. Between 1950 and 1966, 8,561 technical licensing contracts

[34] *Ibid.*

[35] *Ibid.*, p. 9.

[36] "Economic Structure of Japan," *Oriental Economist*, XXXII, No. 641 (March 1964), 44.

[37] *Ibid.*

[38] *Keizai Hakusho: Showa 41 nen* [*White Paper on the Japanese Economy, 1966*] (Tokyo: The Economic Planning Agency, 1966), p. 251.

[39] *Ibid.*, pp. 312–313.

[40] *Kogyō Tōkei Sokuhō* (MITI), p. 2.

were signed between foreign and Japanese firms, for which Japanese firms paid 1.2 billion dollars.[41] Almost 60 percent of the contracts were with American firms.

Japan now leads the world in shipbuilding and is third in the production of crude steel, accounting for over 10 percent of the world's total output. In 1967, Japan's automobile industry outranked West Germany's for the first time, second only to that of the United States. The progress made in other industries, such as the electronic industry, is also well known.

By the mid-1960's, two decades after the catastrophic destruction of World War II, Japan emerged as one of the leading industrial nations of the world, trailing only the United States and the Soviet Union, and vigorously competing with West Germany for third place.

Many explanations have been advanced for the remarkable economic growth in postwar Japan.[42] The factors most often cited include Occupation-sponsored democratic reforms, political stability, sharp decrease in military expenditures, rapid technological innovations, an abundant, well-educated, and industrious labor force, entrepreneurial and managerial skills, the role of the government, and the remnants of traditional institutional arrangements, including the so-called duality in the economic structure. In addition, we should not ignore the fact that the existing international situation, its economic and political aspects, had been favorable to Japan. As Allen aptly notes, "Fortune has certainly shown Japan her engaging and amiable aspect."[43]

The Postwar Political Climate

We shall now turn briefly to an examination of the postwar political climate. The defeat, though it totally repudiated the military, did not result in a political revolution. After the despair and confusion of the immediate postwar era, the conservatives emerged as the dominant force in the political scene. The bureaucracy survived extensive reforms and remained basically intact. Many political leaders — career politicians as well as ex-bureaucrats — were "depurged" and returned to positions of leadership. The Liberal

[41] "1,153 Foreign Technology Cases Were Authorized in Fiscal 1966," *The Japan Economic Journal*, October 24, 1967, p. 7.

[42] For example, see Ichiro Nakayama, *Industrialization of Japan* (Honolulu: East-West Center Press, 1964), pp. 7–25.

[43] Allen, *Japan's Economic Expansion*, p. 249.

TABLE 2

INDICES OF INDUSTRIAL PRODUCTION FOR SELECTED YEARS, 1945–1966
(1960 = 100)

Industry	*1945*	*1950*	*1955*	*1960*	*1961*	*1962*	*1963*	*1964*	*1965*	*1966*
Manufacturing	19.6	20.4	45.7	100.0	119.9	130.1	143.7	169.1	177.2	198.3
Ferrous Metals	13.1	22.9	43.8	100.0	126.1	125.5	140.4	172.8	177.7	204.7
Nonferrous Metals	18.9	25.0	42.2	100.0	119.7	117.1	132.9	161.9	161.2	181.7
Machinery	16.4	11.9	28.5	100.0	129.0	145.0	159.5	194.0	198.8	224.6
Ceramics	8.5	26.2	51.2	100.0	114.4	126.9	136.0	155.6	159.5	174.4
Chemicals	10.3	20.8	49.5	100.0	113.8	130.0	152.7	178.9	208.0	241.9
Petroleum and Coal Products	5.8	11.1	39.7	100.0	120.1	135.0	159.8	184.5	209.7	242.1
Rubber Products	5.8	26.0	40.5	100.0	114.0	126.4	135.8	143.8	140.0	151.0
Leather Products	14.5	26.4	72.7	100.0	129.6	154.3	172.6	180.6	184.3	189.1
Paper and Pulp	5.0	21.4	53.4	100.0	117.4	122.1	135.3	153.0	153.2	169.9
Textiles	5.5	26.4	62.0	100.0	107.9	113.5	122.5	136.9	147.1	162.8
Lumber	20.3	49.9	74.3	100.0	105.9	108.2	114.5	121.2	124.6	130.9
Food and Kindred Products	20.3	33.5	77.4	100.0	108.2	117.2	121.0	127.8	134.4	136.4
Tobacco	28.4	57.8	84.4	100.0	107.5	116.1	118.7	127.2	140.1	143.3
Others	2.7	15.0	32.4	100.0	123.9	136.7	158.8	193.4	206.3	223.3

Source: *Economic Statistics of Japan, 1966* (Tokyo: The Bank of Japan, 1967), pp. 211–212.

Democratic Party, a fusion of conservative elements organized in 1955, has been in power ever since. The LDP is allied closely with big business interests, and its leadership consists of career politicians and ex-bureaucrats who "retired" into politics. Thus, the basic composition of the elite has undergone very little change, except that the military sector has totally lost its power.

The postwar political climate, however, has taken on some distinct features. First, sovereignty now rests with the people, and parliamentary supremacy is guaranteed in the Constitution. Second, the basis for political participation has been substantially widened. As Scalapino notes, one of the most impressive features of the democratic era has been the development of far more substantial social and economic interest groups than any that had previously existed.[44] Included among them are the powerful agrarian cooperative societies, the expanded business pressure groups, and the large-scale unions. These interest groups have provided, to an increasing degree, useful channels of political expression for the major segments of the whole society.[45] These groups now constitute powerful countervailing forces to the political and economic elite.

The LDP, in spite of fierce inner-party factional struggles, has managed to attain a degree of political stability during the past decade, unmatched anywhere in Asia. Moreover, the party, sympathetic to business interests, has definitely created an environment favorable to rapid economic growth through its protective measures, direct and indirect subsidies, and informal encouragements of various kinds. In return, the business community has given the LDP unswerving support.

The Postwar Society

We have examined briefly the nature and extent of the Occupation-sponsored reforms and subsequent developments in the economic and political sphere. Now we shall consider the impact of these developments on Japanese society. Is the postwar Japanese society significantly different from that of prewar Japan? No doubt the massive and deliberate changes introduced in the postwar period inevitably had a major impact in shaping the value system in postwar Japan. The character of the changes introduced in the years immediately after World War II was basically different from

[44] Robert A. Scalapino, "Environmental and Foreign Contributions: Japan," Part A, in Robert E. Ward and Dankwart A. Rustow (eds.) *Political Modernization in Japan and Turkey,* p. 87.

[45] *Ibid.*

those that had taken place in the early Meiji years. In the latter case, as extensive as the reforms were, the basic socioeconomic framework remained relatively unchanged. In fact, the elite, as we have seen, had made deliberate efforts to retain many aspects of the traditional society. In contrast, however, in the immediate aftermath of World War II, the basic framework itself became the main target of the reforms. It is reasonable, therefore, to assume that there was a far greater degree of continuity, at least in the ideological sphere, between the Tokugawa and the Meiji Japan than there has been between prewar and postwar Japan. In fact, there is much evidence to prove that these two periods are indeed separated by a great gulf. Let us now examine the nature and magnitude of social change brought about by the defeat.

First, we should note that the defeat was a profound shock to the masses. The Japanese people, it must be remembered, had been subjected to a most deliberate and effective program of indoctrination for more than half a century. As a result, they became highly imbued with a sense of national superiority and pride. The defeat totally repudiated the past ideology and the traditional values and institutions. Out of the trauma of shock and the humiliation of defeat, the Japanese deliberately sought to reject many of the traditional values. They were labeled "feudalistic" and were to be discarded as rapidly as possible. Out of this disenchantment emerged a strong national consensus that new values had to be found. Thus, the concentrated effort exerted until 1945 to retain traditional values was now replaced by an equally intense effort to reject them.

The rejection of traditional values became somewhat moderated after Japan regained her independence, and particularly so after the Japanese had their self-confidence restored, following their country's phenomenal economic growth. In spite of the often-mentioned reactionary or "reverse" course, the retreat from the reforms of the Occupation has been very slight. This has prompted some observers to claim that many of the more basic and sustained changes were not actually instituted by the Occupation, but could be attributed to the changes that had been taking place in Japanese society for a number of years prior to it. Reischauer, for example, observes that most of the truly significant postwar changes seem to be the acceleration of changes that had already been taking place. The Occupation removed barriers to the forward movement of these forces and stimulated their growth and rapid dissemination.[46]

[46] Reischauer, *The United States and Japan*, p. 292.

Ichiro Nakayama, an eminent Japanese economist, agrees with Reischauer in stating:

> The so-called democratization of Japan did not take place because of the occupation policy. If we understand by democratization all the changes in the characteristics of the traditional society, then they were proceeding everywhere in spite of the apparent persistency of the old order. In other words these reforms merely gave a final blow to the changes that had been going on behind the scenes.[47]

John W. Bennett also makes the following observation:

> The avidity with which the Japanese people and many of their leaders accepted the reforms of the occupation period was an indication of the extent to which social change associated with industrialization had been prepared under cover, so to speak, during the authoritarian epoch. Consequently, the rapidity of current change in Japanese economy and society is due, in addition to many other causes, to a "catching-up" process. That is, it is in part at least a social readjustment, and not merely something new.[48]

Accelerated economic growth, coupled with postwar social reforms, has brought about some important changes in the structure of employment and the pattern of income distribution. Since all this has far-reaching implications for the postwar Japanese society, we shall highlight a few of the more important developments.

There has been a tremendous outflow of workers from the primary sector to the secondary and tertiary sectors. During the decade ending in 1965, the number of those gainfully employed in agriculture declined by four million.[49] Also noteworthy is a significant decline in the number of family workers and a twofold increase in the number of gainfully employed. Still another related development is the acceleration of the trend for urbanization that had started before the war. By 1965, over 68 percent of Japan's population was concentrated in 561 cities, and nearly a fifth of the total population now lived in cities of over one million or more inhabitants. During the five-year period ending in 1964, 1.5 million people poured into the three largest metropolitan areas, accounting for 45 percent of those who reported cross-prefectural moves.[50]

[47] Nakayama, *Industrialization of Japan*, p. 69.

[48] John W. Bennett, "Japanese Economic Growth: Background for Social Change," in R. P. Dore (ed.), *Aspects of Social Change in Modern Japan*, pp. 450–451.

[49] *Kokumin Seikatsu Hakusho: Showa 40 nen do* [*White Paper on National Life, 1965*] (Tokyo: The Economic Planning Agency, 1966), p. 67.

[50] *Ibid.*, p. 68.

One of the most significant factors associated with postwar economic growth is the degree to which the benefits of economic growth have been diffused among the masses. While all segments of Japanese society have shared in the remarkable material advancement of the postwar era, particularly striking has been the gain by wage earners. As noted earlier, the very number of gainfully employed doubled between 1951 and 1965, and the wage level has shown a steady and substantial yearly increase.

The growth in the wage level has been particularly striking during the past several years. In 1960, 60 percent of wage earners had an annual total income of less than ¥300,000, or $833; but in 1965, the percentage of those falling into this category declined to 30 percent. Those earning more than ¥500,000, or $1,290, increased from 31 percent of the total wage earners in 1960 to 36.8 percent in 1965. The number of those earning between one to two million yen ($2,780 to $5,500) increased fivefold during this period.[51]

The extent to which the benefits of postwar economic growth have been distributed may further be seen from the following data: In 1964, over 61 percent of the total personal income was earned by wage earners; unincorporated proprietors' income amounted to about 27 percent; whereas the income earned from rent, dividends, and interest accounted for less than 10 percent.[52] This is a significant departure from the prewar pattern, when the percentages in 1934–1936 for the same categories for instance, were 41.2 percent, 34.3 percent, and 23.4 percent, respectively.[53]

Increasing productivity and land reforms have narrowed the gap in income levels between the urban and rural sectors. Furthermore, a tight labor market has reduced long-standing disparity in the wage levels of large and small enterprises. Thus, rapid industrial growth, coupled with postwar reforms, has now created a truly viable, economically independent middle class, and has achieved by far the highest standard of living in Asia.

The Japanese themselves are keenly aware of this phenomenon. They describe the host of changes brought about by the wide diffusion of benefits from the rapid economic growth in such terms as *Shohi Kakumei*, or consumption revolution. One indication of this consumption revolution can be seen in the rapid increase in

[51] "Salary Earner Income Increasing Steadily," *The Japan Economic Journal*, September 20, 1966, p. 4.

[52] Computed from the data contained in *Hundred-Year Statistics* (Bank of Japan), p. 39.

[53] *Ibid.*

ownership of consumer durables. For example, in early 1966, 94 percent of families owned television sets, 76 percent owned washing machines, 61 percent had refrigerators, and 12 percent drove their own automobiles.[54] Moreover, there has been a significant westernization trend in the mode of living and consumer taste.

Indeed, in postwar Japan we see the emergence of a middle-class-dominated mass consumption society. This is eloquently attested by a nationwide public opinion poll on the standard of living conducted annually by the government. In 1967, the survey indicated that as many as 88 percent of over 16,000 respondents considered themselves belonging to the middle class, in comparison with 72 percent in 1958.[55] Moreover, 60 percent of the respondents reported that they were on the whole content with their present standard of living.[56] As to the future outlook, 44 percent felt that their standard of living would continue to improve.[57]

Also, postwar Japan has enjoyed remarkable progress in mass communication, which has played a significant role as an agent of social change. The very rapid rate of increase in newspaper and magazine circulation as well as in the diffusion of radios and television sets has been simply phenomenal. For example, by the end of 1966, the total circulation of the daily press reached nearly 31 million, 1 copy per every 3.25 persons.[58] The annual advertising expenditure for the year 1966 reached ¥383 billion (1.3 percent of the GNP), recording over fivefold growth between 1956 and 1966, surpassing substantially the growth rate of the GNP for the same period.[59]

All these developments point to the fact that contemporary Japanese society is not merely a continuation of its prewar counterpart. Reischauer, describing the very sweeping social changes taking place in postwar Japan, states, "A great breath of freedom has blown through the tightly knit, cramped society of Japan."[60] He further notes that most of the traditional Japanese values required

[54] *Keizai Hakusho* (Economic Planning Agency), p. 290.

[55] *Kokumin Seikatsu ni Kansuru Seron Chōsa* [*Public Opinion Poll on People's Life*] (Tokyo: The Office of the Prime Minister, 1967), p. 7.

[56] *Ibid.*

[57] *Ibid.*

[58] *Dentsu Kokoku Nenkon, 1967* [*The Dentsu Advertising Annual, 1967*] (Tokyo: Dentsu Advertising Agency, 1967), p. 101.

[59] *Ibid.*, p. 234.

[60] Reischauer, *The United States and Japan*, pp. 306–307.

considerable revision before they could be applied to postwar Japan.[61]

But what is the nature of the change? What is the impact of rapid industrialization and urbanization, combined with extensive social and political reforms, in postwar Japan? On these points, as one may expect, divergent views are found.

One of the most significant studies on this topic is the one undertaken by 17 social scientists knowledgeable about Japan as a part of the large project "Studies on the Modernization of Japan."[62] In this particular study, the participants addressed themselves to social changes in modern Japan. As a basis for this study, they postulated that throughout the period of modernization, Japan experienced a movement toward greater equality, greater individualization, and greater rationality.[63]

The study reports significant changes that have taken place in each of the areas with the progress of modernization. Interestingly, R. P. Dore, the leader of the group, observes that there is more evidence of a move toward greater equality than of a move toward greater individualization.[64] In this study, John W. Bennett specifically examines the impact of rapid postwar growth on contemporary Japanese society. He notes that the following changes appear to be associated with the rapid postwar economic growth:[65]

1. Social recognition of the legitimacy of individual as well as group aspirations for financial and status enhancement.
2. Acceptance, even encouragement, of social mobility to improve one's economic and social position.
3. The above changes appear to be associated with a growing middle class whose culture is defined by the climate of large bureaucratic organization.
4. Close association of cultural attitudes with consumer industries: Consumption patterns have become one of the important criteria for defining social status.

In this study Bennett concludes that contemporary Japanese

[61] *Ibid.*, p. 308.
[62] R. P. Dore (ed.), *Aspects of Social Change in Modern Japan* (Princeton: Princeton University Press, 1967).
[63] *Ibid.*, pp. 4–5.
[64] *Ibid.*, p. 22.
[65] Bennett, "Japanese Economic Growth," p. 412.

society became quite similar to highly urbanized and industrialized societies elsewhere in the world. He notes:

> Whether or not one wishes to explore the meaning of the term "Westernization," it would seem on the basis of various indices of change in contemporary Japan that feudal-familial forms of social structure are changing and the macroscopic social patterns are rapidly shifting toward those associated with high industrialization and urbanization elsewhere in the world.[66]

At the risk of oversimplification, a few of the seemingly more important developments of change that are noted by a number of social scientists are presented. One set of traditional values that has suffered an almost fatal blow is the one pertaining to the family. As Kawashima notes, the traditional family structure had already undergone some important changes even prior to World War II, in the face of growing industrialization and urbanization.[67] The family ideology was perpetuated only through persistent official indoctrination. Now that the political and legal support for the ideology no longer exists, and the pace of industrialization and urbanization has been considerably accelerated, the traditional family ideology has all but disappeared from contemporary Japan. The definition of the family with which the individual now identifies himself has narrowed from the *ie* concept described earlier to the more ephemeral household based on the conjugal family.[68] Indeed, postwar Japan has witnessed a rapid emergence of nuclear families. Furthermore, significant changes have taken place in the pattern of authority within the family. The relationships among family members can no longer be characterized as authoritarian domination and absolute submission. These relationships have taken on a cooperative and democratic character. No longer is authoritarian filial piety considered a virtue. Affection has replaced obligation in governing relationships within the family.

The traditional pattern of interpersonal obligations has also undergone some significant changes. Various forms of particularistic, hierarchically-oriented obligations in interpersonal relationships are still very much evident in almost every sphere of Japanese life, including the large bureaucratic organizations. Indeed, the traditional

[66] *Ibid.*, p. 450.
[67] Kawashima, *Ideology Toshite no Kazokuseido*, p. 125.
[68] Dore, *City Life in Japan*, p. 388.

reciprocal obligations have been given a new meaning and importance in industrialized Japan and one could ignore them only at his own risk. Nevertheless, even these very deep-seated values have been significantly weakened. The rigidity with which they are applied in contemporary Japan has been relaxed and the range of their application has been considerably narrowed. Significantly, some social scientist, notably Vogel, report that even the concept of loyalty, the very core of Japanese values, has undergone a significant change. Vogel notes that the modern value of loyalty stresses social equality rather than hierarchy.[69] Moreover, the range of loyalty relationships has been narrowed, and deviation from their very strict observance is increasingly tolerated.[70]

With these developments, there is a slow but growing tendency to ascribe a greater moral role to personal conscience in contemporary Japan.[71]

Collectivity orientation, though still important, has also undergone a significant change in the postwar period. The postwar reforms and economic progress have greatly accelerated the trend for independence and individualism in personal behavior. The sphere for individual action and independent thought has expanded considerably. On this point, Dore makes the following illuminating comment:

> The word *kojin-shugi* (individualism) was too thoroughly a "bad" word to be easily purified, but other formerly emotionally neutral words which had been the exclusive preserve of metaphysicians — words like "actor-ness" (*shutaisei,* that is, being that in which resides the power of independent action) and "self direction" (*jishusei*) — have been seized on as the slogans of the left-wing writers and educators, and even the counterattack of the more conservative has generally taken the somewhat half-hearted form of stressing the responsibilities of freedom and the danger of confusing liberty with license. These are changes in the values now upheld by the mass communication media. They may be dismissed as changes merely in the ideological superstructure, but they have undoubtedly given an extra stimulus to a long-term trend towards individuation in actual behaviour, a trend which, even before the war, despite the enshrinement of

[69] Ezra F. Vogel, *Japan's New Middle Class: The Salary Man and His Family in a Tokyo Suburb* (Berkeley: University of California Press, 1963), p. 150.

[70] *Ibid.*, p. 151.

[71] *Ibid.*, pp. 147-158.

> the traditional anti-individualist ethic in a position of unassailable supremacy, was nevertheless going forward concomitantly with changes in the structure of society.[72]

There is also evidence that the emphasis on collectivity orientation is gradually shifting from that based on hierarchical ties to collectivity based on egalitarianism.[73]

Of course, not all social scientists are in agreement as to the nature of changes that have taken place in the basic character of the Japanese society. In fact, some claim that the change has been rather minimal. For example, in a perceptive portrayal of the character of the Japanese society, Chie Nakane convincingly argues that beyond superficial changes that are readily observable, the basic character of the Japanese society has undergone little change. She observes that particularly the traditional collectivity orientation and particularistic and hierarchical interpersonal relationships still persist. She goes on to point out that the higher the degree of social integration in a given society, the less likelihood there is of that society undergoing a basic change in a short period of time. She cites the Japanese society as a typical example of an extremely well-integrated society with a high degree of homogeneity.[74]

As may be expected, the Japanese themselves are by no means certain as to the nature of postwar change and they have been earnestly searching for their own national identity. Contemporary Japanese are faced by serious confusion and uneasiness and are not certain what standards of ethics and values should apply to a variety of day-to-day situations. Some of the socioanthropological studies report confusing, ambiguous, and even conflicting results, which may well reflect accurately the lack of uniformity of present-day Japan. If the present condition is uncertain, the future outlook is very much more so.

Some point out that, although many of the traditional values still persist, the rate of change is likely to be accelerated with time. They observe that the momentum and scope of change have been somewhat moderated thus far by the fact that leadership in almost every field is still firmly in the hands of the prewar generation, but as it shifts to the postwar generation, they conjecture that the tempo

[72] Dore, *City Life in Japan*, p. 388.

[73] Yoshiharu S. Matsumoto, *Contemporary Japan: The Individual and the Group* (Philadelphia: American Philosophical Society, 1960), p. 66.

[74] Chie Nakane, *Tate Shakai no Ningen Kankei* [*Human Relationships in a Vertically Related Society*] (Tokyo: Kodansha, 1966), pp. 23–26.

of change will become faster. By 1975, it is estimated, 48 percent of the entire population will consist of people under thirty years of age — a generation not exposed to the war or its aftermath.[75] If the age group up to thirty-five is included, the percentage goes up to 57.[76] This is particularly significant since attitudinal changes appear to be especially pronounced among postwar educated youth. Only the most courageous would dare to predict the exact character of the Japanese society of the future.

The Challenges That Lie Ahead

By the mid-1960's, Japan began to be confronted with problems caused by the rapid economic growth achieved earlier. There has been a mild inflationary pressure. The initial round of active consumer demand in such key industries as synthetic fibres and consumer durables began to taper off. Japanese industries, large and small, began to struggle with a serious labor shortage and rapidly rising labor costs. The so-called "capacity race" among large firms in growth industries has resulted in serious overcapacity. For these and other reasons, the Japanese economy was hit by a serious recession in the mid-1960's. The economy as a whole still showed a handsome gain, but the number of business failures rose to a new high. And though the economy began to show slow but continuing improvement by early 1966, the recession highlighted basic weaknesses and vulnerability — structural and otherwise — of key Japanese industries.

Meanwhile, in April of 1964, Japan joined the Organization for Economic Cooperation and Development (OECD) and accepted the obligations of Article 8 of the International Monetary Fund. With the liberalization of trade for all but a few products, Japanese industries are now being exposed to international competition. At the same time, pressure began to mount for liberalization of restrictions for direct foreign investment. Measures are now under consideration by the government to gradually liberalize the stringent restrictions limiting entry of foreign capital. All these trends point toward one inevitable fact: Japanese industries must now face greater international competition in the heretofore protected domestic market.

[75] Herbert Passin, "The Future," in The American Assembly, Columbia University, *The United States and Japan,* p. 147.
[76] *Ibid.*

Moreover, the economy is still plagued with sectorial imbalances and the inequalities among different regions. Will the economy continue to grow under increasing international competition and will it be able to ease the tensions of various economic and social imbalances? A number of developments are taking place in the political sphere that may have a substantial impact on Japanese business. In terms of per capita income, Japan is still considerably behind most of the western European countries. The per capita income for 1966 was $790; it is about a fourth of that in the United States and approximately one-half of that in West Germany and France. There is also a glaring inadequacy in infrastructure of various types. Also notable is the serious inadequacy of social security and welfare measures.

There is a feeling in the country that the Liberal Democratic Party, which has been credited with providing political stability and a climate favorable to rapid economic growth, has not grappled with these problems effectively. There appears to be a growing discontent and impatience with the LDP and its policies. This is evidenced by the fact that the percentage of LDP votes in the election for the Lower House declined from 54.7 percent in 1963 to 48.8 percent in 1967. Discontentment with the LDP has been further intensified by factional struggles within the party and the corruption and irresponsible behavior of some of its leaders. Growing disenchantment with the LDP, unless checked, will of course result in an increasing popularity of the two Socialist parties and *Komeito*. The Socialists have thus far remained a minority. They, too, have been plagued with factional struggles within their ranks. They are still locked in the ideological battles of classical Marxism, and have not been able to offer effective alternatives to the policies of the LDP. But, with about a third of the seats in the Diet and with strong support from organized labor, their influence cannot be minimized.

Komeito is a political arm of the *Sokka Gakkai* — Value Creating Society — a highly evangelical and action-oriented new Buddhist sect. During the last decade or so, the Sokka Gakkai has attracted a large number of lower class people who failed to benefit from the great postwar economic advance. The political ideology of Komeito is rather ambiguous, but, with its proliferating membership and strongly disciplined leadership, it is becoming a potent political force. In the election of members to the Lower House early in 1967, the Komeito received over 5 percent of the total vote and elected 25 of its 32 nominated candidates.

As a close ally to the LDP, the business community will have to share the burden of defending the present political power structure. Most business leaders believe that their primary political responsibility lies in assuring continued economic growth to ease various imbalances, in securing a greater degree of convergence of interests between the right and the left, and in meeting the rising material expectations of youth.

The most immediate concern in Japan is the so-called crisis of 1970. This will be the year when the United States–Japan Security Pact, which caused such a stir in 1960, comes up for renewal. It is anticipated that the left wing will use this issue as a rallying point for launching an all-out attack on the conservatives. Important as the issue of the Pact is, the real significance of the anticipated "crisis" of 1970 may well lie in the fact that it will mark a quarter of a century since the defeat, the growing influence of postwar educated youth, the worsening of labor shortages, and the intensification of international economic competition. Indeed, it may be safe to conjecture that it will be about that time when the fullest impact of the social reforms and the rapid economic growth of the postwar era will begin to be felt. Undoubtedly, big business interests will have an important stake in these developments.

3

Business Ideologies in Prewar Japan

The Framework of Analysis

Having given an historical overview of Japanese society, we shall now turn our attention to the central subject of this book — the ideologies of the Japanese business leadership.

In analyzing the salient features of Japanese business ideologies, we shall draw heavily on the analytical framework provided by Sutton and his colleagues in their brilliant study of the American business creed. They define ideology as "any system of beliefs publicly expressed with the manifest purpose of influencing the sentiments and actions of others."[1] The central premise of Sutton and his group is that the content of business ideology can best be understood in terms of the strains that businessmen are subject to; that these strains arise from "the emotional conflicts, the anxieties, and the doubts engendered by the actions which their roles as businessmen compel them to take, and by the conflicting demands of other social roles which they must play in the family and community";[2] and that businessmen formulate a specific ideology in an attempt to resolve or, at least, reduce the conflicts and anxieties resulting from these strains.[3] Ideology, according to them, is shaped within the contexts of both cultural heritage and public acceptability.[4]

Sutton and his collaborators further note that business ideology,

[1] Francis X. Sutton, *et al.*, *The American Business Creed* (Cambridge, Mass.: Harvard University Press, 1956), p. 2.

[2] *Ibid.*, p. 11.

[3] *Ibid.*

[4] *Ibid.*

unlike religious or political philosophies, has "no official sacred text,"[5] observing:

> There is no priesthood or political hierarchy to establish an official "line." Business ideology is not a set of ready-made beliefs which potential adherents must take or leave. Rather, it is created and revised by its own adherents.[6]

It follows, then, that business ideology can be viewed, to borrow an apt expression from Clark Kerr, as " 'shared understanding' . . . growing out of common experience rather than a common philosophy, flexible in their adjustment to changing conditions."[7] Considered in this light, business ideology is by no means monolithic. On the contrary, as "shared understandings" it is subject to a variety of interpretations and fairly ready dissent.[8] Nevertheless, it has some common patterns, since it is shaped and revised as "a patterned reaction to the patterned strains of a social role."[9] Sutton and his co-authors note that strains are "normal" in any society. Moreover, the strains experienced by those placed in a particular role in a given society do not vary at random; they follow certain patterns.[10] The reactions to these patterned strains do not vary at random, either; they, too, have a definite pattern.[11] Basing ourselves on this premise, we shall attempt, in the present chapter and the next one, to analyze the ideologies of Japanese business leadership during the past century. In the last hundred years, Japanese business leaders have indeed faced an unusual variety of strains, conflicts, and anxieties. Not unlike their counterparts in other societies, they, too, have attempted to resolve these conflicts by formulating their shared understandings within the context of their cultural heritage, as well as within the realm of public acceptability.

In this chapter, we shall examine developments in Japanese business ideologies during the prewar era, and in the subsequent chapter, we shall discuss the business ideologies that evolved during the postwar years. Because of the complexity and dimensions of the subject matter, one could easily devote an entire volume to it. Given

[5] *Ibid.*, p. 9.
[6] *Ibid.*
[7] Reinhard Bendix, *Work and Authority in Industry* (New York: John Wiley & Sons, Inc., 1956), p. xii.
[8] *Ibid.*
[9] Sutton, *et al.*, *The American Business Creed*, pp. 307–308.
[10] *Ibid.*, p. 307.
[11] *Ibid.*

the space limitation, however, our analysis is, of necessity, selective. We shall focus our attention only on the major ideological developments.

Entrepreneurial Ideology in the Early Period of Japan's Industrialization

There is a long-standing dispute among Japanese business historians as to the social origins of the entrepreneurs who emerged in the early Meiji era. Some argue that the early Meiji entrepreneurial class was almost exclusively drawn from the samurai; others insist that the great majority had come from the commoner classes.

A study recently conducted by Hiroshi Mannari sheds considerable light on this subject. Mannari painstakingly studied the social background of 189 early Meiji entrepreneurs, and he reports the following results (Table 1). The study shows that over three-fourths of the sample came from the commoner classes. This disclosure is particularly interesting in view of the fact that the political elite and intellectual leaders were drawn predominantly from the samurai class. Another noteworthy point in Mannari's findings is that the bulk of entrepreneurs drawn from the commoner classes came from the upper economic and social strata.[12]

However, as Mannari himself points out, certain cautions are needed in interpreting these data. The circumstances prevailing in the late Tokugawa period make the accurate assessment of the social background of business leaders a very difficult task. We have noted earlier that toward the end of the Tokugawa era, class distinctions had become considerably blurred. This change was particularly pronounced in the lower samurai class and in the upper strata of the commoner classes. It was quite prevalent for men to drift back and forth from commoner status to samurai status. This can best be illustrated, as Mannari points out, in the life of Eiichi Shibusawa, a prominent entrepreneur of the Meiji era. Thus, in interpreting these data, we must allow for the fact that the Tokugawa society, toward its end, was much less rigid in terms of class distinctions than is often supposed.

In examining the character of early Meiji entrepreneurs, we should also make a distinction between those who broke with

[12] Hiroshi Mannari, *The Business Elite, Nihon ni Okeru Keieisha no Jōken* [*The Business Elite, the Background of Business Leaders in Japan*] (Tokyo: Kodansha, 1965), p. 57.

tradition and ventured into new types of business and the ones who achieved their success in more traditional types of business activities. Our primary concern here, of course, is with the entrepreneurs in the real sense, that is, the innovators. Unfortunately, Mannari's data do not make this distinction. However, careful examination of the ideology of those who are known to have been more innovative reveals that, with a surprising consistency, these men shared the same mentality regardless of their particular feudal social background.[13] Their thinking was based on the Confucian-oriented samurai ideology. By the end of the Tokugawa era, samurai ideology and training were no longer exclusively for the elite class; this body of thought had penetrated into the ranks of commoners, particularly among commoners of the upper social and economic strata. The reader may recall from our earlier discussion that the Shogunate had deliberately held up the samurai ideology as the ideal ethic for the entire population. This official encouragement reinforced a natural tendency for the socially inferior to emulate the ethical code and behavior patterns of the privileged elite. Thus, to the extent that circumstances allowed, well-to-do provincial merchants and wealthy farmers identified with the samurai ideology and the samurai way of life. At least some of the upper strata of commoners were affected by the basic elements of samurai culture almost as deeply as the samurai themselves.

This phenomenon became more marked toward the end of the Tokugawa era. As a result, it is more meaningful to view early Meiji entrepreneurs of the innovative type as being a product of the samurai ideology rather than as that of a given social class. Of course, we should note here that not all samurai, or those who shared the samurai mentality, were successful in their commercial or industrial endeavors after the Restoration. In fact, because of their inexperience, their insufficient commitment to the new endeavors, the traditional disdain for commercial activities, and a host of other reasons, failures among samurai-turned-businessmen were quite commonplace, even to a point where a new expression was coined that contemptuously described samurai unsuccessfully turned merchants or industrialists. Significantly, the failure rate was

[13] For example, see Mataji Miyamoto, *Kinsei Shonin Ishiki no Kenkyu* [*Studies in the Merchant Mentality of the Early Modern Period*] (Tokyo: Yuhikaku, 1941), pp. 309–312; and Kazutaro Sugano, *Nihon Kaisha Kigyoshi no Kenkyu* [*Studies in the Development of Joint Stock Companies in Japan*] (Tokyo: Toyo keizai Shinposha, 1966), pp. 663–676.

TABLE 1

CLASS STATUS OF EARLY MEIJI LEADERS: RATIO OF THE PROPORTION BY FEUDAL STATUS OF FATHER IN THE LEADER SAMPLE TO THE PROPORTION IN THE POPULATION AS A WHOLE

(Proportional Representation = 100%)

Feudal Status of Father	*Distribution of Population According to Feudal Status**		*Business Leaders* % (N = 189)		*Political Leaders* % (N = 94)		*Intellectual Leaders* % (N = 100)	
Members of Imperial Households and Feudal Lords	0.0†		0.0		12.0		3.0	
Total		0.0†		0.0		12.0		3.0
Samurai								
Upper Samurai	0.1		1.0		7.0		10.0	
Middle Samurai }			8.0		38.0		13.0	
Samurai with Skills }	3.5		4.0		11.0		30.0	
Lower Samurai	2.4		10.0		23.0		14.0	
Total Samurai		6.0		23.0		79.0		67.0
Commoners								
Farmers								
Farmers with Samurai Status	n.a.‡		3.0		4.0		3.0	
Village Officials and Wealthy Farmers	n.a.		14.0		1.0		7.0	
Peasants	n.a.		5.0		1.0		0.0	
Total Farmers			22.0		6.0		10.0	

TABLE 1 *(Continued)*

Feudal Status of Father	*Distribution of Population According to Feudal Status**	*Business Leaders* % (N = 189)	*Political Leaders* % (N = 94)	*Intellectual Leaders* % (N = 100)
Townsmen				
Prominent Merchants	n.a.	19.0	0.0	1.0
Small Merchants	n.a.	31.0	0.0	1.0
Townsmen with Professional Skills	n.a.	3.0	3.0	17.0
Clerks and Artisans	n.a.	2.0	0.0	1.0
Total Townsmen		55.0	3.0	20.0
Total Commoners	94.0	77.0	9.0	30.0
Total	100.0	100.0	100.0	100.0

* The total population was estimated to be about 33 million.
† Actually, the percentage is 0.007.
‡ Not available.
Source: Hiroshi Mannari, *The Business Elite, Nihon ni Okeru Keieisha no Jōken* [*The Business Elite, the Background of Business Leaders in Japan*] (Tokyo: Kodansha, 1965), p. 53.

much higher among those who had gone into traditional types of commercial activities, in direct competition with traditional merchants, than among those former samurai who ventured into modern industrial undertakings.

Let us briefly examine why the samurai mentality played such a vital role in the rise of the entrepreneurs in the early Meiji era. An important characteristic of the samurai mentality was a sense of public consciousness, a concern for public welfare, and a strong nationalistic spirit. These attitudes, as we noted earlier, were a product of the Bushido tradition and Confucian philosophy. This spirit undoubtedly spurred those who shared samurai values to rise to meet national challenges at the time of the great crisis of the need for modernization. In addition to the influence of this very basic ideological orientation, there were a number of other ways in which samurai mentality and training helped them to become an innovating elite not only in the political but also in the economic sphere.

A significant aspect of the samurai mentality was its commitment to education. As we noted in Chapter 1, learning was considered an indispensable status symbol of the samurai class. Those who wanted to identify with the samurai mentality could hardly ignore education.

In addition to formal learning, the samurai class enjoyed other advantages. As noted earlier, the Tokugawa era witnessed a growing trend for bureaucratization in the feudal administrative machinery. The decentralized system of feudal administration provided samurai with ample opportunities for acquiring administrative skills and expertise in the operation of a large bureaucratic organization.[14]

Neither should we overlook the fact that the initial burden of starting and managing modern industrial enterprises fell on the shoulders of the samurai bureaucrats. Moreover, economic deprivation experienced by the bulk of samurai toward the end of the Tokugawa era made them bolder and more aggressive in facing the risks and imponderables of the new era. Given the basic samurai mentality, their long-pent-up discontent with the feudal system found constructive outlets when class barriers to business activities were removed.

[14] R. P. Dore, *Education in Tokugawa Japan* (London: Routledge & Kegan Paul Ltd., 1965), p. 305.

Finally, the former samurai had the advantage of having close connections with the new regime, inasmuch as the Meiji leadership was made up largely of former samurai. "The Meiji leaders," as Hirschmeier succinctly puts it, "were not without sympathy for their former compeers."[15] The Meiji leadership soon became convinced that the best solution for the problems that stood in the way of expeditious industrialization lay in utilizing the talents of former samurai; this leadership was very "aware of the invaluable qualities that remained the distinctive mark of that class, such as education, social responsibility, self respect, and devotion to duty."[16] The Meiji leaders wisely foresaw that once the samurai grew aware of the inevitability of change and of the opportunities of the new era, they would become the key entrepreneurial element in the nation.[17] To reintegrate the former samurai class into the mainstream of the new society, the government introduced a series of measures.

Before we continue our examination of the entrepreneurial ideology of the early Meiji, we should note another significant reason the government had for encouraging former samurai to join in the industrialization effort. Their previous fame notwithstanding, the prominent mercantile families in large commercial centers produced but few outstanding entrepreneurs in the early Meiji era. The reason for this, at least in part, lay in the extreme conservative tradition of these prominent commercial families nurtured during the Tokugawa era, and their close identification with the feudal power structure.

Another factor that prevented members of the traditional merchant class from becoming the industrial leaders of the new era was their contemptuous attitude toward formal education. Industrialization placed business and learning in a new context. Machine technology and modern methods of production required a new type of knowledge, most of which had to be obtained from foreign sources. The merchant class, as a whole, was almost totally unprepared psychologically and educationally for the assimilation of this indispensable knowledge.

Some of the prominent commercial families, such as Mitsui, survived the traumas of the era and later blossomed into prominent Zaibatsu. But they, too, had been on the verge of collapse due to

[15] Johannes Hirschmeier, *The Origins of Entrepreneurship in Meiji Japan* (Cambridge, Mass.: Harvard University Press, 1964), p. 55.
[16] *Ibid.*
[17] *Ibid.*

their inability to adapt themselves to the new conditions. They were saved from total disintegration only through the infusion of progressive new talents into their midst, men whose mentality was basically different from the one shared by the traditional merchant class. We must conclude that, unlike the case of most European countries, feudalism in Japan was not displaced by the emergence of a progressive and liberal merchant class that spearheaded economic and social reforms.

Although the samurai and those who lived by their ideology were undoubtedly best prepared, both intellectually and emotionally, to become the new business leaders, these elements were seriously inhibited from embarking on business activities. They were restrained by the low social status traditionally associated with commercial activities and the low moral regard in which the pursuit of profit and personal aggrandizement were held. Undoubtedly, many of the displaced samurai were anxious, or at least willing, to seek new opportunities in economic activities, but they needed assurance that participating in the business world would not result in a total loss of their former status and honor.

There was still another factor that tended to inhibit the recruitment of former samurai into industrial activities: the enormous prestige and power accorded the government. In the early Meiji era, political activity was the focal point of the progress. It was to be expected, therefore, that government service would be most highly regarded by the capable and ambitious former samurai.

Thus, those determined to modernize Japan industrially faced many problems and conflicts in trying to fulfill their own role and in recruiting capable men to aid them in their endeavor. These strains became increasingly serious as the need for building a viable private business sector became evident. The country was obviously in great need of a new entrepreneurial ideology, suitable to the new socioeconomic demands, the fulfillment of which would further the industrialization of emerging Japan.

Indeed, a new ideology soon began to take shape. The Japanese version of an entrepreneurial ideology found its chief justification in the conviction that industrialization was indispensable to the national interest, and that it was of the utmost importance for Japan to build a powerful industrial base to assure its economic and political independence. Building modern industries was not only a vital goal of the Restoration, but it was essential to the very survival of the newly emerged Japan.

The crusade for industrialization for the sake of the country was quite consistent with both the Confucian-based samurai tradition and the spirit of the early Meiji era. The new ideology exhorted former samurai to regard industrial activity as an honorable way to serve the nation.[18] Significantly, the profit motive was virtually ignored, and the search for profit for its own sake was deliberately deemphasized. Central in the new business ideology was duty to the nation and service in the public interest.

Thus, the earlier Meiji business elite essentially rejected the Anglo-American capitalist creed that emphasized *economic individualism.* In this connection, Byron K. Marshall observes in a very recent study that the failure of the Japanese business elite to arrive at a new social consensus more appropriate for supporting their role in an industrialized society based on private enterprise is one of the most intriguing evidences of the persistence of traditional values in Meiji Japan.[19]

The Meiji entrepreneurial ideology sought to create a new image for businessmen by stressing that the industrialist was now basically different from the feudal merchant. He not only served the national interest but was also engaged in socially and economically productive and useful functions, as contrasted to the unproductive and ethically dubious commercial activities of the merchants of the Tokugawa era. In fact, to distinguish the newly created and enlightened role of the businessman from that of the parasitic *shonin* or merchant of the feudal era, a new term, *jitsugyoka,* was coined, meaning "a man who undertakes a real task."[20]

None was more influential in formulating and articulating the new entrepreneurial ideology of the Meiji era than Eiichi Shibusawa (1840–1931) and Yukichi Fukuzawa (1835–1905).

There is a general consensus that Shibusawa, a bureaucrat turned businessman, was the most outstanding business leader of the era. His life spanned almost the entire century, during which Japan was transformed from an obscure, isolated country to one of the most powerful nations in the world. Without question, Shibusawa played an important role in this transformation. He has been credited with initiating several hundred new enterprises. His busi-

[18] Miyamoto, *Kinsei Shonin Ishiki no Kenkyu,* p. 311.

[19] Byron K. Marshall, *Capitalism and Nationalism in Prewar Japan: The Ideology of the Business Elite* (Stanford, Calif.: Stanford University Press, 1967), p. 3.

[20] Hirschmeier, *Origins of Entrepreneurship,* p. 172.

ness interests cut across a wide variety of industries.[21] But our primary concern is not so much with his accomplishments — outstanding though they were — as with the ideology that he advocated.[22]

Shibusawa was among the first to recognize the need for creating a new status for businessmen and for formulating a viable ideology to guide their beliefs and actions. He was deeply convinced that entrepreneurship was indispensable to the process of industrialization, and was very much aware of the need for attracting capable and ambitious men to the new industries, in order to build a strong private business sector.

Though the son of a wealthy farmer, he received a samurai education, as many wealthy farmers' sons did toward the end of the Tokugawa era. He was deeply impressed by the Confucian philosophy in his formative years. Like many others, Shibusawa was caught up in the highly confusing but dynamic currents of his time.

The young Shibusawa went to France the year before the Restoration; this proved to be an invaluable experience. Upon his return to Japan, he was invited to join the newly organized Ministry of Finance, where he was shortly appointed to a high position. However, in the face of rising militarism and bureaucracy, he soon became disillusioned with government service.

Aware of the inherent danger in these developments, and thoroughly convinced of the need for a strong private business sector, Shibusawa resigned from public service at the age of thirty-four to devote all his energies to Japan's industrial development. By this time, he had become firmly convinced that the role of businessmen was just as vital to the welfare of the nation as that of bureaucrats and political leaders. Indeed, he felt a sense of mission to create a viable private sector and to help develop a modern, progressive entrepreneurial class in his country.

Shibusawa kept stressing the importance of industrial advancement for the new Japan. To him, a modern entrepreneur was a servant of his country as well as a guardian and promoter of eco-

[21] An outstanding source in English on the career and philosophy of Shibusawa in Johannes Hirschmeier, "Shibusawa Eiichi: Industrial Pioneer," in William W. Lockwood (ed.), *The State and Economic Enterprise in Japan* (Princeton: Princeton University Press, 1965), pp. 209–249.

[22] The following discussion on Shibusawa draws heavily from Takao Tsuchiya, *Nihon no Keieisha Seishin* [*Managerial Mentalities in Japan*] (Tokyo: Keizai, Ōraisha, 1963), pp. 126–167.

nomic progress. He constantly pointed out that the new breed of industrial leaders was different from the merchant class of the earlier era. He drew heavily on Confucian philosophy in extolling its concepts of virtue and morality to business leaders. In fact, he defined *jitsugyoka* to mean "someone who works with honesty for the establishment of industry."[23] He took great pains in pointing out that the popular Confucian notion of incompatibility between economic pursuits and morality was a misinterpretation of true Confucianism. He taught that economic activities, as long as they were performed with honesty, were quite consistent with Confucian morality. He stressed that business and morality walked hand in hand. Indeed, to him, productiveness was a way of practicing virtue.[24] As Takao Tsuchiya, a noted business historian, observes, this notion preached by Shibusawa was in fact a radical departure from the traditional interpretation of Confucian philosophy.[25]

Shibusawa sought to build a modern industrial Japan with an abacus and the Analects of Confucius. His speeches and writings were replete with quotations from the teachings of Confucius. Clearly, he felt that Western technology and business institutions alone would not convert Japan into a great industrial nation, for this firm ethical basis of Confucianism was indispensable.[26]

Another important ingredient in Shibusawa's ideology was liberal democratic thought. His liberalism first grew out of his hatred of feudalism and was later strengthened by his exposure to Western liberalism during his sojourn abroad.

He fought against the prevailing climate of *Kanson Minpi* — "the official honored and the people despised" — and was very much opposed to the tendency of business leaders to assume roles subordinate to political leaders. At the same time that he advanced vigorously the notion of industrialization for the sake of the nation, he warned businessmen of the danger of undue reliance on the government. He was greatly disturbed over the prevailing tendency among business leaders to seek special considerations and patronage from the government.

The third key element in Shibusawa's ideology was that of rationalism. The most tangible demonstration of this aspect of his

[23] Hirschmeier, *Origins of Entrepreneurship*, p. 172.
[24] Tsuchiya, *Nihon no Keieisha Seishin*, p. 157.
[25] *Ibid.*
[26] *Ibid.*

thinking can be seen in his enthusiastic acceptance of the concept of the joint stock company.[27] The family-based enterprise had been the prevailing type of business organization in Tokugawa Japan, and the traditional merchants and even the early Zaibatsu builders shunned the concept of the joint stock company. Shibusawa, however, saw inherent limitations for large-scale modern industry in the traditional family-based organization. Consequently, he actively promoted the concept of the joint stock company as a more rational form of modern business organization. Moreover, Shibusawa emphasized that a corporation should be managed according to democratic principles and that profit should not be monopolized.[28]

Closely related to his preference for rationalism was Shibusawa's appreciation of the importance of formal education. He emphasized education as a key requisite for a successful modern businessman. Shibusawa's contribution to the development in Japan of a modern business mentality cannot be overestimated. He did much toward raising the status of business leadership by preaching social responsibility and service to the nation. Although Shibusawa was an idealist — and not everyone shared his ideology wholeheartedly — he was the spokesman for the business community in many matters. Above all, he exemplified his ideology throughout his long life. In this respect, he had few, if any, equals among the Meiji entrepreneurs. He had indeed succeeded in combining the best of two worlds: Western technology, liberalism, and rationalism on the one hand, and the samurai tradition of public service on the other.[29]

Yukichi Fukuzawa, the great Meiji educator, contributed both to the evolution and the dissemination of the new ideology through his writing and teaching. He was described as "a man of self-reliance and self-respect with a world wide vision."[30] Born into a samurai family of lower rank, he, too, had opportunities to travel abroad in his youth. Upon returning to Japan, he wrote extensively on the conditions of the West. One of his well-known books, *Gakumon no Susume* (*An Exhortation to Learning*), sold 3.4 million copies in the five-year period between 1872 and 1876.[31] This book was an attack on Japan's traditional views on learning. Fukuzawa emphasized pragmatism in learning and taught that learning had

[27] *Ibid.*
[28] *Ibid.*
[29] Hirschmeier, "Shibusawa Eiichi: Industrial Pioneer," pp. 242–245.
[30] William T. De Bary, *Sources of the Japanese Tradition* (New York: Columbia University Press, 1964), p. 116.
[31] Hirschmeier, *Origins of Entrepreneurship,* p. 166.

to be liberated from a highly theoretical orientation and applied to daily life, particularly in the field of business.[32]

Seiyo Jijo (*Conditions in the West*) was another well-known Fukuzawa book in which he described what he had observed among Western nations. He strongly emphasized the respectability accorded to business in the West. For two reasons, Fukuzawa's influence as a writer and educator was greater than that of any of his contemporaries. He was able to maintain independence from the government, and his writings were couched in a practical and popular style.[33] Like Shibusawa, he was strongly imbued with Western liberalism and was deeply disturbed over what he thought was an excessive prestige accorded to public office, and the businessman's tendency for overreliance on political connections and patronage. He, too, strongly urged business leaders to be independent of the government.

Fukuzawa founded Japan's first modern institution of higher learning — Keio University. This school was designed to train potential business leaders. He thus contributed much to the early emergence of professional managers in Japan, and had much to do with shaping their ideology. His men were later to occupy key positions in various Zaibatsu groups.

In summary, the prevailing entrepreneurial ideology of the early Meiji years was a strange but tremendously effective fusion of intense but enlightened nationalism, Confucian morality, and an abiding partiality to Western liberalism, rationalism, and technology. It drew heavily on traditional samurai ideology with its emphasis on morality and duty. The new business ideology was steeped in Confucianism. Yasuzo Horie notes that in the early Meiji years, Confucianism played a role similar to that of the Protestant ethic in the West in helping to breed the entrepreneurial spirit.[34]

Hirschmeier, in his outstanding study of Meiji entrepreneurship, draws an interesting parallel between American Puritanism and Meiji business ideology. He states that the former was rooted in faith in God, the latter in faith in the nation. Puritanism was individualistic; its ethic centered on God and the individual. The Japanese business ethic centered on society and the individual, or the state and the individual; in other words, it sought the subordi-

[32] *Ibid.*

[33] De Bary, *Sources of the Japanese Tradition*, p. 117.

[34] Yasuzo Horie, "Entrepreneurship in Meiji Japan," in William W. Lockwood (ed.), *The State and Economic Enterprise in Japan*, p. 196.

nation of individual interests to the common good.[35] Thus, as Gustav Ranis observes, Japanese entrepreneurs in the early Meiji era were "community-centered," in contrast to autocentered entrepreneurship characterized by Schumpeter.[36]

Of course, it must be admitted that not all early Meiji entrepreneurs were in complete agreement with this ideology. We should not overstate the case — obviously not all of them were motivated by patriotism.

Just as the social backgrounds of the new entrepreneurs differed, so did their motives for choosing business careers. As Kozo Yamamura cautions in a recent article, there is a great danger of misinterpretation in indiscriminately attributing community-centered business thinking to every Meiji entrepreneur.[37] Some, like Shibusawa, gave up promising government positions to enter private business largely out of patriotism. Some chose business careers rather than government service only because they lacked proper connections in any of the several dominant factions of the Meiji political elite. There is no doubt, however, that the bulk of early Meiji entrepreneurs differed little in their basic motives from their counterparts in other times, other places, and other circumstances. Their primary motivation was the quest for personal gains and power. The ethical standards of some were indeed questionable.

Many of the so-called *seisho,* or businessmen with political influence, were not above exploiting fully their close ties with the government and extracting an enormous profit from their business dealings. They vied vigorously for government patronage and connections. In fact, many of the Zaibatsu gained their initial prominence by means that would hardly be ethically acceptable to contemporary business. Thus, the professed ideology of the early Meiji entrepreneurs, the ideology exemplified by Shibusawa, was not always practiced. Some accepted only those aspects of the ideology that happened to suit their purpose. For example, many Zaibatsu leaders looked upon the concept of the joint stock company with contempt. The most outspoken among them was Yataro Iwasaki, the founder of Mitsubishi. The House Rule of the Mitsubishi Zaibatsu clearly

[35] Hirschmeier, *Origins of Entrepreneurship,* p. 205.

[36] Gustav Ranis, "The Community-Centered Entrepreneur in Japanese Development," *Explorations in Entrepreneurial History,* III, No. 2 (December 1955), 80.

[37] Kozo Yamamura, "The Founding of Mitsubishi: A Case Study in Japanese Business History," *Business History Review,* XLI, No. 2 (Summer 1967), 160.

stated that, though it assumed the name of company, it differed from one in the ordinary sense. Everything, including praise, blame, and profit, belonged to the head of the family and every key decision was to be made by him. This orientation certainly differed from the notion of the joint stock company advanced by Shibusawa. Nevertheless, the Mitsubishi House Rule contained such admonitions as "Operate all enterprises with the national interest in mind," and "Never forget the pure spirit of public service and sincerity."

It is exceedingly difficult, if not futile, to attempt to measure the extent to which a particular Meiji entrepreneur was motivated by the quest for personal gains or by a sense of mission for the good of the country. Some undoubtedly professed the Shibusawa brand of ideology to conceal their selfish motives and gain public acceptance. Although the pursuit of profits was undeniably the single most important goal of the majority of early Meiji entrepreneurs, it is significant to note that the climate of the early Meiji era was such that the development of Shibusawa's brand of entrepreneurial ideology was required. Moreover, the pursuit of private gains alone was not adequate in explaining the conduct of most of the early Meiji entrepreneurs.

Before we blame the apparent discrepancy between the actual conduct of some early Meiji entrepreneurs and their public pronouncements on their hypocrisy and deceitfulness, we should take into account the circumstances of that era. It is important to note that to Meiji leaders a commitment to national goals did not preclude the quest for personal gains and power. As long as the overt ideology stressed the goals of the national collectivity, neither the government leaders themselves nor the public saw any conflict between the pursuit of national interests and the quest for personal gains.

The very circumstances of the early Meiji era were such that national needs and personal ambitions of the innovating business elite coincided to an amazing degree. The development of modern industry, though promoted largely for the sake of private gains, did, in fact, contribute significantly to the national goals of the country. Before concluding this section, let us examine the positive contributions made by the early Meiji entrepreneurial ideology.

First, the new ideology was successful in reestablishing the traditional status ascribed to men engaged in business activities. This helped resolve the intense conflict faced by many business leaders and those contemplating adopting business as a career in a highly status-conscious society. It helped recruit capable former samurai into industrial activities.

Second, in contrast to the tradition-bound merchants, former samurai, known for their initiative, ability, and experience, were very much needed in building Japan's key industries. The new ideology helped transform capable, educated, ambitious, but somewhat hesitant samurai, and those who subscribed to the samurai mentality, into a class of highly motivated *entrepreneurs*. The new ideology aided the process of national integration by giving displaced samurai (and those who had become disappointed with the new regime) opportunities to direct their energies and ambitions toward a positive end.

Third, though the new ideology was formulated by a small number of Meiji business leaders, the new entrepreneurial ideology became an ideal for businessmen to follow. Moreover, it inspired otherwise highly independent and individualistic entrepreneurs to cooperate in a number of key ventures. Indeed, on many occasions, individual differences were reconciled in the name of the society-oriented ideology — that is, for the sake of the country.

Fourth, this period saw the appearance of many overly optimistic and adventurous entrepreneurs. However, to the extent that the new ideology emphasized rationalism, it had a restraining effect on some of those who otherwise would have been overly enthusiastic and unrestrained, and helped achieve a healthy development of Japanese industries.

Fifth, early Meiji entrepreneurs had to learn by trial and error. Many made some costly mistakes. In the agony of failure and frustrations, the idealism of the new business ideology undoubtedly gave them strong moral support and courage to go on.

Sixth, as noted by Marshall, the strong bent for nationalism articulated in the new business ideology provided a rationale for government guidance of and assistance to private business. In this context, nationalism explicitly rejected the ideology of *laissez-faire* economics.[38]

Finally, because of the new ideology, some Meiji entrepreneurs were moved to initiate business enterprises that were important to the nation's development, regardless of their justification strictly from a business point of view. The ideology gave them a much

[38] Marshall, *Capitalism and Nationalism*, p. 18.

longer time span and a broader perspective in initiating new ventures. In essence, the entrepreneurial ideology of the early Meiji era was quite consistent with the economic and political climate of the day and was enormously helpful in resolving some of the basic conflicts and strains faced by the rising entrepreneurial class. The new entrepreneurial ideology was to exert a profound influence on Japanese business leaders for decades to come.

The Rise of Industrial Paternalism

With the rapid progress of industrialization, business leaders began to face conflicts and strains of quite a different nature. By the end of the Meiji era, the main ideological concern of business leaders had shifted in emphasis from that of creating a respectable self-image to that of finding an effective ideological justification and legitimacy to assure the continued loyalty and subordination of a growing industrial labor force.

The rapid pace of industrialization had brought about several important changes by the end of the Meiji era. It had resulted in an increase in the size, organizational complexity, and bureaucratization of business enterprises. It had changed skill requirements and qualifications of the work force. Industrialization, with an accompanying trend for urbanization, had created a distinct industrial proletariat class and had contributed to a weakening of the traditional authoritarian social structure that the early Meiji leaders had so painstakingly built.

These developments rendered antiquated the traditional relationship between employers and employees and began to threaten the absolute authority that management had been able to command vis-à-vis the workers. Throughout industrial history, a similar problem was faced by business leaders in other societies in the course of their industrialization. A lucid analysis of this development in a number of Western societies is provided by Reinhard Bendix in his outstanding book, *Work and Authority in Industry.*[39] The pattern of response to this challenging problem varied considerably among societies.[40] Significantly, Japanese business leaders, after considerable soul-searching, turned to the traditional family ideology for their solution of this very difficult problem. In the case of Japan, therefore, the traditional family system and ethic provided the

[39] Bendix, *Work and Authority in Industry,* pp. 22–116.
[40] *Ibid.*

ideological framework for achieving what Bendix has called "... the civic reintegration of the newly created industrial work force."[41] The application of the traditional family ideology in the modern industrial context gave rise to the well-known Japanese version of industrial paternalism, with its accompanying personnel practices.

What, then, was the evolutionary process of the Japanese version of industrial paternalism? What were its distinct features and subsequent adaptations? While the following analysis is based on a wide variety of sources, it owes much to an outstanding recent work on this general subject by Hiroshi Hazama.[42]

To gain an historical perspective, we shall begin by examining the ideologies governing employer-employee relationships in preindustrial Japan. Toward the end of the Tokugawa era, there were three distinct types of commercial and industrial activities: (1) the work of artisans, (2) merchants and their commercial house, and (3) large factories initiated and managed either by the Shogunate or by fief governments. Each had developed its own ideological basis for structuring employer-employee relationships.

In the artisan class, future craftsmen were recruited as young apprentices and received rigorous training from the master. Here, status was highly differentiated into three major categories: masters, craftsmen, and apprentices. The position of apprentices was further differentiated according to the length of apprenticeship to the master. It was customary to structure the relationship between senior and junior apprentices in a way similar to the older and younger brother relationship. Apprentices were not tied to their masters for life. Upon completion of their training and a period of obligatory services to the master, they were free to seek employment elsewhere. In the world of artisans, individual skills and craftsmanship were of prime importance. Skilled craftsmen often shifted from one master craftsman to another to gain further experience, to improve their skills, and to find better opportunities. The relationship between the master and his apprentices could best be characterized by the traditional teacher-pupil relationship. A craftsman was indebted to his master for his entire life for the training he received as an apprentice, and he was fully expected to pay homage and respect to his former master on various formal

[41] *Ibid.*, p. 434.

[42] Hiroshi Hazama, *Nihon Romu Kanrishi Kenkyu* [*Studies in the History of Japanese Labor and Management Relations*] (Tokyo: Diamond Co. Ltd., 1964).

occasions. Nevertheless he did enjoy considerable independence and freedom in changing his employment.

In the commercial house — the second category — the traditional concept of *ie,* or "House" (see Chapter 1), was applied for the first time in a business establishment. The "house" served as the basic organizational framework for commercial activities, arranging for unrelated persons to function together in an artificial or simulated kinship group. This was not surprising, because practically all commercial houses had initially been established by a real family. There was, at least at first, little distinction in this regard between economic and noneconomic activities.

Employment in the commercial house was clearly divided into two basic categories. In the first category were the apprentices, who were for the most part drawn from related or friendly families; they were considered members of the house and were given the status and privileges of kin, retaining this relationship for life. The second category consisted of servants who, unlike apprentices, were not considered members of the house; usually they were not allowed most of the privileges associated with house membership.

The emphasis in apprenticeship, in commercial houses, was on learning through practical experience. Apprentices were highly differentiated in status according to length of service; they made very slow progress up the clearly defined hierarchical ladder. After many years of faithful service to a house, they were given an opportunity to set up their own business as a branch of the main enterprise, with the main house supplying, in most cases, much of the needed capital and business connections. The branch house was allowed to operate under the name of the main house. In fact, the offshoot was a branch of the main establishment in every respect, regardless of the fact that in the great majority of cases, no blood relationship existed between the head of the main house and that of a newly created branch. At least for the first several generations, a close business and ceremonial relationship was maintained between the main enterprise and its branch houses. As a result, the simulated kinship tie established when an apprentice was first taken into the business lasted well beyond his lifetime, involving his descendants.

As commercial activities expanded toward the end of the Tokugawa period, it became increasingly common for apprentice clerks to stay on in the master's house as managers, instead of branching out on their own. They served in the master's house until their retirement, after which their economic needs were fully taken care of by the house. In some cases, these managers gained considerable influence not only over the business but also over the master's household. The master himself usually presided over the commercial house with absolute authority, but if he was found incompetent, the chief clerk was placed in actual charge of the operations. In such cases, the power of the chief clerk was considerably greater than that of the nominal head. Bellah points out that in commercial houses at this time, the collectivity goal was uppermost, and, when necessary, status was superseded by performance.[43] Not infrequently, the manager in charge married into the house to become the legitimate heir.

The third type of economic activity in the late Tokugawa period was a factory managed by feudal authorities. The organization of these factories paralleled closely that of the feudal bureaucracy. The managerial posts were filled by officials appointed by the fief government; workers were drawn exclusively from among commoners. Since most officials lacked the technical competence to train and supervise factory workers, this task was largely performed by foreign experts and by first-line supervisors selected from among the workers themselves.

Generally, the samurai administrators maintained a proper but detached attitude toward their workers. The relationship between the managers and the managed in fief-owned factories did not have the closeness and intimacy found in commercial houses; it was conditioned by official feudal class distinctions and formal standards of behavior prescribed for each class.

Their superior status automatically entitled the samurai officials to loyalty and obedience from the workers recruited from the inferior class. This was entirely in accordance with Tokugawa class relationships characterized by authoritarian domination on the one hand and absolute submission on the other. Managerial status was legitimatized by the official code of class distinctions.

The preceding examination of late Tokugawa economy reveals that Japanese entrepreneurs in the early Meiji era had three quite distinct types of traditions to draw on in formulating their ideology toward workers. As we shall see later, all three of these patterns exerted considerable influence.

According to Hazama, the first half-century of Japan's indus-

[43] Robert N. Bellah, *Tokugawa Religion: The Values of Pre-Industrial Japan* (Glencoe, Ill.: The Free Press, 1957), p. 50.

trialization may be divided into three relatively distinct stages from the point of view of the ideological developments governing employer-employee relationships.[44] Although the specific years selected to identify each of these three stages may be somewhat arbitrary, it is important to note that the Japanese industrial system had gone through two quite different stages before it turned to the third, the traditional family ideology, to structure employer-employee relationships.[45]

The first stage, as seen by Hazama, corresponds to the initial phase of Japan's industrialization, in which the government was preeminent as promoter, owner, and manager. At this time, the organization and management of factories largely followed the pattern established during the late Tokugawa era: Managerial posts were filled by samurai turned bureaucrats, and workers continued to be recruited largely from former commoners. Foreign technical experts and supervisors selected from among skilled workers continued to perform many of the day-to-day managerial and supervisory functions. While feudal class distinctions were officially abolished shortly after the Restoration, they still persisted in practice. A fundamental status difference between managers and workers continued to exist, and the management's attitude toward workers remained much the same as that of the late Tokugawa era.

Working conditions during this period were considerably better than what followed in the next stage. Because of government ownership, profit was not a critical consideration in the first stage. Moreover, the widespread participation of foreign experts in day-to-day management helped to create a satisfactory working atmosphere. During this period, virtually none of the forthcoming paternalistic personnel practices were in evidence. A considerable degree of employment mobility was enjoyed, particularly by workers. With the gradual emergence of private enterprise, competition for skilled workers trained in government-owned factories became intense, and many were lured away to private enterprises by the offer of higher wages. The wage level in government-owned factories was determined largely on the basis of ability, as evaluated by the foreign experts. Welfare facilities of various sorts were lacking. Thus, during the first two decades of industrialization, the relationship between managers and the managed in these government-owned factories differed little from that of the late feudal era.

[44] Hazama, *Nihon Romu Kanrishi Kenkyu,* p. 32.
[45] *Ibid.*

The government's decision, in 1880, to sell all but a few of its factories to private interests marked the end of the first stage and ushered in the second stage of industrialization. This second stage roughly covers the period between 1880 and the end of the Meiji era in 1912. Hazama labels this stage as the "primitive" era in the history of Japanese industrialization.[46]

This second stage differed from the first in several important respects.[47] During this period, the pace of industrialization became greatly accelerated. The successful assimilation of Western industrial technology and the accumulation of capital greatly contributed to a rapid rise of industrial output. The scale of enterprises greatly expanded, and the level of technology became more sophisticated. While light industries still remained predominant, the wars against China (1894–1895) and Russia (1904–1905) greatly stimulated the development of heavy industries. Since most of the industries were now in the private sector, profit became the dominant goal of management. Entrepreneurs ruthlessly pursued profit opportunities. Though the government continued to extend its protection and patronage to large-scale enterprises, the competitive pressures, on both the domestic and international markets, began to mount. During this period, a hard core of Japanese workers skilled in Western technology began to emerge. Japanese managers replaced most of the foreign experts in the management of large-scale enterprises, thus precipitating the rise of a managerial class. Education rather than feudal status had become increasingly important for entry into managerial ranks.

During this period, the industrial labor class consisted of three main categories. Because of the importance of the textile industry, the largest segment of industrial workers were young unmarried women recruited from rural areas. These girls were hired on a short contract basis, as they were not expected to remain permanently in industrial employment.

The second category consisted of those referred to as *dekasegi*, workers whose roots were on farms but who participated in wage labor activities intermittently. This group supplied the bulk of unskilled male workers.

The third category was made up of skilled workers affiliated with independent labor contractors, commonly called *oyakata*, or master workmen. *Oyakata* provided workers for factories on a short-term

[46] *Ibid.*
[47] *Ibid.*, pp. 32–34.

contractural basis, as they were needed. Most of these *oyakata* had learned their skills from foreign experts or skilled Japanese workers in fief- or government-operated factories; they later became independent labor contractors.[48] Some influential *oyakata* had as many as several hundred workers under them. Thus, skilled male workers were not direct employees of the enterprise; they were hired through an independent labor contractor. The latter performed all the key personnel functions, including recruiting, training, supervising, and rewarding the men. In this respect, the *oyakata* system differed little from subcontracting. The *oyakata* maintained a highly personalized and particularistic relationship with his cadres of skilled workers; and the ideology governing their relationship closely resembled that of the feudal master-artisan relationship. Individual skills and craftsmanship continued to be important.

Only a very small number of the skilled male workers were employed by the same employer for an extended period of time. The great majority drifted back and forth, either between farm and factory or from one factory to another.[49]

In any of the above three categories, the management hardly felt a need for having to formulate its own firm ideological basis for directing and controlling workers. The female textile workers and the unskilled *dekasegi* were only partially and temporarily involved in industrial employment. In the case of skilled workers, they were not directly employed by the enterprise, and the management had little direct commitment to them; independent labor contractors assumed the entire responsibility for personnel management and maintained tight discipline through a particularized and personalized relationship. Under these circumstances, the attitude of any of the three categories of workers was of little concern to the management. At the same time, their managerial authority was not challenged. Workers were, on the whole, respectful of managerial authority, diligent, and obedient. Thus, having no need for a new ideology, management simply held on to the traditional authoritarian ideology of the previous era.

Management continued to hold authoritarian views and to seek justification for its absolute control over workers through the clearly defined status distinctions. By virtue of status superiority, manage-

[48] For a detailed English description of this system, see Solomon B. Levine, "Labor and Collective Bargaining," in William W. Lockwood (ed.), *The State and Economic Enterprise in Japan,* pp. 642–648.

[49] *Ibid.*, p. 642.

ment fully expected the socially inferior workers to remain loyal and obedient.

We must therefore conclude that the managerial ideology toward workers during this period was based primarily on the concept of reciprocal obligations based on status differences between the superior and the inferior. It resembled closely the feudal master-servant relationship and had a strong regulatory orientation.[50] With the general lack of concern for the welfare of workers, and in the face of mounting competitive pressures, it is readily understandable why Japan began to experience the evils of industrial revolution experienced earlier in Europe. These evils became particularly virulent in Japan around the last decade of the nineteenth century and culminated in the first decade of the twentieth century.

Describing the process of Japan's industrial development, Lockwood observes that Japanese industrialization, in spite of the contrary impression often given, brought its share of human suffering and social evils. People were pushed as well as pulled to the urban industrial centers, where the conditions were no better than in the poverty-stricken rural sector.[51] After noting that the factory owners experienced great difficulties in recruiting efficient and reliable workers, Lockwood describes the plight of industrial labor as follows:

> Peasant daughters, many of them under sixteen, furnished a large share of early recruits. In 1896, for example, 261,000 out of 435,000 operatives in private plants employing ten or more workers were women. Prisoners and vagrants were also extensively employed. The iron discipline, the working conditions, the false representations in hiring, the long hours — typically eleven, twelve, or more — all made for reluctance to enter factory industry even in this overpopulated country. The turnover of labor was constant, and labor piracy gave employers much difficulty. One investigator in the nineties concluded that half of the factory workers deserted every six months.[52]

Taira cites a study that indicated that, in the cotton textile industry, the leading sector during Japan's "takeoff" period (1880–1900), the average employment contract was for three years. In many

[50] Hazama, *Nihon Romu Kanrishi Kenkyu*, p. 45.
[51] William W. Lockwood, *The Economic Development of Japan: Growth and Structural Change, 1868–1938* (Princeton: Princeton University Press, 1954), pp. 484–485.
[52] *Ibid.*, p. 485.

factories, however, one-third to one-half of the workers deserted before the end of six months. In half of the factories studied, none had remained on the job at the end of the contract period.[53]

The deplorable conditions that existed in the nation's factories shortly after the turn of the century are revealed in the following data provided by a large textile mill with over 4,000 employees. During the year 1900, the mill recruited 6,085 new employees (1,323 male and 4,762 female), but during the same year it lost a total of 7,701 employees (1,877 male and 5,824 female). The reasons given for the workers' departures were strongly suggestive of the existing conditions—82 percent escaped, 14 percent were dismissed, 3 percent had to return home because of illness, and 1 percent died.[54]

Extensive exploitation of workers continued even after the turn of the century. Working conditions remained most primitive. Raw abuses of the sweatshop — child labor, slum living, long hours, unattended illness, and high accident rates — were commonplace in the nation's factories. There were no protective labor standards of any kind. This was, indeed, the primitive era in the history of Japanese industrialization.

What were the factors responsible for the deplorable labor conditions? What had become of the benevolence that management, as a superior class, traditionally owed to the workers as an inferior class? A key negative factor was, of course, the overabundant supply of labor. The overpopulated and poverty-stricken rural sector provided an almost unlimited reservoir of cheap labor. The mounting competitive pressure and the drive for profit were other important factors. "The cold calculations of industrial capitalism,"[55] to borrow Lockwood's apt phrase, tended to supersede all other considerations, including humane concern for employees.

Employers consciously or unconsciously shifted the burden of competition to the working class, who had little choice but to bear the strain as best they could. Many entrepreneurs, though basically sympathetic to the plight of the workers, were simply too involved with the challenges of meeting the unfamiliar problems of expansion, new machine technology, and strong competitive pressure.

[53] Koji Taira, "The Labor Market in Japanese Employment," *British Journal of Industrial Relations*, II (July 1964), 216.

[54] Hiroshi Hazama, *Nihon teki Keiei no Keifu* [*Evolution of Japanese Management*] (Tokyo: Nihon Nōritsu Kyōkai, 1963), p. 102.

[55] Lockwood, *The Economic Development of Japan*, p. 557.

The rapid growth in the scale of enterprises was still another factor causing the dismal labor conditions. With the growth in the size of enterprises, it became necessary to recruit employees from different and distant parts of the country. This, of course, resulted in a lesser bond of understanding and empathy between employers and employees than had existed when both had shared close local ties. Moreover, rapid growth in the size of enterprises demanded a new type of leadership and administrative skills. Some managers, who had been benevolent in a small organization, where it was possible to maintain close person-to-person relationships, ceased to be similarly effective in a larger and more bureaucratic organization. It was during this period that an industrial proletarian class began to emerge. It consisted of former samurai, artisans, and merchants who failed to adapt themselves to the drastically changed environment, and of unskilled workers who were drawn to urban centers from poverty-stricken rural areas. As this class became the major source of the labor supply, whatever empathy had existed earlier between the managers and the managed steadily eroded. The increasing importance attached to education as an avenue for entry into the managerial ranks also tended to accentuate this cleavage. Many of the managers had been, by this time, directly recruited from colleges, and, by and large, they possessed neither on-the-job experience nor close emotional ties with the working class.

At the same time, the government, too, was almost totally unconcerned with the welfare of the rising industrial labor class and was unresponsive to its needs during much of the period. Workers expressed their protest against maltreatment and deprivation through a variety of means, including violence. However, their protests were sporadic and ineffectual, for they lacked organizational skill and did not have a leadership to represent their case effectively. Neither had they developed a close class consciousness and unity.

Around the turn of the century, the plight of the industrial workers began to attract the attention and engage the sympathies of liberal-minded intellectuals, journalists, and politicians. Their points of view and convictions differed considerably, but the majority looked upon the problem from the vantage point not of labor-management relations, but of humanitarian considerations. They viewed the mistreatment of workers as a social evil and called for a more compassionate attitude toward them. Several books, written to expose the miseries of factory employees, stirred up public opinion and criticism against employers.[56]

Gradually, the government began to show some concern about the appallingly primitive working conditions. Though the rising public sympathy for the workers was partially responsible for this trend, the government's concern was largely prompted by fear that the maltreatment of workers would have serious adverse effects on the achievement of the national goal of "building a wealthy nation and a strong army." The continued harsh exploitation of labor, it feared, might too seriously deplete human resources and thus slow down Japan's industrial progress.[57] Also, the government became aware of the need to protect the health of young female factory workers — the future mothers of the country's soldiers — from industrial abuses and maltreatment.[58]

As a consequence, in 1911, at the close of the Meiji era, the Factory Act was enacted to regulate industrial working conditions. True to industrial history, the Factory Act was strongly opposed by the business community. It contended that such legislation would be a serious encroachment on managerial prerogatives and freedoms. Furthermore, it claimed that the Act would slow down the industrial progress of Japan and thus subvert her national interests. Consequently, the business community launched a most vigorous campaign against the passage of the legislation. In the course of this abortive campaign against the Factory Act, we detect the first formal articulation of the paternalistic ideology. Management began to extol the virtues of the traditional family ideology and to emphasize that the problems of employer-employee relations could be approached much more effectively through the application of the familial concepts of benevolence and reciprocity, rather than through labor legislation or organized labor movements. They insisted that the employer-employee relationship in a large modern factory could be modeled after the pattern of the parent-child relationship in the traditional family system. Management now also began to insist that Japanese employers, unlike their Western counterparts, had always shown benevolent attitudes toward their employees. They further advocated that the paternalistic approach

[56] Hazama, *Nihon teki Keiei no Keifu,* pp. 102–103.
[57] *Ibid.*
[58] *Ibid.*

based on the familial virtues was inherently superior to the impersonal approach commonly used in the West, and that it was infinitely more congruous with Japanese tradition.

It is highly worth noting that industrial paternalism began to be advocated by business leaders only when their managerial authority and legitimacy was seriously questioned, and when a new ideology was being sought to serve as a basis for structuring employer-employee relationships under a set of new conditions. It is equally significant to observe that, for the solution to this problem, business leaders turned to one of the key traditional sets of social values by resurrecting the virtues and ideals of the traditional Japanese familial ideology.

Meanwhile, another significant development was taking place that further increased the usefulness of the evolving paternalistic ideology. By the end of the first decade of the twentieth century, the Japanese economy had reached a new level of development. As we noted in the previous chapter, it was during these years that capital-intensive and technically oriented industries came into their own. The pace of industrialization was further accelerated during the decade of the 1910's. Significantly, this was the period in which the Zaibatsu became firmly established in the Japanese industrial system. The Zaibatsu pressed actively for diversification and expansion into capital-intensive and technically oriented fields. Thus, the structure of the Japanese industry began to undergo a rather basic change, which, in turn, forced management to revise its traditional personnel practices.

First of all, the high labor turnover and absenteeism that were characteristic of the earlier era were no longer tolerable because of the operating requirements of heavy industry. Heavy industry, dependent on sophisticated technology, needed a well-trained, skilled, and stable corps of employees. It could not be operated by young female workers employed on a short-term basis. Neither could it be run by unstable, unskilled workers who drifted back and forth between their farms and industrial employment. Moreover, the ubiquitous introduction of machine technology rendered the *oyakata* system antiquated.

To build a stable corps of workers with sufficient technical background, the management of large-scale modern enterprises now took two steps.[59] First, it tried to persuade the *oyakata* and their

[59] Levine, "Labor and Collective Bargaining," pp. 645–649.

workers to join the ranks of company employees in order to reduce the undesirable mobility of skilled workers. Second, it began to recruit company employees directly from the secondary schools and established a system of in-plant training to teach the young recruits specific skills needed in the plant's production process. The cooperation of *oyakata* and their skilled workers was also needed in this process. The managers, most of whom by this time were college graduates, possessed neither the technical skills nor the experience for providing technical training to new recruits.

To induce *oyakata* and their workers to become employees of their firms, managers offered a series of incentives, including the status of full-time employees, guarantees against dismissal, set salaries and salary advancements. The status hierachy of the *oyakata* system was recognized, and *oyakata* were given supervisory positions. As noted earlier, *oyakata* maintained a very particularistic and personal relationship with their retinues, whose status in the system was determined according to the length of attachment to the *oyakata*. Thus, as Levine points out, the pre-existing system of the *oyakata* wage relationship became fused with the new technological and production requirements for skilled labor.[60] Fresh recruits started at the bottom of the *oyakata*-craftsman hierarchy and progressed slowly up its long ladder. Since the young recruits were to become employees of the firm, and were expected to stay with the firm permanently, management began to stress personal qualities, such as obedience and dependability, in selecting these young men.

The skilled workers had developed a highly particularized and loyal relationship with their *oyakata*. Now this loyalty had to be transferred to the company. Management had to turn men formerly tied to different *oyakata*, through a highly particularistic relationship, into a cohesive work force closely identified with the enterprise. In essence, management faced the task of creating what Bendix has called an "internalized ethic" of work performance.[61] In general, management now began to pay much greater attention to the needs of employees than before.

Against this background emerged the personnel practices that are considered distinct features of the Japanese managerial system: lifetime employment, a seniority-based reward system, and heavy involvement of management in the lives of the workers. Nor did

[60] *Ibid.*, p. 647.
[61] Bendix, *Work and Authority in Industry*, p. 204.

management neglect the ideological front. The traditional familial ideology was used as a model for factory organization, with the purpose of eliciting workers' loyalty to, and close identification with, the company. The company was regarded as one vast family, with management playing the benevolent "father" role and the workers accepting the submissive role of "children." Moreover, management justified the new personnel practices on the basis of the virtues of the family ideology. Permanent ties to the enterprise, status differentiation on the basis of length of attachment to the firm, and the firm's involvement in the private affairs of employees were ideologically justified in terms of Japan's unique familial tradition, and they were hailed as unique virtues of the Japanese managerial system. By linking these personnel practices to the family ideology, management sought to maximize its emotional appeal to the workers.

The traditional family ideology was also quite effective in meeting another very serious problem of the period. We noted in the previous chapter that the decades of the 1910's and the 1920's witnessed some significant changes in the social fabric of the nation. The tight authoritarian social control of the Meiji era had loosened considerably. New values began to erode the groundwork of the traditional loyalty and solidarity system, especially in the urban industrial proletariat. The new class consciousness led to social unrest, challenging the traditional authoritarian order. This social unrest, influenced by Western doctrines of anarchism and communism, reached a new intensity. Significantly, for the first time, Japan now began to experience serious problems of class struggle. Whereas sharp class distinctions had been an integral feature of the Japanese society for many years, conflicts between classes were virtually unknown; the lower classes, who were always controlled by the authoritarian elite, had been content with their subordinate role.

The labor movement, now better organized and under much more militant and sophisticated leadership, had gained in strength and had begun to compete seriously with management for the worker's loyalty. Beginning in the 1910's, this surge of organized labor activities resulted in a significant increase, in both number and intensity, of disputes with labor.

Managerial authority was thus threatened. Here, again, the paternalistic ideology was well suited to combat such a trend. Emphasizing that an enterprise was one vast family, management sought to establish rapport with employees as well as to elicit their close identification with, and solidarity to, the enterprise. Employees were repeatedly told that their real security and opportunity lay not with labor movements in the Western style, but with the enterprise managed in the best tradition of the Japanese familial virtues.

Thus, the stressing of familial paternalism as the central aspect of the Japanese managerial ideology of this period was not fortuitous. That familial paternalism was used as a deliberate means to solve economic, political, technological, and social problems specific to the era of intense industrialization and urbanization cannot be overemphasized. The ideology of industrial paternalism was articulated only after a desperate search by management for viable ideological appeals to meet these problems. Paternalism proved eminently suited to the prevailing climate of the era.

As we have already noted, the family system represented the very core of traditional Japanese social values. It had become highly institutionalized and intrinsically linked to the legal and political system of the period. The attributes of an ideal family were clearly articulated and received the highest official sanction. Moreover, the Japanese had developed, with a consistency almost unparalleled in any other society, a tradition of structuring nonfamilial social groups on the pattern of the family.

It is also significant to note that, beginning around the turn of the century, there was a parallel movement led by conservative *political* and *educational* leaders to reemphasize the family system in order to arrest the tide of social unrest. They, too, were appalled by the rising trend for loosening the tight authoritarian social structure, and they turned almost instinctively to the family ideology for reassurance.[62]

One should also take into account the fact that this was the period in which the Zaibatsu system attained its preeminence and gained monopolistic control of Japan's large-scale industries. The Zaibatsu was structured and organized after the pattern of the traditional family system, making itself consistent with the traditional paternalistic ideology.

A handful of Zaibatsu, having gained almost complete control of Japan's large-scale industries, were now financially more than ca-

[62] Takeyoshi Kawashima, *Ideology Toshite no Kazokuseido* [*The Family System as an Ideology*] (Tokyo: Iwanami Shoten, 1964), p. 51.

pable of providing their employees with the tangible benefits promised by paternalism. The high-sounding promises would have held little appeal to employees without benefits and privileges.

However, the family ideology of these later decades differed in emphasis from that of the early Meiji era. In the earlier years, strong authoritarian relationships and obligatory filial piety, such as in the idealized samurai family, were stressed. This was to be expected, since the feudal tradition was still strong and the ruling oligarchy was determined to have a docile and submissive populace, responsive to their authoritarian control.

With the burgeoning of industrialization and urbanization, however, the traditional family structure had begun to disintegrate, slowly but surely, and the established authority structure began to fall apart. We should also note that, despite the many years of concentrated effort on the part of the political elite to indoctrinate the masses with the belief in the virtues of the traditional family system, by far not every aspect of it had been accepted by the masses. A certain disparity had always existed between the idealized image of the family and the character of the family in reality. This distortion of the ideal image was prevalent particularly among families in the lower social strata. Contrasting the ideal family system of the upper classes with that of the commoners, Kawashima notes that in the latter, especially in the typical rural family, the relationship between members was much more cooperative and there was far less insistence on absolute authority and piety.[63]

This difference was further widened with the advent of industrialization and urbanization. Reflecting these developments, the official family ideology underwent a subtle change in emphasis, beginning around the first decade of the twentieth century. Without undermining the ideological virtues of the ideal family, the emphasis gradually shifted from the strong authoritarian orientation to that of family solidarity, harmony, and cooperation.

Complete interdependence between the interests of the family and that of the individual member was stressed. The individual member was to identify himself completely with the family collectivity. In fact, he was required to lose himself in the attainment of the goals of the family collectivity. The preservation of close emotional ties between family members was also emphasized. With the stress on close intrafamily solidarity and intensive identification

[63] *Ibid.*, pp. 122–123.

with the family collectivity, individual freedom and independent actions were denied. It also emphasized that each family member was given a definitely ascribed status in the family hierarchy, and he was to be content with his station within this hierarchical structure and was expected to do his part to the best of his ability.

The ultimate objective of the ruling elite was to arrest the tide of social unrest and the developing class struggles by inducing the entire society to live according to the traditional family ideology. The masses were indoctrinated to extend family solidarity to a complete identification with the nation; the individual was to devote himself totally to the fulfillment of his nation's goals. Viewing the entire country as one vast family, the ruling elite exhorted the masses to reject the class struggle above all — especially when it showed a Marxian orientation — as completely alien to the best traditions of Japan. The rich and the poor, the educated and the uneducated, the socially superior and the socially inferior should be equally content with the conditions of their lives and should do their part to the best of their ability for the good of the whole society.

This ideology, as applied by management, emphasized that an enterprise, regardless of its size, was like one family. Management argued that whereas hierarchical differentiation was necessary in any large organization, in Japanese industrial relations the hierarchical distinctions differed from the class distinctions between management and labor in Western business enterprises — in Japan, every permanent employee was a member of the enterprise family and, as such, there could be no conflicting interests and goals among them.

From the company president down to the humblest worker, all employees must be united in purpose and in their devotion to the enterprise. Each member of the enterprise must be content with his station in the organization and do his utmost for the good of the enterprise. Close emotional ties, solidarity, and harmony among members of the enterprise were also stressed.

It is important to recognize that the Japanese management ideology differed basically from the Western concept of cooperation between labor and management. While the latter is based on explicit recognition of management and labor as two distinct entities, Japanese industrial paternalism does not recognize such a distinction.

We should also note that the new ideology was a significant departure from that of the previous era. The basic premise of the ideology of the earlier era was the categorical status difference between the managers and the managed. It drew heavily on the feudal Confucian-oriented superior-subordinate relationships. It was highly authoritarian in character and had a strong regulatory element. In contrast, the new ideology sought managerial legitimacy in family-like harmony, unity, and solidarity, as well as in emotional ties among members of the enterprise.

We should point out, however, that the material sharing of family members was not extended to all of the factory employees. The primary reason for the industrial paternalistic ideology was to achieve work force stabilization. Built into this paternalistic system, however, was a danger of overachieving the original objective.[64] Management was keenly aware of the extreme rigidity that such a system, with its perpetuation of employment, would impose on its operations. To retain operating flexibility, the firms chose to restrict the extension of paternalistic privileges only to a cyclically justifiable minimum level. The rest of the labor force was to be supplied by temporary workers who served as a buffer. These were hired and dismissed depending on personnel requirements. The temporary workers were in no sense members of the enterprise "family," and they did not enjoy any of the privileges associated with industrial "family" membership.

The paternalistic ideology would have been futile had it not been accepted by the employees. It is relevant, therefore, to examine the prevailing attitude of the workers. For several reasons, they enthusiastically responded to this ideology. We should note that industrial paternalism was primarily offered to male workers who had become increasingly important in the nation's industrial system. It had a great deal of appeal to them. They were, themselves, heads of their own families, or at least potentially so. Unlike young female workers, they were permanently committed to industrial employment. Although they had close rural ties, once they left their villages, the poverty there precluded their returning permanently to the protective umbrella of the family collectivity. They somehow had to sustain themselves in the unfamiliar industrial environment.

To these men, paternalistic personnel practices — the guarantee against dismissal, regularized wage increases to meet the rising needs of a growing family, and fringe benefits — held a great deal of appeal. The men found a new type of security in the industrial collectivity. In addition to these tangible benefits, paternalism held

[64] Taira, "Labor Market in Japanese Employment," p. 218.

a strong emotional appeal as well. The great majority of this new proletariat, as recent migrants from the rural areas, still closely identified with the rural value system in which the family ideology occupied a central place. In fact, the very insecurity and isolation of urban life made the security provided by familial ideology all the more important to them. Against this background of dislocation, it is readily understandable why these men found the paternalistic management ideology very attractive. Industrial paternalism undoubtedly facilitated the very difficult process of transition from a rural life to industrial employment. This ideology appealed even to urban-bred workers whose number was gradually increasing. The reason for its appeal was that by this time, compulsory six-year schooling had become widespread, and, as noted earlier, ideological indoctrination stressing the virtues of the family tradition, loyalty to the nation, and diligence was the core of this elementary educational program.

The fact that paternalistic privileges were extended to workers on a selective basis enhanced their value in the eyes of the fortunate minority who received them. Once they attained this enviable status, the men worked diligently to retain it.

We should observe, however, that the paternalistic ideology, though enthusiastically espoused by the great majority of business leaders, was not unanimously accepted by management. A small group of progressive businessmen and liberally inclined opinion leaders were reluctant to accept it. Some questioned the practical value of applying the familial tradition to large-scale enterprises. Others objected on ethical grounds, claiming that the familial virtues were used as a means to "buy" employees' loyalty. A number of progressive businessmen called for the recognition of the basic rights of individual workers. In their opinion, paternalism, by its very definition, suggested the hierarchical superior-inferior relationship between management and worker. Paternalism as articulated by the business leaders of the time consisted of condescending measures to employees meant to placate discontented workers. These progressive elements within the managerial class felt that real cooperation could only be achieved when management and workers enjoyed equal status and rights.[65] The proponents of these views were obviously influenced by Western liberalism and democratic thought. But they were a very small minority.

The prevailing climate was, on the whole, much more compatible

[65] Hazama, *Nihon Romu Kanrishi Kenkyu,* pp. 50–56.

with and hospitable to familial paternalism. In summary, we should like to emphasize that the paternalistic management ideology based on the familial tradition was a deliberate and rational response on the part of Japanese business leaders to the specific economic and social strains they faced. This point can hardly be overemphasized. Although the nature of the problems facing them was basically similar to that encountered by management in other nations in the process of industrialization, the pattern of management response in Japan was uniquely Japanese; it was consistent with the country's historical legacy and the existing social and political climate. Some of the personnel practices associated with this ideology may appear impractical when judged by Western standards and experience, but they were eminently suited to the conditions that existed in Japan *at the time.* Judging by the results, they were, indeed, very effective.

4

Today's Japanese Executives and Their Ideologies

The Emergence of a New Business Leadership

Postwar Japan has witnessed the emergence of a new business leadership, which has played a significant role in promoting the rapid postwar growth of the Japanese economy. In this chapter, we shall first review the circumstances under which the postwar business leadership emerged and analyze its background, power, and role in contemporary Japanese society; an examination of the ideologies of postwar Japanese executives and the factors contributing to their formulation will follow.

Among a number of significant developments in the immediate aftermath of World War II, three factors deserve special mention in our discussion of the rise of a new business leadership.

First, the Occupation-directed economic reforms, among other things, dissolved the entrenched Zaibatsu system, which subsequently led to the wide diffusion of corporate ownership. This resulted in the separation of ownership and management in Japan's leading corporations. The real control of these corporations then shifted to, and continues to remain in the hands of, professional managers who had come up from the ranks.[1] A major revision of Japan's Commercial Code, in 1950, further assured the dominant position of professional managers in the corporate organization. Among a number of other significant changes, it reduced the power of the shareholders and significantly increased the power of the board of directors. The Code revision even opened a way for non-shareholders to become directors of a corporation.

[1] Professional managers are defined as those who attain managerial positions on the basis of alleged or demonstrated competence rather than because of their kinship to a family or partisanship to a political regime.

Although it is true that Japan witnessed the rise of a professional managerial class relatively early in the process of her industrialization, it was not until this later period that the professional managers attained preeminence. In the prewar Zaibatsu, *banto,* or hired executives, played an important role in the management of their far-flung enterprises. In fact, in some instances, the Zaibatsu families totally withdrew from the active management of their enterprises, and instead hired executives who were carefully selected on the basis of personal qualifications and competence. The high prestige enjoyed by Zaibatsu firms enabled them to attract the most capable graduates from the nation's leading universities. The *banto* were imbued with the spirit of hard work, perseverance, and unfaltering loyalty to the enterprise as well as to the Zaibatsu family. And they were abundantly rewarded for their services.

Although the role of *banto* in the Zaibatsu system must not be minimized, these hired executives nevertheless had to work under the strict house rules as well as under the general direction of the family. Professional managers in contemporary Japan work under no such restrictions and therefore enjoy far greater power and freedom in management of their enterprises than did their prewar counterparts.

Secondly, the Occupation's sweeping personnel purge of wartime leaders, including prominent business executives, suddenly created key vacancies in the top managerial echelons of Japan's leading corporations. Through two successive measures, it is estimated that a total of over 3,600 key executives in Japan's leading corporations and 56 members of the Zaibatsu families were purged, creating a crucial leadership gap in these companies. The gap was quickly filled, for the most part, by men from the upper-middle level of management who, at the time of the defeat, were serving in such functions as department heads, plant managers, divisional heads, and so on. They were comparatively young men, most of them in their forties. Indeed, upon the shoulders of these men fell the burden of postwar reconstruction and recovery, to be achieved under the most trying conditions. A few of them were obviously poor choices as successors to the purged leaders in the midst of despair and confusion; they were unable to meet the challenges of the time. But, surprisingly, most of the new top managers rose to the new challenges admirably. In fact, out of this group emerged such outstanding executives as Chikara Kurata (Hitachi, Ltd.), Shigeki Tashiro (Toyo Rayon, Ltd.), Taizo Ishizaka (Toshiba Co., Ltd.), just to mention a few. Indeed, the immediate postwar era demanded strong and gifted leadership, and these men were able to provide it.

Freed from the control of the holding company and from stringent government regulations that had constricted Japanese industry for almost a decade and a half, the long-pent-up energies of these young men found fresh outlets. Despite the generally conservative character that Zaibatsu had acquired toward the end of the prewar era, many of these younger executives were endowed with an entrepreneurial spirit. Thus, within two or three years after their ascendancy, these men had established a firm control over the enterprises they managed. This is evidenced by the fact that, despite the reversal in the policy of the Occupation after 1949, resulting in the cancellation of purges, few of the prewar managerial leaders returned to their former posts. Consequently, it was under the leadership of these younger men and with their fresh ideas and vitality that Japan's major corporations achieved the initial postwar recovery and the subsequent phenomenal growth.

Thirdly, postwar Japan witnessed the rise of a number of very successful founder-type entrepreneurs who were able to seize upon newly created opportunities. Under their brilliant leadership, their firms have achieved a preeminent position in postwar Japan. Some of these outstanding entrepreneurs included Kōnosuke Matsushita (Matsushita Electric), Sazo Idemitsu (Idemitsu Kosan), Shōjiro Ishibashi (Bridgestone Tires), Masaru Ibuka (Sony), and Soichiro Honda (Honda Motors). Whereas the first three had already achieved some degree of success before the war, the last two owe their success entirely to the postwar era. The accomplishments of these exceptional entrepreneurs have been widely publicized and have even become a sort of myth in contemporary Japan.

Among a number of factors that have favored the rise of these entrepreneurs, three are particularly noteworthy. First, the dissolution of the Zaibatsu resulted in a substantial lessening of the once formidable barrier to entry into the Zaibatsu-dominated industries. Second, the stringent government control over economic activities, which had prevailed over the Japanese economy for almost a decade and a half until 1945, was removed, allowing much more freedom for entrepreneurial activities. Finally, the most important element was the rapid growth of the Japanese economy itself. Particularly significant was the shift in the demand structure from the military to the consumer's market. As noted in Chapter 2, the postwar era witnessed, for the first time in Japanese history, the emergence of a truly viable mass consumer market. Many of the established firms had been geared primarily to the needs of the military, and they naturally experienced difficulties in reorienting themselves to a consumer market. This inability of many of the established firms to respond quickly to the new type of demand offered tremendous opportunities to the entrepreneurs uninhibited by past ties and inspired by fresh visions. It was largely their new outlook in marketing that brought such firms as Matsushita and Honda to their present prominence.[2]

The Background of the Typical Postwar Japanese Executive

We shall now examine the personal backgrounds of the Japanese managerial elite, since we perceive that some appreciation of their personal backgrounds is important, if not essential, in understanding their ideologies and activities.

A number of empirical studies have been undertaken during the past several years on the personal backgrounds of key Japanese managers. The subsequent analysis draws heavily from these secondary sources. Particularly useful, in terms of its scope and coverage, is a recent study by Yoshimatsu Aonuma.[3] Aonuma investigated the backgrounds of a total of 1,500 executives in the 250 largest manufacturing firms (largest in terms of 1962 sales) and in 125 non-manufacturing firms. He chose for his sample the four highest ranking executives in each of these corporations. Therefore, the 1,500 men may certainly be considered as representative of the executives of Japan's leading corporations. To provide an historical perspective, Aonuma included in his investigation 420 business leaders who were active in 1900, and 500 for each of the years 1928, 1936, 1944, and 1953. Whenever relevant, we shall draw from these comparative data.

One of the most significant facts revealed by Aonuma's study was that out of his 1,500 executives, only 90, or 6 percent, were considered to have achieved their present positions through ownership. Out of this small number, 39 were the founders of the

[2] This does not imply that the newly burgeoning consumer market was the exclusive domain of these founder-type entrepreneurs. A number of newly emerged professional managers in some Zaibatsu firms as well were able to seize successfully upon these new opportunities.

[3] Yoshimatsu Aonuma, *Nihon no Keieiso* [*The Managerial Class in Japan*] (Tokyo: Nihon Keizai Shinbun Sha, 1965).

enterprises. The remaining 94 percent, or 1,410 executives, were professional managers.[4]

This very low percentage of owner-managers in the contemporary scene becomes particularly significant when it is compared with historical data. In 1900, 80 percent of the executives in Aonuma's sample were owner-managers, and even in 1925, almost 50 percent of the executives surveyed were also considered to belong to this category. Aonuma further reported that there was no single executive among the 1,500 examined who held 30 percent or more of the company's stocks. All of the above data clearly demonstrate the degree to which the separation of ownership from management and the professionalization of managers have progressed in postwar Japan.

Aonuma's data further revealed that among the 1,410 professional managers in the sample, 46 percent, or 649, had spent their entire working careers with a single company.[5] This indicates that there is some mobility among top management despite the traditional practice of lifetime employment. Of course, wartime dislocation and the special circumstances in the immediate postwar era partially account for this relatively high mobility rate among top management. Of the 54 percent, or 761, of the 1,410 professional managers in the sample who had moved from elsewhere, 19 percent came from financial institutions and 9 percent had been in government service prior to assuming their current positions.[6] (It has been quite common in Japan for high-ranking bureaucrats to move, upon retirement, into top management positions in private corporations. For example, it is reported that, in the year 1966 alone, 140 senior government officials accepted high managerial positions in private corporations upon retirement from government service. Interestingly, this practice is known as *amakudari,* literally translated as "descending from heaven." Unlike in the United States, the reverse flow of personnel from business to government service is practically unknown.)

Another noteworthy characteristic of the Japanese managerial elite is that virtually all of them are in a relatively high age bracket. Aonuma's study revealed that nearly 87 percent of the 1,500 executives studied were fifty-five years of age or older; nearly 50 percent

[4] *Ibid.,* p. 140.
[5] *Ibid.,* p. 141.
[6] *Ibid.*

were in their sixties.[7] This is, of course, due to the fact that seniority has been a major consideration in career advancement. A more recent study of the personal backgrounds of the presidents of 1,150 of Japan's major corporations, undertaken by the Toyo Keizai Publishing Company, reveals that approximately 70 percent were sixty years old or older.[8]

Perhaps the most significant characteristic of the Japanese managerial elite is their high level of educational achievement. Aonuma's data show that nearly 90 percent of the 1,500 executives studied were graduates of institutions of higher learning, including government and private universities and college-level technical institutes.[9] Although a very strict comparison is not possible, Aonuma's data do point to some interesting historical trends. Out of 420 business leaders studied in 1900, less than 5 percent were graduates of universities or higher technical institutes. By 1928, however, out of 500 executives studied, nearly two-thirds had a college degree or its equivalent.[10] This indicates that formal education became an important factor in entry into the ranks of professional management relatively early in Japan's industrialization.

Another significant factor relating to the educational background of those surveyed is that a handful of prestigious universities have provided a large proportion of leading executives. Aonuma's data reveal that over a fourth of the 1,500 executives studied were graduates from the University of Tokyo.[11] Significantly, as many as 60 percent of the 1,500 executives of the Aonuma sample were graduated from the most highly rated universities (four state universities — Tokyo, Kyoto, Hitotsubashi, and Tokyo Technical — and two private institutions, Keio and Waseda).[12] The aforementioned survey by the Toyo Keizai Publishing Company of the presidents of 1,150 leading corporations yielded similar results. It reported that 273, or 26.5 percent, were graduates of the University of Tokyo; 81, or 7.9 percent, 75, or 7.3 percent, and 67, or 6.5 per-

[7] *Ibid.*, p. 161.

[8] "Gendai Shacho no Shinjō Chōsa" ["A Study of Personal Backgrounds of Corporate Presidents"]. *Business*, July 1966, p. 10.

[9] These were known as Senmon Gakko; they gave three to five years of college-level instruction to prepare skilled technicians in such fields as agriculture, industry, commerce, fisheries, and others. To be admitted to these institutes, the applicants had to have eleven years of primary and middle-school education.

[10] Aonuma, *Nihon no Keieiso*, p. 117.

[11] *Ibid.*

[12] *Ibid.*

cent, received their degrees from Keio, Kyoto, and Hitotsubashi Universities, respectively.[13]

Aonuma's study also revealed that 16.5 percent of the college graduates majored in law, 13 percent in economics, 22 percent in commerce, and 23 percent in engineering.[14] As may be expected, the educational backgrounds of the founder-type executives are quite diverse. Some, like Matsushita, Honda, and Ishibashi, had only a minimum of formal education, whereas others, like Idemitsu and Ibuka, had a college degree or its equivalent.

From the foregoing analysis of the backgrounds of Japan's present-day managerial elite, one factor stands out: They are, as a whole, quite homogeneous as to age, educational background, and work experience.

The Role of the Managerial Elite in Contemporary Japan

We noted in Chapter 2 that the business community, as represented by Zaibatsu interests, enjoyed an important influence over the ruling oligarchy of prewar Japan. Throughout much of the prewar era, however, it had been placed in a somewhat subordinate position to the military and the government elite. Understandably, the defeat in World War II was followed by a substantial change in Japan's power structure. For one thing, it totally discredited the military as a power elite. Further, the postwar democratization measures resulted in the weakening of bureaucratic power. Coupled with these changes, the rapid postwar economic growth greatly enhanced the relative prestige and influence of the business leadership, propelling the business elite to a dominant position in the power structure of contemporary Japan. In postwar Japan, a managerial career in a large corporation has carried as much or greater prestige than government service or professional activities, and it attracts the most capable graduates from Japan's leading universities.

The power of the managerial elite in Japanese society is not merely confined to its role in directing and controlling the means of production. The managerial elite occupy a central place in contemporary society. In the last decade or so an abundance of books on business leaders and their philosophies has appeared, and many

[13] "Gendai Shacho no Shinjō Chōsa," p. 28.
[14] Aonuma, *Nihon no Keieiso*, p. 131.

of them have enjoyed a wide readership. In fact, a number of these publications, including some written by business leaders themselves, have appeared on best-seller lists. In opinion polls, the names of prominent business leaders, such as Kōnonsuke Matsushita, are cited among those most respected or admired.

The *Zaikai*, literally translated as "financial circle," has become a major power center in the postwar political scene. The postwar version of the Zaikai differs from its prewar counterpart in two important respects. The prewar variety, as may be expected, was dominated by the Zaibatsu; in fact, the Zaibatsu and Zaikai were virtually synonymous. The postwar Zaikai, however, is more diverse and broader in its composition. Its other major characteristic now is that it consists almost exclusively of professional managers who derive power from their high positions in large corporations. Their power definitely does not stem from personal wealth. In fact, these high-positioned managers are men of modest means. Their financial compensations, though high by Japanese standards, are not substantial enough to enable them to accumulate personal fortunes. Although there are many fringe benefits that are difficult to quantify, the annual gross cash compensation, including bonuses, for high-ranking professional executives of leading corporations usually ranges from $20,000 to $50,000.

A recent government survey on compensation of top management in corporations with capitalization of ¥1 billion or more indicates that there were only 512 directors whose reported yearly income exceeded ¥10 million (approximately $28,000); 2,837 directors reported an income ranging between ¥5 million to ¥10 million, and the reported earnings of 11,453 directors fell within the range of ¥2 million to ¥5 million.[15] Although these figures do not include the extensive fringe benefits, which range from membership in country clubs and chauffeured automobiles to housing accommodations, the cash income of professional managers of large corporations in Japan is considerably less than that of their American counterparts. In terms of real income, owner-managers of small- to medium-size enterprises frequently earn considerably more than professional managers of large corporations, although the latter enjoy infinitely more prestige.

The Zaikai wields considerable political power and has been the major and the most staunch supporter of the Liberal Democratic

[15] "Juseki no Wari ni Sukunai Hōshū" ["Inadequate Financial Reward for Heavy Responsibilities"], *Nihon Keizai Shinbun*, May 15, 1967, p. 5.

Party, Japan's conservative party. The power of the business community vis-à-vis the LDP is largely derived from the fact that the LDP, lacking a broad basis for financial support, must depend on the business community, particularly big business, for a large portion of its political funds. Large corporations contribute liberally not only to the coffers of the LDP but also to individual party leaders and to their factions. Of course, the fusion of big business and political interests is nothing new in Japan. In the prewar era, two major rival political parties — Seiyukai and Minseito — received much of their financial support from two rival Zaibatsu, namely, Mitsui and Mitsubishi.

In the best Japanese tradition, business leaders prefer to exercise their political influence through behind-the-scenes arrangements and personal contacts, avoiding direct participation in political activities. The highest ranking political leaders, including the Prime Minister, informally and regularly meet with key business leaders. Rare is the important political leader who does not have a particular group of business executives to whom he turns for advice and material assistance. Through these informal channels, as well as by means of formal policy pronouncements made by a number of business associations, the business community lets its wishes be known to the political leadership. The latter makes but few important decisions, certainly none on economic policy, without prior consultation with key business leaders. In fact, it is generally believed that no political figure aspiring to premiership could win the post without close support from the mainstream of business leadership.

By the foregoing we do not mean to give the impression that all leading executives of Japan's major corporations are active in the political scene. In fact, the core of politically active and vocal business leaders is quite small. There are many who maintain contact with political leaders only through occasional meetings. Others, though willing to have their firms make political monetary contributions, prefer to keep their relationships with politicians correct and detached.

Although, in the main, the relationship between big business interests and political leadership is a close one, and the two groups share a fundamental consensus in support of the present power structure, this does not imply that their interaction is always harmonious. They have their share of conflicts of interests. Neither is the business community itself homogeneous in its political attitudes and ideologies. This is particularly true of the postwar business community, which is itself divided into factions and cliques, each vying for dominance.

One way to define the diversity of interests among the various groups within the business community is to examine these groups in the context of their business organization and their philosophy. Among the large number of trade and business associations, four deserve special attention — each of these four has a wide membership and wields considerable power and influence.

The most powerful business association is, without doubt, the *Keidanren*, or the Federation of Economic Organizations. The Keidanren is somewhat similar to the National Association of Manufacturers in the United States, but its membership is far more encompassing and it enjoys greater power and prestige. The Keidanren was established in August 1946, incorporating five major wartime economic organizations. Today, it consists of 102 organizations, most of which are trade associations, and 750 leading corporations in almost every field of industry and commerce. Some of its leading members include the Japan Iron and Steel Association, the Japan Machinery Federation, the Japan Petroleum Association, the Japan Shipbuilders' Association, the Japan Synthetic Fibre Association, to mention just a few. The organization has 31 standing committees, including committees on economic research, industrial policy, international relations, economic cooperation, small- to medium-size enterprises, agriculture, and taxation. Even this limited enumeration of Keidanren committees speaks for the diversity of its interests. Through these committees, the organization frequently makes policy recommendations to the government.

The Keidanren leadership, as is to be expected, is in the hands of some of the most powerful and prominent business leaders. In fact, in terms of power and prestige, they represent the crest of the Japanese business power structure. Understandably, the organization is conservative in its political ideology, is firmly committed to the free enterprise system, and prefers to keep governmental intervention in the private business sector to a minimum. Its leadership exerts considerable influence on government policies through both formal and informal channels. In matters of policy, this association has been the most important spokesman for big business in Japan.

The second major business association is the Federation of Employers' Associations, or *Nikkeiren*. Although the scope of its activities covers a broad front, its primary function is to represent the employers' interests vis-à-vis labor unions. Its predecessor was first organized shortly after World War I to combat the rising labor movement and socialistic ideology. It subsequently lost much of its *raison d'être* when the government itself began to suppress the labor movement. But, in the face of serious labor problems in the immediate aftermath of World War II, it was reactivated. In its inaugural declaration in 1946, the Nikkeiren called on management to insist on its prerogatives and exhorted it "to be right and strong." This orientation has characterized much of Nikkeiren's subsequent activities. This association continues to exert a powerful voice in matters relating to labor and labor-management relations.

The third major business association is the *Nissho*, or the Chamber of Commerce and Industry of Japan, representing 448 local Chambers of Commerce, with a combined membership of some 350,000. (Its predecessor was first organized in 1892.) The Nissho, in contrast to the Keidanren, represents the interests of the nation's small- to medium-size enterprises. Because of its very size and due to the fact that its members are often prominent citizens in their respective areas, the Nissho has been a political and economic force to reckon with.

Finally, there is the strategic *Keizai Doyukai*, or the Japanese Committee for Economic Development, which we shall now examine in detail.

Managerial Ideologies in Postwar Japan

Having looked at the salient characteristics of the business leadership that emerged in postwar Japan, we shall now examine its ideologies. In doing so we shall rely on the framework employed in the preceding chapter; that is, a business ideology is formulated by business leaders to resolve strains they face in the performance of their functions.[16] We should remember once more that business ideology is not monolithic. Nor is it a set of preconceived notions. Rather, as Sutton and his colleagues point out, business ideology is shaped and revised by its proponents.[17]

During the past two decades, Japanese business leadership has, indeed, experienced a variety of strains. To resolve them, the busi-

[16] Francis X. Sutton, *et al., The American Business Creed* (Cambridge, Mass.: Harvard University Press, 1956), p. 11.
[17] *Ibid.*

ness community has evolved a number of distinct ideologies. (The postwar ideologies, though they have had some basic similarities to their prewar prototypes, have taken on a number of very important new aspects.)

A most useful way to assess the major trends in postwar ideological developments in Japan is to analyze the statements on business philosophy made by the Keizai Doyukai.

The Doyukai was established in the spring of 1946 — the darkest days of the postwar era — by a group of young and progressive executives of leading corporations. These men, dissatisfied with past business leadership and with traditional ideology, and confronted with the mounting economic crisis, sought out those who shared their own sense of urgency. The charter membership, consisting of no more than 70 executives, perceived as the primary task of the Doyukai the formulation of a managerial ideology viable in the postwar situation. From this rather small nucleus, the organization has grown into a major business association with considerable power and prestige.

Although the Doyukai is not the sole articulator of significant business ideologies in postwar Japan, and its ideological position is not universally accepted, a careful examination of what it stands for is justified on the following grounds:

1. The Doyukai, unlike the other prominent business associations, has always viewed its chief function as that of articulating a business ideology congruent with the new era.
2. The membership of Doyukai consists almost exclusively of the postwar type of professional executive; thus, it represents the point of view of the new class of managerial elite that emerged in the postwar era.
3. Every major ideological statement officially adopted by the Doyukai is a product of careful deliberations, not only by its leadership but by its rank and file members as well. As a result, it represents serious and carefully formulated opinions of Japan's thoughtful business leaders.
4. As the chief ideological spokesman for the new type of professional executive, the Doyukai has had a considerable impact in shaping his thoughts and ideologies. Its impact has steadily been enhanced as its membership has increased and as its leaders have advanced to key top management positions in their respective corporations, thereby improving their standing in the Japanese

business community. The fact that the Doyukai's membership grew from about 70 to nearly 1,000 key executives of Japan's leading corporations is eloquent proof of the degree to which postwar professional managers have found the Doyukai philosophy congenial and acceptable.

Although somewhat diffuse in terms of ideological development, the postwar era may be divided into three quite distinct periods. The first phase was the crisis-ridden immediate postwar years, when the very survival of Japan's capitalistic private enterprise system was at stake; a sense of urgency pervaded the scene. The second phase covers the period of recovery and rapid postwar growth. The ideology articulated during this period clearly reflects unbounded optimism in the Japanese economy and a growing awareness of the responsibilities of the business elite to the society at large. This period was also characterized by an enthusiastic acceptance of the American managerial ideology, concepts, and techniques. The third period began in the early 1960's. Faced with the growing strains of rapid economic growth and the prospect of growing international as well as domestic competitive pressures, the business leadership turned to critical self-examination of past practices and a search for a new ideological stand. We shall now examine each of these three postwar phases somewhat in detail.

An account of the desperate conditions that prevailed in immediate postwar Japan can be found elsewhere, and the subject needs no detailed elaboration by us. Suffice it to say here that Japan's once-mighty industrial system was in a state of almost total collapse. The economy was in chaos, beset with serious shortages of materials, disrupted transportation and communication systems, and a galloping inflation. Moreover, the threats of impending reparations to the victorious nations and the Occupation's reform programs meant confusion and despair for Japanese management.

Perhaps the single most serious threat to Japanese business management was the great offensive waged by the newly organized labor movement. Not only the encouragement given to it by the Occupation but also the chaotic conditions of the immediate postwar period greatly spurred the labor movement. To the great majority of workers who were desperate to keep their jobs in the face of rampant inflation and to maintain at least a subsistence living standard, the organized labor movement appeared to be their only salvation. The spectacular response of the masses of industrial workers to the call for unionization is well known. By 1947, more than five million workers, representing nearly half of the total of wage and salary earners, had joined unions.

The labor movement became increasingly militant as control over many unions passed into the hands of the determined and disciplined minority of Communists and their sympathizers. The incessant demand of the union leadership for wage increases and greater fringe benefits led to a further deterioration of the already chaotic Japanese economy. In a number of instances, unions ousted existing managements and took over the running of plants in the course of a labor dispute. The temper of the labor movement during this time was to call for a basic revolution in Japan's political, economic, and social structure. The traditional image of the self-effacing, obedient worker had all but disappeared. Many of the business leaders were helpless in coping with this overwhelming and unprecedented problem, and management lost nearly all initiative in dealing with the militant union movement.

This is the background against which the Doyukai was established. The fact that the Doyukai was born out of this wholesale crisis has had a far-reaching impact on its subsequent evolution and development. The group viewed as its first task the articulation of a business ideology that would be consistent with the demands of the new era and would help resolve the tremendous tensions on business leadership caused by the defeat. It was fully aware that the traditional Zaibatsu-oriented business ideology was no longer viable.

Early in 1947, the Doyukai proposed a "Tentative View of Democratization of Business Enterprises." It must be noted that, in the fall of 1946, the left-wing labor leadership was pressing for a massive offensive to achieve both political and economic objectives. (This offensive culminated in an abortive general strike set for February 1, 1947, in which 2.6 million workers were to participate.) Indeed, all of Japan was in the grip of social unrest and chaotic economic conditions. The proposal of the Doyukai must be viewed in this general context. The ideology of *shusei shihon shugi,* or revised capitalism, ran through the entire proposal. It sought to promote the separation of ownership and control of an enterprise, to curb the preeminent position of shareholders in corporate government, and to improve the position of workers. The "Tentative View of Democratization of Business Enterprises" advanced the following major points:

1. It unequivocally stated that the assets of a corporation belonged to three parties — the shareholders, the management, and labor. The control of a corporation was to be shared equally among these three groups. It called for the creation of a board consisting of representatives of the three sectors as the ultimate policy-making and governing body of the corporation. To select representatives to the ultimate policy board, both management and labor were to establish their own committees, whose power was to equal that of the shareholders.
2. The Doyukai declaration called for a guarantee of a minimum income both for management and for labor. It also stipulated that profit was to be divided equally among the three groups. It was thus advocated that the fruits of a productive enterprise were to be shared *equally* among shareholders, management, and labor, thus denying the dominant ownership rights traditionally assigned to shareholders.
3. The proposal stated that the foregoing principles would alter the basic character and role of the labor union. The union would retain its entity not as an agent external to the firm but as an integral part of the key decision-making body in the corporate organization. The primary task of the union under this concept was to promote the welfare of the workers by means of its contribution to increased efficiency and improved productivity of the enterprise.

This was the solution that the young leaders of the Doyukai offered after an agonizing search for a viable ideology in the face of the great strains the immediate postwar situation imposed on the Japanese economy. This ideology, although it was, indeed, a radical departure from traditional Japanese business thinking, was by no means extreme when viewed in the context of the times, when the existing political and economic power structure was seriously threatened. On the contrary, the Doyukai proposals were a carefully considered and pragmatic response to the threatening conditions. It made major concessions to the rapidly growing militancy of labor unions in order to maintain a climate half-way hospitable to management.

The "Tentative View of Democratization of Business Enterprises" was made public, and it immediately stirred up much controversy. Reactions among business leaders were strongly divided — some hailed it as the business ideology of a new democratic Japan, praising the Doyukai leadership for taking such a bold stand; others were clearly skeptical, for various reasons; still others were violently opposed. There was criticism on the grounds that the proposals were too radical, and their future effectiveness and viability were questioned should normality return to the scene. Doubt was expressed as to whether the militant unions would accept such a highly idealistic ideology of cooperation between management and labor at the time that union leaders felt they were gaining an upper hand. Some opponents of the "View" pointed out that the unions could be expected to look upon such a radical departure by management with suspicion, and that they might see ulterior motives in its proposals — motives seeking to weaken the unions' power by devious offers of sharing corporate profits and participating in management.

For the aforementioned and other reasons the Doyukai proposals, though widely circulated, were never adopted as an official view of the association. Nevertheless, the proposals proved highly significant in three respects. They were the first attempt to articulate ideological guidelines in the midst of confusion and imminent catastrophe in the immediate aftermath of the war. They were made public in the darkest days of the postwar period, when most business leaders either were at a complete loss because of the overwhelming difficulties or were preoccupied with day-to-day problems of survival. Whether or not they agreed with the "View," it gave many executives who were desperately groping for an ideological stand food for thought. Secondly, the proposals marked a radical departure from the traditional ideology and clearly denounced the traditional Zaibatsu-oriented business mentality, thus producing an impact on the evolution of the subsequent business ideology. Finally, the "View," radical as it appeared to some, put the spotlight on the Doyukai as a progressive business organization and a champion of a new orientation to the solution of Japan's many economic quandaries.

Soon after the "Tentative View of Democratization of Business Enterprises" was made known, the deepening crisis in the Japanese economy persuaded the Occupation to revise its economic policy. The change, of course, became accelerated as postwar relations between the United States and the Soviet Union deteriorated. The United States soon became firmly committed to the rapid economic recovery of Japan. Thus, by the spring of 1950, Japan regained a measure of stability both politically and economically. The sudden outbreak of the Korean war touched off an economic boom in Japan, ushering in a new era. In the following year the Peace Treaty was signed, restoring full sovereignty to Japan.

With the conclusion of the Korean war, the economic boom in Japan subsided and a deflationary pressure set in. At about this time, the political climate of the country began to deteriorate. The pro-business conservatives were badly divided. Not only were the two conservative parties feuding, but within each party leaders were enmeshed in severe factional struggles. Political morality hit a low ebb, and public resentment against the ruling political leaders was mounting. All these factors contributed to the popularity of the Socialist Party.

Consequently, the Doyukai began to show a growing concern about the deteriorating political situation and began to exert its influence toward the stabilization of the country's socioeconomic and political life. In spite of repeated efforts on the part of the Doyukai and other economic associations, such as the Keidanren, the political situation continued to worsen to the point where the very survival of the parliamentary democracy was in question. In 1955, the Doyukai passed a resolution calling for the defense of parliamentary democracy in Japan and urging the political leadership to heed its advice.

It was against this background that the Doyukai gradually evolved its ideology, which was stated in an official resolution to be passed at its annual conference of 1956. Significantly, this coincided with the tenth anniversary of the association's founding. The resolution was entitled "The Social Responsibilities of Business Leadership." The preamble to the resolution gave the essence of the declaration and read as follows:

> The function of management in a modern corporation goes far beyond that of a search for profit. From the moral as well as practical point of view, it is vital that modern corporate managers strive to supply products of highest quality at the lowest possible prices through the most effective utilization of productive resources consistent with the welfare of the whole economy and the society at large. It is indeed the social responsibility of modern executives to serve as an effective instrument to develop a managerial system capable of accomplishing this mission.[18]

The declaration of 1956 contained several key points:

[18] *Keizai Doyukai Jugonen Shi* [*The Fifteen-Year History of the Doyukai*] (Tokyo: Keizai Doyukai, 1962), p. 391.

1. It acknowledged that a modern corporation was a public instrument. Management was entrusted with the stewardship of the enterprise, not only by the shareholders but by other participants as well — employees, suppliers, customers, and the public; an important responsibility of management, therefore, was to bring about a harmony of interests among the various key participating groups.

2. It emphasized the social responsibilities of modern corporate managers. In a highly complex industrial economy such as Japan's, the overall welfare of the national economic system could no longer be assured merely through the proper functioning of individual firms. It could be achieved only through the concerted, deliberate efforts of the congregate of socially responsible managers of the corporate community. Unless management were willing to fulfill its social responsibilities (as expressed in the above-mentioned preamble), it would face increasing encroachments on its independence and managerial prerogatives by the government. Indeed, the welfare of the whole economy depended, to a large measure, on the effectiveness with which management could fulfill this responsibility.

3. It called for the removal of social and economic imbalances and injustices; specifically, it called for the removal of the evils of monopoly and ills of duality in the economic structure.

4. It emphasized the creation of a climate for fair competition and the strengthening of countervailing power to achieve a proper balance among major sectors of society.

5. It stated that modern corporations should seek a fair and stable profit extended over the long run through technological innovations and market development. It urged that corporate earnings be distributed in a more equitable manner, and that management see to it that all the key elements participating in the productive process were rewarded fairly for their efforts.

6. It emphasized the need for improvement of managerial practices and of the training of future generations of managers — particularly stressed was the need for systematic efforts in management development.

During the preceding ten years, the Doyukai had made a number of ideological pronouncements, but this declaration, made in 1956, was considered a milestone in the ideological development of postwar business leaders. It was certainly formulated in an environment very much different from that of 1946. By 1956, Japan had completed her economic recovery, and management had regained control over the economic process. Japan's major industries had been reequipped and were growing rapidly. The militant labor movement had been contained. With the military deposed and the bureaucracy somewhat weakened, the business community was emerging as a major power center in Japanese society. Political leaders, particularly those of the ruling Liberal Democratic Party, now had to be responsive to the wishes of the business community, because they were receiving most of their financial and ideological support from big business. Management no longer allowed itself to be regarded as an equal partner with shareholders or union leaders, as advocated in the earlier Doyukai declaration. Its role now was that of the ultimate harmonizer of diverse and often conflicting interests among various claimants of the fruits of productive activities.

Another significant fact about the 1956 Doyukai resolution was that the American managerial ideology, particularly the managerial view as analyzed by Sutton and his colleagues, exerted a great deal of influence on its formulation. By this time, Japanese business leaders had been exposed to American business concepts and managerial practices. Particularly significant was the fact that, in 1955, the Japan Productivity Center had sent its first top management study team to the United States. The team, consisting of leading Japanese business executives and scholars, came home much impressed with the managerial strand of business philosophy articulated by professional managers in the United States.[19] It was no coincidence, therefore, that the resolution of 1956 resembled in its major tenor the so-called managerial strand of U.S. business ideology. Thus, the Doyukai resolution of 1956 was often called the Japanese version of American managerial ideology.[20]

The thinking contained in the resolution, however, was not totally inconsistent with traditional Japanese business beliefs and attitudes. It must be noted that the search for a viable new ideology grew out of the concern of business leadership for the future of the nation. Here, one could see a close parallel to the tradition of community-centered entrepreneurs of the earlier era. Certainly, as we have seen in the preceding chapter, the concern for the public

[19] For details on the managerial strand of business philosophy, see Sutton, *The American Business Creed,* pp. 347–383.

[20] Yasuo Takeyama, *Nihon no Keiei: Sono Fudo to Tenbō* [*Japanese Management: Its Climate and Perspective*] (Tokyo: Kashima Kenkyūjo Shuppankai, 1965), p. 87.

welfare was not a new element in Japanese business orientation. Neither is it surprising to find an aversion to the profit motive as the sole goal of the business enterprise. As noted earlier in this study, disdain for the ruthless pursuit of profit, stemming from Confucian doctrine, had been well ingrained in the Japanese business mentality.

Thus as Takao Tsuchiya, a leading historian of Japanese business, tersely noted, the ideology embodied in the Doyukai declaration of 1956 was a fusion of modern American business philosophy and the traditional Japanese business mentality.[21]

As was to be expected, the responses from various sectors of Japanese society to the declaration of 1956 again varied widely. It was praised by some for its progressiveness, whereas others, even in the business community, viewed it with more restrained enthusiasm. The more conservatively oriented business leaders declared it unrealistic and impractical. The intellectuals, always suspicious of the motives of the business community, simply dismissed it as "window dressing."

But the declaration's ideology appealed to most of the country's professional managers and helped resolve their basic strains. Because of their very training and background, these men were dissatisfied with traditional capitalism and now felt much more comfortable in the role prescribed to them by the resolution. To a certain degree they took seriously the Confucian-oriented concept of public consciousness, which they inherited from their predecessors. Moreover, their reluctance to be totally committed to old-line capitalism stemmed partially from the training and ideological orientation that they had been exposed to in their youth; most of the business leaders of this generation had experienced in their earlier years the impact of both the liberal movement of the 1920's and the depression of the early 1930's. These were the reasons why the declaration's position on the social responsibility of executives was accepted by professional managers with considerable enthusiasm. Particularly appealing was the declaration's denial that the pursuit of profit was the principal goal of business, and they met with approval the idea of a balanced sharing of the fruits of a business enterprise by all participants.

Moreover, the Doyukai resolution of 1956 modified the definition of what constituted personal achievement in one's business career.

[21] Takao Tsuchiya, *Nihon no Keieisha Seishin* [*Managerial Mentality in Japan*] (Tokyo: Keizai Ōraisha, 1960), p. 106.

Management implied a lot more than a stewardship to stockholders. Following the managerial strand of American business ideology, the resolution of 1956 sought to establish business management as a profession embodying a set of ethical norms that comprised the approved means to professional managerial success. This vision of the manager's occupation as a profession further discouraged the measuring of success only in terms of profit.

When the Doyukai's new managerial ideology was announced, Japan was at the threshold of unprecedented growth. Japanese management was eagerly importing the new technology of the West and successfully commercialized it in the rapidly growing market.

The spectacular growth of the Japanese economy between the late 1950's and early 1960's is well known and needs little elaboration here. Confronted with unprecedented growth opportunities, Japanese business pressed for continued expansion and diversification. Enterprises, particularly those in the growth industries, competed in a race for advantageous market positions. In the process of this rapid expansion, management became understandably engrossed in the development of productive capacities and the attainment of a greater market share for its products; this, in turn, triggered an investment race. The supply of goods gradually caught up with what appeared to be an insatiable demand. By the early 1960's, a number of industries began to be plagued with excess capacity. The pressure to utilize this excess capacity soon led to what has become known as *kato kyōsō*, or excessive competition. By this time, the unprecedented economic growth began to show signs of slowing down. Also imminent was the liberalization of trade restrictions.

The Doyukai's repeated calls for voluntary restraint in the investment race went unheeded by many firms still preoccupied with the increase in their market share regardless of the danger signals. Interfirm agreements to avoid the consequences of excessive competition were often violated by aggressive corporations maneuvering for a better competitive position. Not unexpectedly, the earlier stress on social responsibility was ignored in the face of strong competitive pressures. At this time the government intervened to curb the evils of excessive competition. In fact, not being able to restore order in the market on their own initiative, industrial groups now frequently sought government intervention on their behalf.

Faced with an excess capacity and the pressure of intense competition, the performance of many leading firms began to deteriorate. Their worsening performance often brought to light poor management, which had gone unnoticed under the mantle of aggressive strategies and rapid growth. This deterioration of large firms was a real test not only of the ability but also of the integrity of their managements. To improve their situation, even some of the leading enterprises did not hesitate to shift the burden of the recession to subcontractors, dealers, or temporary workers.

Some executives, for the sake of self-preservation, attempted to conceal the deteriorating condition of their companies through accounting "adjustments" of dubious nature. Though the managers resorting to such extreme measures were in a definite minority, the behavior of other executives also left much to be desired from the point of view of the Doyukai declaration of 1956. Moreover, preoccupied with the pursuit of aggressive corporate policies, even some of the major firms failed to carry out their assumed community responsibilities. The pressure of rapid construction of new plants or the expansion of the existing facilities often led to the neglect of such responsibilities, resulting in strained community relations. Thus, as one prominent executive admitted, Japanese business leadership repudiated by its own behavior the high-sounding idealism embodied in the Doyukai resolution of 1956.

Perhaps it would be helpful to pause here and examine why the Doyukai ideology, which had appeared to be so widely accepted among Japanese business leaders, did not take firmer root. For one thing, as Takeyama appropriately notes, a basic difficulty lay in the fact that the resolution of 1956 had not been totally indigenous to the thinking of Japanese business leaders; it drew heavily on the managerial strand of the American business ideology.[22] As a result, it was unable to stand the acid test of crisis. Another difficulty was the intrinsic nature of the managerial strand of the American business ideology: It assigns to business leadership responsibilities that are too numerous, conflicting, and broad. As Eells summarizes it, the managerial definition of business responsibility leaves businessmen at sea without a compass.[23] The codes of prescribed managerial behavior as articulated in the managerial strand of the American business ideology are very vague, and there are no operationally

[22] Takeyama, *Nihon no Keiei,* p. 190.

[23] Richard Eells, *The Meaning of Modern Business: An Introduction to the Philosophy of Large Corporate Enterprise* (New York: Columbia University Press, 1960), p. 24.

meaningful norms by which to measure business performance when responsibilities are so diffuse.[24]

Disappointed with the imported version of managerial ideology, some executives turned to Japanese tradition for guidelines. The popular cry was for a search for answers in Japan's tradition. In the process, the American managerial philosophy, its concepts and practices, were almost totally rejected on the grounds that they were not suited to Japanese society. The emphasis now shifted to the search for *Nihonteki Keiei,* or a Japanese way of management. This rather sudden about-face was a result of quite diverse reasons. It partially stemmed from the resentment against indiscriminate and almost blind adoption of American managerial ideology and practices. Other factors explaining the sudden about-face included national pride in the brilliant economic accomplishments of the past and sheer frustration arising from the current inability to solve new and complex problems.

In the meantime, more thoughtful business leaders were seeking ways to resolve new strains and challenges. The first official response came in the form of a resolution of a *Kansai* Chapter (Osaka) of the Doyukai in the fall of 1964. The pronouncement was made public under the title "Managerial Ideology in a New Environment." Although this pronouncement resembled in many of its aspects the declaration of 1956, closer examination reveals subtle and important differences.

First, the pronouncement in 1964 called for a critical self-appraisal by business leadership of its past practices. It recognized that the current economic condition suffered from a series of distinctive strains. It frankly admitted that the business leadership was partially responsible for these strains because of its pursuit of an overly aggressive expansionary policy and ruinously excessive competition. This overzealous expansionary policy, it pointed out, had not only resulted in the deterioration of public confidence in the business leadership, but had invited government intervention to a degree that was endangering the private enterprise system. The pronouncement pointed out that, in view of growing international competition, Japanese management should reexamine its ideology and pattern of functioning. Specifically, the pronouncement exhorted business leadership to recognize (1) that some of the traditional managerial practices had become obsolete and in-

[24] *Ibid.*

efficient in the present-day business environment and that they needed to be replaced by modern and more efficient practices; (2) that the principle of fairness should govern the competitive behavior of firms; and (3) that the private enterprise system is most suited for promoting economic growth.

Based on the foregoing premises, the pronouncement made the following five proposals: (1) that management recognize the vital role of profit in the private enterprise system and establish the pursuit of profit as its key goal; (2) that management deal with individual workers in such a manner that each employee could realize fully his or her creative potential on the job; (3) that management correct unfair and excessive competition and strive for the creation of a climate favorable to fair competition; (4) that a corporation be aware of its responsibilities to the local community in which its facilities are located — management does its utmost to solve social ills and problems created by its industrial activities; and (5) that in a highly industrialized society such as Japan, the responsibilities of management go far beyond those strictly related to the management of enterprises — management has direct as well as indirect responsibilities to the whole society.

The most striking feature of the pronouncement of 1964, in contrast to the earlier ones, was its bold assertion of the legitimacy of the profit motive in the private enterprise system.

In Chapter 3, we saw that the Confucian-inspired Meiji business ideology had *deemphasized profit as the central goal of business.* This tendency persisted. Throughout the 1920's and 1930's, the dominant business doctrine stressed that the primary motivation of business was promoting the welfare of the society rather than obtaining personal material gains. Moreover, the very condition prevailing in Japan throughout much of the prewar era was such that the pursuit of profit did not have to be the paramount concern of executives. Operating under close patronage and the protection of the government, much of the business of the prewar Zaibatsu came from the government, particularly the military sector, in which a satisfactory profit was all but guaranteed. The favorable postwar economic environment and its protected market again assured most large firms of profitable operations.

Moreover, the very orientation of professional managers in the postwar period was such that they tended to emphasize growth, diversification, and expansion rather than profit. This was quite understandable in an economy abundant with growth opportunities. Also, the public tended to evaluate the performance of business leaders and their firms in terms of technological advances, innovative organizational and personnel policies, the rate of growth, the degree of diversification, and so on; it was less inclined to apply the single criterion of profit. Furthermore, the emphasis on management's social responsibilities tended to dim the profit consciousness of postwar executives.

It should be noted here that the managerial strand of the business ideology of the United States had developed as a reaction to the classical or traditional view in order to counteract its overriding commitment to the pursuit of profit as the central goal of business. In the case of Japan, however, the managerial strand was superimposed upon a business mentality that had deemphasized the pursuit of profit as the goal of business. The pronouncement of 1964 sought to instill profit consciousness as an important and legitimate goal of private enterprise in the face of increasingly keen competition and the deteriorating profitability of operations of many leading corporations.

The pronouncement of 1964, of course, defined profit in the manner acceptable both to the business leadership and to society as a whole. Profit, it emphasized, must be obtained through the innovative and creative functions of management, that is, through technological innovations, market development, rationalization of business practices, and higher productivity. In this respect, the pursuit of profit was not regarded as inconsistent with the concept of social responsibility. In fact, the pronouncement pointed out that an earnest but fair search for profit, and its equitable distribution among the various groups of participants, does contribute to economic growth and stability. The pronouncement stressed that this actually constitutes the fulfillment of social responsibilities on the part of managers.

Another significant public pronouncement recently made by the Doyukai is the policy statement made early in 1965 by the Committee on Management Policy, under the chairmanship of Haruo Suzuki, executive vice-president of Showa Denko Company, Ltd. The Committee was established earlier for the express purpose of searching for a set of managerial guidelines viable in the new economic environment. After many careful deliberations it made public a declaration entitled "A New Managerial Ideology: A Managerial Philosophy in the Japanese Climate." The declaration of 1965 stated at the outset, as its basic ideological premise, that of utmost importance was the creation of a highly industrialized democratic society based on the recognition of the individual's dignity, freedom, and creativity. In achieving this overriding goal, the modern corporation and its managers have momentous responsibilities. Then the declaration focused on another central issue—that the Japanese industrial system was entering a new era, and that the environment in which Japanese industries now operated was radically different from that of an earlier period. The new environment required the development of a new ideology and a revision of at least some aspects of traditional managerial practices. Among the numerous recent developments in the corporate environment, the declaration singled out four as most critical: (1) growing international competition; (2) the rapid rate of technological change; (3) the growing complexity in organizational and human relationships; and (4) changes in the traditional Japanese value system, particularly noticeable among the younger generations.

In line with the above basic premises, the pronouncement of 1965 offered the following guidelines:

1. Emphasis on the independence and self-determination of business leadership: It recognized that the past sociopolitical and economic climate had not been conducive to the development of a truly independent business sector. The spirit of independence and self-determination on the part of business leaders had been lacking, particularly in their relationship with the government. This managerial attitude had increased the already pervasive government influence vis-à-vis the private sector and had resulted in a considerable erosion of managerial prerogatives. The 1965 statement warned against further erosion of management rights and against the danger in the tendency of business leaders to be overly dependent on the government. It reaffirmed that the key moving force in the development of the economy rested with private enterprise, rather than with the government.

2. The need for new organizational philosophy: It was widely recognized that paternalism—the emphasis on harmony and the traditional family concept—had been the salient feature of Japanese management. The statement recognized that, historically, the fusion of traditional values with modern technology had made an important contribution to Japan's rapid industrialization. However, in the face of the rapidly changing environment, the statement questioned the continued effectiveness of at least some of the traditional

managerial practices, including the traditional view of corporate organization. The declaration stated that the new organizational philosophy should emphasize *functionalism*, *flexibility*, and *professionalism*. We want to stress, however, that the statement did recognize that some of the traditional practices might continue to be effective. As an example, it pointed out that the reward system based on seniority had outlived its usefulness in a corporate environment where a premium is placed on flexibility and creativity. Nevertheless, it cautioned that the lifetime employment pattern should not be lightly discarded, because the intense loyalty to and close identification with the firm that lifetime job security inspires may more than offset the costs associated with such a practice. The statement exhorted Japanese management to retain and refine the positive elements of traditional managerial practices.

3. Social responsibilities and profit: The statement of 1965, like the one made by the Kansai Chapter in 1964, emphasized the legitimacy of profit. It stated: "The managers should discuss profit more boldly and should strive for its attainment." It reassured business leaders that the pursuit of profit, provided that it was done in a socially acceptable manner, was legitimate and consistent with the social responsibilities of business. The statement also asserted that profit consciousness was essential to overcome the ills of excessive competition.

4. The role of the manager in modern society: The declaration explicitly recognized that a modern corporation was a major driving force for economic development and industrialization, and modern corporate managers had public responsibilities as innovators, organizational leaders, and promoters of economic growth.

The statement urged business leaders to recognize the importance and role of a modern corporation as a system of power of great importance in a highly industrialized society, but at the same time, it cautioned management of large corporations to be aware that in a complex, pluralistic modern society, it is only one element. It urged business leaders to cooperate with those in other fields such as politics, religion, and education for the development of the ideal society. As an important element in their society, the declaration insisted that business leaders must possess not only a high degree of ability, knowledge, and initiative, but integrity and moral character as well.

Both the declarations of 1964 and of 1965 were articulated against the background of an increasingly demanding business environment. The two had several points in common. First, a strong sense of urgency characterized both statements. Second, both explicitly recognized the role that large corporations and professional managers must play in a highly industrialized modern society such as Japan. Third, both focused on recent significant developments in the corporate environment and questioned the continued effectiveness of some of the traditional managerial practices. Fourth, both stressed the importance of the independence of the private business sector vis-à-vis the government and warned against the danger of complacent reliance on the government for the solution of economic problems. Fifth, both emphasized the critical role of profit in the private enterprise system and its legitimacy as long as it was obtained in a socially acceptable manner. Finally, like the earlier pronouncements, both were highly idealistic.

We have now briefly examined the major ideological developments in the postwar era, as reflected in the important public resolutions, declarations, and pronouncements made by the Doyukai. Although the Doyukai ideology has represented the philosophy of an important segment of Japan's managerial elite, we want to emphasize that it has not been unanimously accepted. On the contrary, there have been a number of important executives who have both publicly and privately disagreed with the Doyukai ideology. Some leading executives have considered the Doyukai as no more than an exclusive club of idealistic intellectual business leaders, whose pronouncements have been unrealistic, vague, and impractical pieces of verbal exercise. Some have delighted in their discovery of discrepancies between the Doyukai's ideological stand and the actual, less edifying conduct and performance of the firms managed by Doyukai leaders. Others have pointed out that the Doyukai leaders are major executives in such basic and stable industries as banking, steel, and public utilities, where they have not been exposed to the full rigor of competitive pressure. Still others have felt that the Doyukai has overplayed the "crisis" psychology.

We would violate objectivity were we to claim that the above criticisms are completely unjustifiable. But, despite the limitations and weaknesses of the Doyukai, its ideological formulations have made important contributions to needed changes in the business ideology of postwar Japan. At each of the critical moments, the Doyukai did offer alternatives that, to a degree, served as guidelines for executive action. Clearly, considerable numbers in the postwar generations of executives saw in the Doyukai pronouncements a clear articulation of their own ideas. Many executives have internalized or have attempted to internalize the criteria set in the Doyukai declarations. However, there were those who regarded the Doyukai statements as nothing more than convenient and high-sounding ideological pronouncements for public consumption. Although it is impossible to assess accurately the impact of the various Doyukai ideas and ideals on individual executives and on their practical reactions to them, the Doyukai has played a vital role of ideological spokesman for Japan's professional managers.

Let us now turn to the examination of managerial attitudes toward labor in postwar Japan. In Chapter 3, we noted that the traditional familial values and concepts had served as the ideological base for employer-employee relationships in the large Japanese industrial enterprises of the prewar era. Did the prewar paternalistic ideology apply to the postwar scene? Or have postwar economic and social changes prompted management to alter its view of appropriate employer-employee relationships?

Because of the continuation of such personnel practices as lifetime employment, the reward system based on seniority, and the extensive provision of fringe benefits, one is inclined to conclude that the traditional paternalistic pattern of the previous era still persists. However, closer examination reveals that during the past two decades, at least some of the basic premises and values that had supported the paternalistic ideology appear to be eroding. There are indications that the well-entrenched paternalism is slowly but surely losing its viability and appeal to workers.

The process and manifestations of this change are indeed complex, and an entire volume could be devoted to the analysis of this topic. Our objective is merely to identify major postwar developments that have tended to weaken the paternalistic ideology.

One important factor has been the very rapid emergence of labor unions in postwar Japan, which has reduced considerably the prerogatives once enjoyed by management. As we noted elsewhere, the labor movement, in the face of severe economic distress and with the open encouragement of the Occupation, experienced a sudden upsurge in the immediate aftermath of World War II. Extremely militant labor unions entered the scene in a number of industries, reversing, at least for a time, the power relationship between management and labor.

To the newly emerged militant union leaders there was nothing more irritating than the patronizing and paternalistic employers. They vehemently asserted the inalienable rights of workers and demanded that employers honor these rights. Moreover, management, whose productive assets had been all but destroyed and whose future prospects were very dim, were not in a financial position to meet extensive paternalistic obligations. In fact, in a series of rationalization movements, managements of many firms dismissed or attempted to dismiss their workers, and this disregard of the protective traditional pattern of lifetime employment often became a major cause for labor-management conflicts.

Although the radical militant union leadership soon lost its ascendancy, the labor movement and its unions have become firmly established. By 1965, union membership exceeded the ten million mark, representing approximately 36 percent of the entire work force.[25] With rare exceptions, the employees of large corporations are now unionized. Of course, we should recognize here that most Japanese unions are organized on an enterprise basis (rather than along the lines of craft, industry, or region), thus reflecting the collectivity-oriented particularistic tradition of Japan's social structure. Moreover, union jurisdiction covers nonsupervisory white collar employees as well as permanent blue collar workers, the former providing an important share of union leadership. Therefore, unions are committed primarily to the protection and promotion of the interest of permanent employees within the enterprise per se, and they are little concerned with their members' relative position in the industry, craft, or national economy.[26] This peculiar organization pattern has tended to limit the scope of collective bargaining in Japan, inhibiting the development of class consciousness and solidarity among union members. This limitation notwithstanding, labor unions have become a potent force in most large Japanese corporations. Bilateralism, though somewhat limited, has been achieved, and mechanisms and institutions for collective bargaining based on egalitarian ideology have been established, allowing for "frank, open and direct confrontation of different value systems to a degree not tolerated before."[27] Management can now make few key decisions affecting workers without first consulting

[25] *Rōdō Hakusho, Showa 41 men ban* [*White Paper of Labor, 1966 Edition*] (Tokyo: The Ministry of Labor, 1966), p. 301.

[26] Solomon B. Levine, "Postwar Trade Unionism, Collective Bargaining, and Japanese Social Structure," in R. P. Dore (ed.), *Aspects of Social Change in Modern Japan* (Princeton: Princeton University Press, 1967), p. 257.

[27] *Ibid.*, p. 277.

with the unions. Wage and salary increases, semiannual bonuses, and fringe benefits now have to be negotiated.

The rapid surge of unionization has resulted in a change in the workers' attitude toward their employers. As far as workers are concerned, their wages, salaries, bonuses, and fringe benefits no longer represent something to be dispensed by paternalistic and patronizing employers and accepted by the recipients with gratitude. Workers now have at their disposal means for registering formal protests against unilateral actions by management. No longer can management insist on personalized harmony and loyalty.[28] The trend toward the greater independence and self-determination of labor is likely to strengthen with the passage of time.[29] The progress of unionization has definitely reduced the ideological and emotional attachment of workers to the enterprise. The enterprise can no longer take the employee's loyalty for granted; it must compete for the worker's devotion with his loyalty to the union.

The second significant development that has contributed to the weakening of the paternalistic ideology has been the substantial increase in labor-management legislation, restricting the unilateral control of employers. The government's participation in shaping labor-management relationships has guaranteed certain basic rights to workers and has correspondingly reduced their dependence on the whims of their employers. Many of the workers' benefits are now legally prescribed.

The third key factor in the changed labor-management picture has been a growing labor shortage. As the reader may recall from our discussion in Chapter 3, the paternalistic ideology had functioned in a setting with an abundant labor supply. The rapid postwar economic growth resulted in a serious labor shortage for the first time in Japan's industrial history. Especially serious has been the shortage of younger workers. Hiring competition for new graduates of junior and senior high schools, in particular, has increased considerably during the past several years. The demand has yearly surpassed the supply by three to four times since 1961. The labor market for younger workers, especially, is expected to become tighter in the future, with an anticipated marked decline in the supply to begin in the later 1960's.

With the availability of abundant employment opportunities, the guarantee of lifetime tenure and the seniority-oriented reward sys-

[28] *Ibid.*
[29] *Ibid.*, p. 278.

tem no longer hold much appeal to these young men. So basic a change in the labor market's supply and demand ratio cannot but have a major impact on their attitudes.

Fourth, as we have already noted, the postwar economic and social reforms and the subsequent economic growth have resulted in a considerable weakening of traditional values that had supported the paternalistic managerial ideology. Most certainly, the contemporary educational system of Japan does not provide the support for the traditional values nurturing the paternalistic ideology that the prewar educational orientation supplied.

Fifth, the paternalistic ideology presupposes a very definite status difference between managers and the managed. But the postwar democratization measures considerably closed the status gap that had existed between the managerial class (*shokuin*) and the working class (*koin*). In the prewar Zaibatsu corporation, leading executives, though they were technically hired executives, received large compensations; the bonuses for top management often amounted to as much as 10 percent of the net profit; senior executives were regularly entitled to "status shares" of company stocks. Postwar democratization reduced considerably the relative size of executive compensations and prerogatives. This, coupled with the relative gain in the earnings of workers, has also helped to substantially reduce the status gap. As noted previously, the jurisdiction of unions extends to nonsupervisory management personnel (*shokuin*) as well as to blue-collar workers (*koin*). Moreover, the crises of the war's immediate aftermath induced the two elements to develop close ties. In the face of serious economic distress, both *shokuin* and *koin* found it pragmatically useful and even necessary to close ranks for survival.[30] This necessity was coupled with the appeal of democratic ideology in promoting egalitarian unification.

Furthermore, the postwar ideology of management has been basically averse to the paternalistic philosophy. As shown in the declarations of the Doyukai, professional managers have been deliberately trying to abandon paternalism and to recognize the dignity and rights of the individual worker. Managers, of course, still acknowledge that they have responsibilities to employees, but not the old paternalistic kinds. In the Doyukai statements, employees are recognized as an important and independent sector contributing to the productive process, and, as such, they are believed to have a

[30] *Ibid.*, p. 259.

just claim on the fruits of the business enterprise. The attitude of postwar professional managers, as expressed in the postwar Doyukai ideological pronouncements, is unquestionably considerably different from that of their prewar counterparts.

Practical considerations of the increasing need for operating flexibility have caused management to begin to question the continued value of the paternalistic philosophy and its personnel practices. Few would deny that paternalism was supremely useful in the past, when Japan was undergoing rapid transition from agrarianism to industrialization. To be sure, paternalism always involved certain costs to management, but previously, the benefits more than justified the costs incurred.

A growing number of Japanese managers now acknowledge that, for the reasons noted, paternalism has had its day and lost most of its appeal to workers — particularly to younger ones — at the same time that both the direct and indirect costs of sustaining paternalistic personnel practices (without which the ideology itself is meaningless) are constantly mounting. Clearly, the intrinsic benefits of paternalism are becoming less and less real, so that regardless of one's emotional commitment to it, practical necessity may well force Japanese management to abandon gradually both the paternalistic ideology and its accompanying personnel practices.

Of course, paternalism is still visible in Japan's business scene. It has been too strongly entrenched for too long a time to have yet become obsolete. A certain degree of paternalism may well linger on for some time, but we should recognize that the forces are mounting that are weakening its ideological and practical relevance. Unquestionably, management must now evolve a new set of attitudes toward labor upon which to structure more viable management-employee relationships. This task is very likely one of the most vital challenges now facing Japanese management.

5

Industrial Structure and New Enterprise Groupings

In this chapter we shall examine the organization and structure of Japanese industries, with special emphasis on the major types of business groupings that have appeared in the postwar economy. Modern Japan's industrial organization has some distinctive characteristics, bearing imprints of the country's economic, social, and political history and traditions. An important and unique feature of Japan's contemporary industrial organization is the *kigyo shudan*, or enterprise grouping. In such a grouping, a company is connected with other firms through a web of intricate relationships. We shall first analyze the salient features of Japanese industrial organization as a whole, and then we shall examine several major forms of enterprise groupings (*kigyo shudan*).

Industrial Structure

The Prewar Pattern

The prewar industrial structure of Japan was shaped under historical circumstances radically different from those that shaped Western capitalism. For reasons indicated in Chapter 2, a modern industrial sector had to be developed rapidly in the early Meiji era to provide adequate national defense. This modern sector was created and superimposed on the traditional sector, initially, through government effort, but it was later turned over to the private sector. Although the government maintained monopolies over a few key industries, such as iron and steel, armaments, railroads, telephone, and telegraph, throughout the pre-World War II period, the great majority of industries remained in the private sector. Moreover, ownership and control of private industries were highly concentrated in a few Zaibatsu families.

The term "Zaibatsu" has often been used without sufficient discrimination. Actually, Zaibatsu should be classified in three different categories. First, there were the Big Four: Mitsui, Mitsubishi, Sumitomo, and Yasuda. The first three were particularly prominent, having well-diversified industrial, financial, and commercial interests; the Yasuda Zaibatsu largely confined itself to financial and banking operations. The group second in importance to the Big Four consisted of half a dozen or so combines, including Furukawa, Ōkura, Asano, and others. Most of these lesser combines tended to confine their activities to relatively narrow fields. The third-ranking group comprised those Zaibatsu that emerged in the 1930's to meet the specific needs of the military — a group known as *Shinko* (newly emerged) Zaibatsu. They included Nissan, Nisso, Nakajima, and others. Within the more strict definition of "Zatibatsu," their total number did not exceed twenty or so. The Zaibatsu in aggregate, however, wielded great economic power, as can be seen from the following facts.

At the end of World War II, over a third of the total paid-in capital in Japan was held by the ten largest Zaibatsu. In banking, the four largest Zaibatsu held nearly half of the paid-in capital. In heavy industry, the Big Four alone held over a third of the total paid-in capital. Table 1 summarizes the proportion of the total paid-in capital held by Zaibatsu interests at the end of World War II.

The share of production of key products by Zaibatsu was equally significant. The Big Four produced 51 percent of all the coal, 69 percent of all aluminum, 69 percent of locomotives, 50 percent of pulp, 88 percent of caustic soda, and 43 percent of sulfuric acid, just to mention a few key products. The banks of the Big Four extended over 70 percent of the total bank loans, and their trading companies were responsible for one-third of Japan's total foreign trade. In shipping, the Big Four had 60 percent of the total market.[1]

Despite this high degree of concentration of economic power in the Zaibatsu, few cases of outright monopoly were found in the private sector. In most of the key industries the prevailing pattern was oligopoly.[2] Table 2 summarizes the degree of concentration

[1] Hitoshi Misonō, *Nihon no Dokusen* [*Monopoly in Japan*] (Tokyo: Shiseido, 1965), pp. 37–38.

[2] For reasons, see William W. Lockwood, *The Economic Development of*

TABLE 1

PERCENTAGE OF TOTAL PAID-IN CAPITAL HELD BY THE TEN LARGEST ZAIBATSU IN SELECTED INDUSTRIES PRIOR TO THEIR DISSOLUTION, 1946

Area of Activity	*Big Four** (*% of Total*)	*Smaller Six*† (*% of Total*)	*All Ten Zaibatsu* (*% of Total*)
Finance			
Banking	48.0	2.4	50.4
Trust	85.4	—	85.4
Insurance	51.2	9.1	60.3
Heavy Industry			
Mining	28.3	22.2	50.5
Metals	26.4	15.4	41.8
Machine Tools	46.2	21.7	67.9
Shipbuilding	5.0	7.5	12.5
Chemicals	31.4	7.1	38.5
Light Industry			
Paper	4.5	0.2	4.7
Ceramics	28.4	27.4	55.8
Textiles	17.4	1.4	18.8
Agriculture, Forestry, Fishing, and Food	2.7	6.5	9.2
Sundry	9.7	6.5	16.2
Other			
Gas and Electric	0.5	0.03	0.53
Land Transport	4.9	0.7	5.6
Ocean Transport	60.8	0.6	61.4
Real Estate and Warehousing	22.6	6.7	29.3
Commerce and Foreign Trade	13.6	6.7	20.3

* Mitsui, Mitsubishi, Sumitomo, Yasuda.
† Ayukawa, Nissan, Asano, Furukawa, Ōkura, Nakajima, Nomura.
Source: Adapted from Hitoshi Misonō, *Nihon no Dokusen* [*Monopoly in Japan*] (Tokyo: Shiseido, 1965), pp. 38–39.

measured in terms of value of output controlled by the largest firms in 1937. The pattern may be taken as somewhat representative of the situation existing at the end of several decades of rapid economic modernization and growth.

Another significant factor in the prewar industrial organization was the prevalence of collusive actions, particularly in the form of

Japan: Growth and Structural Change, 1868–1938 (Princeton: Princeton University Press, 1954), pp. 223–235.

TABLE 2

PERCENTAGE OF VALUE OF OUTPUT CONTROLLED BY LARGEST FIRMS, 1937

Industry	*Single Largest*	*Three Largest*	*Five Largest*	*Ten Largest*
Coal	15.1	35.4	44.4	66.06
Petroleum	67.2	91.1	95.5	—
Iron	83.9	97.8	—	—
Primary Aluminum	52.9	91.8	—	—
Shipbuilding	35.4	67.5	86.8	—
Automobiles	59.0	100.0	—	—
Ball Bearings	47.9	100.0	—	—
Sulfuric Acid	22.5	60.7	78.0	—
Sheet Glass	73.5	100.0	—	—
Cement	23.1	40.1	54.3	78.5
Paper	71.7	83.1	90.0	99.3
Rayon Yarn	13.0	36.5	53.4	76.1
Flour	34.6	71.7	—	—
Beer	63.6	99.4	—	—
Celluloid	59.5	77.7	35.1	—

Source: Adapted from Hitoshi Misonō, *Nihon no Dokusen* [*Monopoly in Japan*] (Tokyo: Shiseido, 1965), pp. 41–42.

cartels. They became especially prevalent after World War I. Though not always effectively enforced, both Zaibatsu and non-Zaibatsu firms participated extensively in collusive actions; there were no legal measures prohibiting them. On the contrary, cartels and other forms of collusive actions were formed often at the explicit encouragement of the government. As Misonō notes, cartels became permanent and highly institutionalized in a number of industries. The cotton spinning industry, for example, developed an extensive network of cartel arrangements encompassing a large number of firms. Similar arrangements were found in the sugar, copper, and cement industries.[3]

Finally, we should note that the traditional private sector, with its numerous small, unaffiliated business establishments, remained important throughout the pre-World War II era (Table 3). In fact, the importance of small business establishments was even greater than the figures indicate, because there were a large number of extremely small workshops, too small to be classified as factories.

With the rapid emergence of the modern sector, there developed a clear-cut dichotomy between the modern, capital-intensive, tech-

[3] Misonō, *Nihon no Dokusen*, pp. 35–36.

TABLE 3

NUMBER OF FACTORY ESTABLISHMENTS ACCORDING TO SIZE OF LABOR FORCE, IN SELECTED PREWAR YEARS

Year	Number of Factory Estab-lishments	Number of Employees	Factories with Given No. of Employees (%)*				
			5–29	30–99	100–499	500–999	1000 & over
1909	32,032	821,383	86.0	10.7	2.8	0.3	0.2
1914	31,458	1,009,456	82.7	13.0	3.6	0.4	0.3
1919	43,728	1,808,412	81.4	13.5	4.3	0.5	0.4
1924	48,097	1,968,026	82.3	12.7	4.0	0.6	0.5
1929	59,430	2,055,557	84.2	10.3	3.6	0.5	0.3
1932	66,810	1,921,156	85.3	10.4	3.2	0.4	0.2
1935	84,625	2,620,178	85.1	11.1	3.2	0.4	0.3
1937	105,349	3,253,002	86.2	10.1	3.0	0.4	0.3
1942	125,680	4,736,868	86.9	9.7	2.7	0.4	0.3

* The percentages do not always add up to 100% due to rounding.

Source: Kogyō Tōkei Gojūnenshi, cited in Imai *et al.*, *Gendai Nihon no Dokusen Shihon: Dokusen Keitai* [*Monopolistic Capital in Contemporary Japan: Monopolistic Patterns*] (Tokyo: Shiseido, 1966), pp. 14–15.

nologically-oriented sector, dominated by large enterprises, and the traditional sector, consisting of a large number of small workshops. This phenomenon, often referred to as industrial dualism, was by no means unique to Japan, but the special circumstances of Japan's industrialization significantly heightened this tendency and its importance.

An important consequence of the marked duality in the Japanese economy was the appearance of a substantial disparity in the wage scales and working conditions between large and small enterprises. Mainly due to the almost inexhaustible reservoir or labor, the labor market became highly differentiated between large and small enterprises, resulting in the substantial wage disparity. To take advantage of the lower wage scales prevailing in small- to medium-size enterprises, the modern sector made extensive use of the traditional sector as subcontractors. This practice became particularly extensive after World War I with the rapid development of the modern sector. Thus, through the system of subcontracting, often combined with financial control, a considerable number of small- to medium-size establishments performed indispensable supporting functions for large firms.

The Postwar Pattern

The Occupation initially sought two major goals in its economic reforms: to deprive Japan of the industrial capacity to wage war and to create an economic climate hospitable to democracy. To achieve these goals the Occupation took four key steps. It sought (1) to dissolve the Zaibatsu system, (2) to achieve deconcentration of economic power by breaking up high concentration in key industries, (3) to purge senior executives of major concerns, and (4) to pass the Anti-Monopoly Act.

For the reasons noted in Chapter 2, in time these very ambitious initial goals of the economic reforms and the means of accomplishing them became substantially moderated, particularly after 1948. As a result, the Occupation measures were carried out with varying degrees of effectiveness. The most spectacular progress was made in the dissolution of the Zaibatsu structure. Family ownership and control were removed, the holding companies were dissolved, and each subsidiary became an independent corporation whose ownership was now widely diffused.[4]

To maintain a competitive economy, the Occupation had the Japanese government pass the country's first Anti-Monopoly Act, which in many respects was more stringent than its American counterpart. The law specifically prohibited the following actions: "private monopolization, unreasonable restraint of trade, unfair methods of competition, undue disparities in bargaining power, and certain intercorporate practices affecting directorates and stock holdings."[5] The Fair Trade Commission was created to implement the Anti-Monopoly Act.

The Occupation's program of dissolving highly concentrated individual firms was carried out only to a very limited extent. A total of 325 large firms was designated for dissolution, but only 11 firms were actually dissolved. The main reason for this paucity of decentralization was the change in American policy toward Japan brought on by the cold war; however, other reasons were also present.

For one thing, many of the prewar giant industrial firms were too important in the immediate postwar economy. Practical considera-

[4] For details on the dissolution of Zaibatsu, see T. A. Bisson, *Zaibatsu Dissolution in Japan* (Berkeley: University of California Press, 1954), particularly pp. 33–179.

[5] *Ibid.*, p. 182.

tions forced the Occupation to proceed slowly with its dissolution measures to avoid total disruption of the economy. As Bisson notes, the working elements in Japan's immediate postwar economy moved parallel to the deconcentration measures,[6] and he goes on to observe:

> During the occupation era with the exception of foreign trade firms, the great corporate units of the combines were being shored up, and this under conditions that enabled them to obstruct new competitors. Drastic as the changes forced by SCAP [Supreme Commander of Allied Powers] in combine structure and personnel might seem, their divorcement from economic practice lent them at times an air of unreality.[7]

To implement its reform measures, the Occupation chose, from the very outset, to work through the Japanese bureaucracy. Traditionally sympathetic to big business interests, the bureaucracy offered subtle but quite effective resistance to the weakening of Japan's big business, in which former Zaibatsu-controlled firms had occupied a central position.

We must also note that the conservative political leadership, in power during much of the Occupation period, was also closely identified with the interests of big business. The government channeled a huge sum of capital to large firms in strategic industries such as coal, iron and steel, fertilizer, and shipbuilding for the purpose of reconstruction through various agencies, such as the Reconstruction Finance Bank. The government also favored big business by awarding leading firms important public projects for the Occupation as well as for reconstruction. For these reasons, the structure and organization of the large Japanese enterprises, though their physical assets were destroyed and their senior executives were purged, remained virtually unaltered.

When we proceed to the later years of the postwar period, what do we find to be the salient features of Japan's industrial organization? As in the prewar days, we find little public ownership of industry. In fact, government ownership of industries has even declined. The government still operates the revenue monopolies of tobacco and salt, the telephone and telegraph industry, and the nation's key railroad lines. It also controls a dozen or so financial institutions that are engaged mostly in financing private enterprises. However, key industries, such as oil refining, shipbuilding, steel,

[6] *Ibid.*, p. 198.
[7] *Ibid.*

shipping, as well as power generation and distribution, are now totally in the private sector. Once more economic power has come to be highly concentrated in a relatively small number of firms. According to a study conducted by the Fair Trade Commission in 1966, the aggregate capital of the 100 largest corporations (exclusive of banking and insurance firms) listed in the first section of the Tokyo Stock Exchange as of March 31, 1964, represented 39.4 percent of the total corporate capital in Japan. It is also significant that the rate of concentration steadily climbed from 32.1 percent in 1953 to 35.4 percent in 1958, and then to nearly 40 percent in 1964.[8]

Another common feature of the postwar industrial structure is the absence of product monopolies. Oligopoly is the prevailing pattern in almost all industries. Table 4 presents the degree of concentration as measured by value of output in selected industries.

As in the prewar period, small- and medium-size enterprises have continued to be an important source of employment and income. Industrial dualism has persisted, as indicated in Table 5.

The disparity in wage levels between large and small enterprises still exists, as shown in Table 6. It is important to note, however, that this disparity has been narrowing during the past several years.

Another feature, familiar from the past, is the resurgence of collusive arrangements. The Anti-Monopoly Act was weakened considerably through its two successive revisions, in 1949 and 1953. Though it still remains on the statute books, enforcement has been weak. As early as 1952, only a few years after the economic reforms of the Occupation were instituted, cartel-like arrangements to restrict output again became part of the industrial scene. (The nature of postwar cartels and their effectiveness will be discussed in detail in the next chapter.)

Coexistent with the similarities between the prewar and postwar eras, we find some notable differences. One noteworthy postwar development has been the striking change in the composition of industry. Heavy industry made considerable strides in the 1930's and showed further progress during the war. After the initial setback in the immediate postwar period, it again began to experience a very rapid pace of growth, so that by 1956, the heavy and chemical industries combined were responsible for a little over 50 percent

[8] "Corporate Mergers Are Progressing: Trend Moving Toward Oligopoly," *The Japan Economic Journal,* January 3, 1967, p. 11.

TABLE 4

Percentage of Value of Output Controlled in Selected Industries, 1966

Industry	*Top Firm*	*Top Three Firms*	*Top Five Firms*	*Top Ten Firms*
Sugar	13.0	37.0	52.8	79.8
Butter	58.5	82.1	—	—
Cheese	65.5	77.8	—	—
Beer	47.7	96.2	100.0	—
Pure Cotton Yarn	5.8	16.4	26.1	46.4
Rayon Staple	13.0	32.7	47.8	80.4
Vinylon	67.1	100.0	—	—
Vinyliden	75.2	100.0	—	—
Polyethylene	47.6	75.0	88.5	95.9
Polypropylene	43.7	80.1	95.1	99.8
Pulp	12.8	31.6	42.6	62.6
All Paper	16.0	40.9	50.7	65.4
Newsprint	29.0	62.5	77.4	94.8
Paperboard	9.5	20.5	27.6	41.9
Ammonium Sulphate	12.9	35.9	51.9	—
Calcium Cyanamide	45.1	83.5	95.6	—
Superphosphate of Lime	16.5	34.0	46.6	—
Concentrated Fertilizers	11.6	30.6	47.3	—
Sulfuric Acid	7.5	21.1	32.3	—
Sheet Glass	53.2	100.0	—	—
Cement	16.6	44.5	59.7	79.4
All Petroleum	17.5	42.4	58.4	84.0
Lubricating Oil	20.8	50.4	66.7	92.4
Gasoline	18.0	42.1	58.7	88.6
Naphtha	20.9	51.7	70.5	94.8
Jet Fuel	29.2	58.3	73.2	92.2
Pig Iron	24.0	59.0	83.9	99.5
Crude Steel	18.6	43.7	64.2	79.0
Hot-Rolled Ordinary Steel Products	19.8	45.0	64.6	78.1
Large Shapes (Steel)	29.2	63.7	81.7	96.6
Medium Shapes (Steel)	25.5	49.6	64.0	82.7
Small Bars (Steel)	8.8	18.8	26.1	38.7
Hot-Rolled Special Steel Products	14.6	38.6	54.7	76.6
Galvanized Iron Sheets	12.7	34.8	53.2	74.8
Electrolytic Copper	26.2	64.2	89.4	99.7
Lead	33.1	74.4	96.3	100.0
Zinc	34.0	74.9	97.3	100.0
Aluminum Ingot	38.5	90.6	100.0	—
Ordinary Trucks	23.3	64.0	88.7	100.0

TABLE 4 (*Continued*)

Industry	*Top Firm*	*Top Three Firms*	*Top Five Firms*	*Top Ten Firms*
Small Trucks	33.0	74.1	87.8	100.0
Light Trucks	21.9	57.6	82.1	100.0
Buses	24.0	55.3	81.9	100.0
Ordinary Passenger Cars	48.7	100.0	—	—

Source: Adapted from "Production Concentration in Japanese Industries," *Oriental Economist*, XXXIV, No. 669 (July 1966), 412.

TABLE 5

SIZE DISTRIBUTION OF ESTABLISHMENTS IN MANUFACTURING INDUSTRIES, 1964*

Size of Establishment (No. of Employees)	*Number of Establishments (%)*	*Number of Employees (%)*	*Value of Shipment (%)*	*Value Added (%)*
1–3	74.01	17	1	7
4–9			5	
10–29	16.60	16	10	11
30–99	7.02	20	16	16
100–299	1.73	16	17	16
300–999	.50	15	21	19
1,000 & over	.13	17	30	31

* The percentages do not always add up to 100% due to rounding.

Source: Adapted from *Chūshō Kigyō Hakusho* [*White Paper on Small- to Medium-Size Enterprises*] (Tokyo: Ministry of International Trade and Industry, 1966), pp. 582–585.

TABLE 6

WAGE LEVELS ACCORDING TO SIZE OF ESTABLISHMENT*—MANUFACTURING INDUSTRIES

Sizes of Establishment (No. of Employees)	1957	1958	1959	1960	1961	1962	1963	1964	1965
4–9	30	30	32	33	37	40	31	—	—
10–29	39	39	42	44	48	52	53	—	—
30–99	47	47	50	52	57	61	63	64	65
100–299	58	57	59	60	64	67	69	70	72
300–999	73	71	73	75	76	79	81	81	83

* The wage level at establishments with 1,000 or more employees = 100.

Source: *Chūshō Kigyō Hakusho* [*White Paper on Small- to Medium-Size Enterprises*] (Tokyo: Ministry of International Trade and Industry, 1966), p. 586.

of the total industrial output.[9] And a decade later, this combined sector accounted for nearly 62 percent of the total industrial output (in factories with 30 or more employees).

Another significant postwar change has been the wide diffusion of corporate ownership. Unlike the prewar pattern, all but a few large corporations are now publicly owned. According to a report published by the Ministry of Finance, there were over 19,750,000 stockholders at the end of 1966, and 45 percent of the total shares outstanding were in the hands of individual stockholders. Equally significant is the fact that 55 percent of the nearly 20 million stockholders owned more than 1,000 but fewer than 5,000 shares. Examination of ownership patterns in a few leading corporations further reveals the extent of this wide diffusion of corporate ownership in postwar Japan. Mitsubishi Heavy Industry Company, Ltd., a prominent member of the former Mitsubishi Zaibatsu, now has approximately 380,000 stockholders. The ownership of Yawata Steel, formerly a part of the government steel monopoly, is now distributed among nearly 400,000 shareholders. Hitachi, Ltd., a diversified manufacturer of electric machinery and equipment, has 420,000 stockholders.

The emergence of new types of business groupings is also a significant postwar development; in some respects these groupings take the place of the tightly knit prewar Zaibatsu system. A number of unique factors in the postwar economic environment gave rise to several types of corporate groupings. These intercorporate relationships have had an overriding importance in Japan's postwar industrial system. We shall devote the rest of this chapter to their examination.

Two distinctive types of enterprise groupings are dominant in postwar Japan. The first type consists of the corporate groups of large independent firms. There are several different categories within this type; we have singled out the two most important and unique categories for careful examination: (1) corporate groupings based on former Zaibatsu ties and (2) those formed around major city banks. There is a certain degree of overlapping in these two groupings, but, for the purpose of our analysis, we shall treat them separately.

The second basic type of enterprise grouping is a loose, vertical

[9] *Kogyō Tōkei Sokuhō: Showa 40 nen* [*The Preliminary Report on Factory Statistics, 1965*] (Tokyo: Ministry of International Trade and Industry, 1966), p. 14.

hierarchy of small- to medium-size enterprises organized around a single giant firm. The large firm has a network of intricately related subsidiaries, affiliated firms, and subcontractors, which it fosters and directs. In this respect, a number of leading Japanese corporations constitute a powerful enterprise grouping of their own.

Enterprise Groupings Among Large Independent Firms

Corporate Groupings Based on Prewar Zaibatsu Ties

The results of Zaibatsu dissolution were not equally effective in all aspects. Family control and ownership of the Zaibatsu was totally severed, and the once-so-powerful holding company was destroyed. However, the initial deconcentration measures, intended ultimately to be applied to the dissolution of many of the chief subsidiaries of the gargantuan Zaibatsu, were not fully implemented, and in all but a few cases, these major operating subsidiaries of the former Zaibatsu remained virtually intact.

As Japanese industry embarked on reconstruction after World War II, executives of the newly independent (former) Zaibatsu subsidiaries faced a number of very trying difficulties. On this point, Allen makes the following observation:

> The underlying conditions that had led to the emergence of the Zaibatsu were still present, even in an exaggerated form. At a time when the country was deeply concerned with modernizing its industrial equipment and with closing the wide technical gap between itself and the West, capital was scarce and technical and administrative expertise was still concentrated in relatively few undertakings.[10]

It appeared quite natural to top management of former Zaibatsu firms to cooperate with their erstwhile colleagues in solving these almost unsurmountable problems. By their very disposition, as well as for reasons of advantages to business resulting from cooperation, they began to reestablish their prewar ties as soon as it was feasible to do so.

The period since 1953 has witnessed the reconstruction of the Zaibatsu, though in a definitely altered form. The formal acts of dissolution and personnel purging were ineffective in annihilating the deeply rooted loyalties and solidarity nurtured by the prewar Zaibatsu system. It must be remembered that the family-oriented

[10] G. C. Allen, *Japan's Economic Expansion* (London: Oxford University Press, 1965), p. 185.

prewar Zaibatsu were much more than impersonal financial or industrial combines in the Western sense.

By the early 1950's, the trend for Zaibatsu regroupings became clearly discernible. In 1952, when the ban against the use of the old Zaibatsu names was lifted, most ex-Zaibatsu affiliates, though no longer controlled by the holding company, quickly resumed their former Zaibatsu names and trademarks. The Korean war supplied an added and strong impetus to the reemergence of former Zaibatsu firms. Subsequently, the recession that followed the Korean war wiped out or struck a severe blow to many of the new enterprises unassociated with the former Zaibatsu, which had emerged in the midst of the immediate postwar dislocation and confusion. The worsening of the position of the unassociated enterprises gave former Zaibatsu firms a chance to regain their preeminence in a number of key industries.[11] They now began to strengthen their intercorporate ties by increasing cross-holdings of stocks. This was done more often out of practical necessity than by deliberate intent. The need for funds greatly increased with the progress of reconstruction, but capital was scarce and highly concentrated. The stock market was not yet well developed at the time.

It is not surprising, therefore, that former Zaibatsu firms sought to obtain needed funds from erstwhile sister firms and financial institutions. This procedure was made easier by two successive revisions of the Anti-Monopoly Act that greatly facilitated cross-holdings of stock. Thus, ownership ties among former subsidiaries of the prewar Zaibatsu steadily increased throughout the 1950's. Consequently, we find that cross-holdings of stock among firms within the Mitsui, Mitsubishi, and Sumitomo groups, for instance, were 6.2 percent, 1.3 percent, and 7.0 percent, respectively, in 1953; two years later, the percentages went up to 10.8 percent, 15.1 percent, and 14.0 percent; and by 1957, they reached 11.0 percent, 16.4 percent, and 21.2 percent, respectively.[12]

Former Zaibatsu banks played a very important role in the reunification of the Zaibatsu groups; they were the major suppliers of both short- and long-term funds. The banks and other former Zaibatsu financial institutions, important in the prewar Zaibatsu system, came to occupy an even more crucial position in the postwar era. Throughout the latter period of reconstruction and growth, former Zaibatsu banks channeled a substantial portion of their

[11] *Ibid.*, pp. 185–186.
[12] Misonō, *Nihon no Dokusen*, p. 182.

funds to their sister firms. The trading companies also contributed to the reestablishment of former ties by facilitating reciprocal transactions among member firms.

Once again, a considerable degree of mutual dependence in normal business transactions, as suppliers and customers, developed among firms belonging to the same prewar Zatibatsu groups. The dissolution measures had greatly restricted reciprocal dealings among former Zaibatsu firms, but when they were removed, transactions within the group greatly expanded. In the midst of rapid economic growth, opportunities for reciprocal dealings were plentiful, and the old personal ties, mutual trust, and community of interest played their important roles. The relative importance of reciprocal dealings within the member firms has varied from group to group. One prominent Mitsubishi executive estimates that a fourth to a third of the total business of the Mitsubishi group is done among the twenty or so *major* member firms. If the secondary affiliated and related firms were to be included, as much as a half of the total business could be reported as being done within the total group. It is also estimated that about a third of the total business done by the Mitsubishi Shoji (the group's trading company) consists of transactions within the Mitsubishi group. Although these are crude estimates, they are nevertheless indicative of the degree of mutual dependence in day-to-day business transactions among firms with common prewar Zaibatsu ties.

But the cooperation among member firms of prewar Zaibatsu groups goes much beyond day-to-day business transactions. One of the major challenges facing former Zaibatsu firms in the postwar period has been the need to diversify into new growth fields, such as chemical, petrochemical, and atomic energy. Because of the very nature of these industries, entry into these fields was often beyond the financial, technical, and managerial capacities of single firms. Moreover, a close technical linkage in these industries often makes cooperation of a number of enterprises highly desirable, if not indispensable, for successful entry into them. Again, former Zaibatsu firms cooperated with one another. Significantly, three of the four petrochemical complexes initially established in Japan were formed through joint actions of associated firms within each of the three dominant prewar Zaibatsu—Mitsui, Mitsubishi, and Sumitomo. Likewise, in entering the atomic energy field, 23 major Mitsubishi industrial firms and financial institutions jointly established Mitsubishi Atomic Energy Industries, Ltd. Also, 37 Mitsui-related firms collaborated in forming Nippon Atomic Energy Industry, Ltd. The Sumitomo atomic energy venture, as well, was established through the cooperation of 17 Sumitomo-affiliated firms.

Another potent force in strengthening the interfirm bond in former Zaibatsu groups has been the role of regularly scheduled council meetings of the chief executives of member firms. Sumitomo, the most compact and cohesive of the major Zaibatsu, established as early as 1949 an informal group composed of the chief executives of former main subsidiaries. It later developed into the council of chief executives of the 15 leading Sumitomo firms, which met to discuss major issues affecting the group and to coordinate major decisions among the member firms. Mitsubishi soon followed suit, early in the 1950's, by establishing its coordinating council consisting of the chief executives of 21 major Mitsubishi firms. Regular meetings were also held at the operating level to coordinate activities in various areas — advertising, for example. The chief executives of the 26 major Mitsui firms subsequently set up regular group meetings. With increasing cross-holdings of stock, interlocking directorates among member firms have reemerged, though not to the degree seen in the prewar Zaibatsu.

The degree of solidarity, of course, has varied from group to group and from time to time, and even within a given group. Sumitomo and Mitsubishi have been, on the whole, more cohesive than Mitsui. The latter, the largest prewar Zaibatsu, has experienced some difficulties in attaining intragroup solidarity to the extent achieved by Mitsubishi or Sumitomo. This has been due, in part, to its prewar organization and tradition, which stressed independence and individual action. Mitsui was also traditionally weak in heavy industries, which handicapped its postwar growth. Moreover, as the largest prewar Zaibatsu, Mitsui suffered most from the dissolution measures. Particularly devastating was the severe blow dealt to the Mitsui Bank. As a result, this bank has been unable to exert as strong a leadership as either the Mitsubishi or Sumitomo Banks in the reunification efforts. The experience of Mitsui in this regard provides telling evidence of the very crucial role played by financial institutions in the regrouping of the former Zaibatsu.

It was thus that the three major Zaibatsu — Mitsui, Mitsubishi, and Sumitomo — evolved in their new form during the past decade and a half. Each group is now well diversified and is a very potent force in contemporary Japan, as evidenced in Table 7.

Among these three dominant reconstituted Zaibatsu groups,

TABLE 7

THE THREE MAJOR ENTERPRISE GROUPINGS BASED ON PREWAR ZAIBATSU TIES

Enterprise Groupings	*No. of Major Member Firms*	*Total Paid-In Capital** (¥ *in millions*)	*Combined Annual Sales*† (¥ *in millions*)
Mitsubishi	25	273,900	1,555,800
Mitsui	17	113,000	588,500
	(27)‡	(135,100)	(835,600)
Sumitomo	17	158,600	736,900

* As of March 1, 1967.

† The combined annual sales are for fiscal year 1966 and do not include member firms engaged in banking, insurance, trading, real estate, and warehousing.

‡ Member companies that belong to Getsuyokai.

Source: Adapted from "Nihon no Kigyō Shūdan" ["Enterprise Groupings in Japan"], *Nihon Keizai Shinbun*, April 25, 1967, p. 23.

Mitsubishi has the broadest and strongest industrial base. The Mitsubishi group claims combined annual sales of over $4.3 billion, or over 11 percent of the total sales of the entire manufacturing sector, which, in turn, represents slightly over 4 percent of the nation's gross national product. Firms in this group are engaged in a multiplicity of industries: shipbuilding, machine tools, electrical equipment, automobiles, petroleum refining, chemicals, petrochemicals, synthetic fibres, glass, cement, ceramics, textiles, primary copper and zinc, and home appliances. The Mitsui group, though much weaker in heavy industries than Mitsubishi, includes enterprises that are active in the mining and processing of primary copper and zinc, in shipbuilding, in chemicals, petrochemicals, and paper and pulp industries, in the production of synthetic fibres and machinery, and in food processing. The Sumitomo group had been traditionally strong in the field of primary raw materials. This group is active in the following industries: copper, steel, aluminum, chemicals, petrochemicals, electric equipment, electric wire and cable, glass, machinery, ceramics, and textiles. All three groups, of course, have strong financial and banking institutions. The enterprises belonging to the three groups combined are reported to represent nearly 40 percent of the total paid-in capital of all the firms listed in the first section of the Tokyo Stock Exchange.

Even some of the lesser prewar Zaibatsu — though with a varying degree of success — have regrouped themselves. It is interesting to note that increasing efforts have been made in recent years among these groups to establish closer cooperation. Prominent among these are the Furukawa, Kawasaki, and Nissan groups. For instance, the presidents of 28 Furukawa firms meet regularly. The executive committee, consisting of the presidents of 10 leading member firms, has a major voice in directing the group's activities. The Kawasaki group, though considerably smaller than the others and lacking a diversified base of operations, is known for its close group solidarity. This group also convenes regularly a meeting of the presidents of its 6 leading firms. Likewise, the Nissan groups, which include such prominent firms as Hitachi, Ltd., and the Nissan Motors Co., Ltd., have taken steps to increase intragroup closeness. In 1966, 13 leading firms of this group formed a central coordinating organization.

Compared with the Big Three, however, enterprise groups of lesser prewar Zaibatsu have faced certain basic limitations in their regrouping efforts. In addition to being considerably smaller, they lack a broad diversified basis. Nor do they have strong financial institutions or trading firms that can play a key role in their reunification programs.

Particularly serious has been the absence of banks of their own, which has forced these groups to seek ties with the banks of the Big Three or the non-Zaibatsu city banks. For example, both the Kawasaki and Furukawa firms depend considerably on the Daiichi Bank, and some of the major Nissan firms have established a close tie with the Fuji bank.

The prewar Zaibatsu regrouped themselves under their former names and resumed some of their former characteristics, yet their postwar form and functioning are significantly different from their prewar prototypes in several important respects. Family ownership has been completely severed, and the holding company has been dissolved. Each former subsidiary is now an independent concern, with its own stockholders and board of directors. Reflecting these changes, the term *group* is being applied with increasing frequency to describe the postwar pattern, rather than the term *Zaibatsu.* Moreover, cross-holdings of stock among the firms within each of the groups have not only substantially declined (from the prewar figures), but they are now widely diffused. For example, at the end of the first half of fiscal year 1965, cross-holdings of stock among the Mitsui, Mitsubishi, and Sumitomo groups were 10 percent, 17 percent, and 19 percent, respectively;[13] these proportions of holdings

[13] *Ibid.*, p. 72.

were considerably lower for these groups in 1965 than during the prewar period. Furthermore, in the postwar years, the proportions held by *individual* firms within these groups have been quite low. For instance, in 1965, firms that owned 1 percent or more of the stock of all the firms in the group numbered only two for the Mitsui, four for the Mitsubishi, and five for the Sumitomo groups;[14] the rest owned only a fraction of 1 percent. Thus, the pattern of interlocking of stock ownership as it emerged in the postwar era is very different from the prewar pattern, in which the majority of the stock of major subsidiaries was held by the families, the holding company, or other subsidiaries.

For example, in the case of Mitsubishi Heavy Industries Co., Ltd., in 1966, the largest stockholder was the Mitsubishi Trust Company, which owned 4.13 percent of the total shares. This is a significant contrast with the prewar days, when over 60 percent of the company shares was held by the holding company and a few major subsidiaries. Furthermore, no Mitsubishi industrial or commercial firms appear among the ten largest stockholders; instead, the trust companies belonging to major rival groups, Sumitomo Trust and Mitsui Trust, are the seventh and ninth largest stockholders, owning 2.24 percent and 1.38 percent, respectively, of the total shares outstanding.

A similar situation is quite commonly found among a number of other large former Zaibatsu firms. Thus, unlike the tightly knit and centrally controlled and directed prewar pattern, the postwar groups are a loose confederation of independent enterprises sharing common former Zaibatsu ties and a certain community of interest.

The council of chief executives also differs in its power, structure, and function from the prewar holding company. The present organization is, in fact, no more than a council of peers with equal power, each representing an independent firm. No doubt such a council is useful for exchange of information, informal coordination, and even promotion of reciprocal transactions within each group, but it lacks the ultimate authority and power once vested in the holding company and its executive council; on more than one occasion, the policy decision or advice of the group council has been ignored by the top management of a member firm. True, in some respects banks have exerted strong leadership within the group and have assumed a central coordinating role similar to the holding company, but they have been restrained in such efforts by their

[14] *Ibid.*

limited financial and managerial resources. The former Zaibatsu banks have also been inhibited in fully committing themselves to the sister firms by their desire to strengthen their ties with a number of prominent firms that have emerged in the postwar scene outside their group. Consequently, the former Zaibatsu banks, though their influence vis-à-vis the member firms is by no means to be discounted, are basically different in their function and structure from the prewar holding companies.

We have seen that the practice of interlocking directorates has been resumed. But we should note a rather basic change in the nature of this practice in the postwar setting. In the prewar Zaibatsu, directors of subsidiaries were generally appointed by the Honsha, or the all-powerful holding company, thus giving the directors a major controlling influence. In contrast, in the postwar pattern, interlocking directorates have been drawn from the top management of sister firms, which are basically equal in status to the firms on whose boards these executives serve. It is true that those who serve on the boards of member firms are usually influential within a particular group, but they certainly lack the power once enjoyed by their counterparts in the prewar Zaibatsu.

Another important postwar development is the emergence of intense rivalry among some associated firms. (Although intragroup rivalry was not totally absent in the prewar Zaibatsu, it was restrained by close ownership ties and as a result of the control exercised by the holding companies.) Competition among firms sharing the same prewar Zaibatsu ties is particularly notable in growth fields such as petrochemicals and synthetic fibres. The rivalry that exists among several Mitsui chemical and petrochemical concerns is well known. Three Mitsubishi heavy industry firms also competed vigorously in a number of product lines prior to their recent merger.

The officers of these firms quite understandably place the interest of their own company over that of the group. They are willing to cooperate only insofar as such collaboration will be beneficial to their own firm. Significantly, some executives of leading former Zaibatsu enterprises deliberately seek to minimize the importance of their affiliation with the former Zaibatsu group and are very careful to carve an independent role for themselves. Another important factor that has tended to weaken intragroup solidarity is the drive to diversify into new fields; the postwar composition of the former Zaibatsu has been such that they could no longer confine themselves to their own group in their search for partners. We pointed out earlier that the former Zaibatsu firms cooperated with one another in entering into new fields such as petrochemicals and atomic energy, but it should be noted that in many of these cases, they have collaborated with companies that were only very distantly related, or even with complete outsiders.

We have thus far examined the internal structure and cohesiveness of the former Zaibatsu groups as they reemerged in the postwar scene. In concluding this section, we shall discuss another significant postwar development — the decline in relative importance of the former Zaibatsu firms in Japan's overall industrial economy. They no longer enjoy the preeminence that they had prior to the war. The dissolution measures were partially responsible for this. More basically, however, as the Japanese economy grew both in scale and complexity, a number of non-Zaibatsu firms came to occupy key positions in new industries. Zaibatsu companies have always been strong in traditional industries, but in entering new fields they had to compete against dynamic non-Zaibatsu firms. In nearly every strategic industry, Zaibatsu groups are now pitted against powerful non-Zaibatsu rivals. There is no question that businesses belonging to the prewar Zaibatsu are individually and collectively a potent force in the Japanese economy, but they are not omnipresent in every phase of it. Also, typically, the firms associated with the former Zaibatsu are not the largest within many of the industries — they are usually second, third, or fourth in importance.

Significantly, of the ten biggest industrial firms ranked by sales in 1966, only one bears the name of one of the prewar Big Four Zaibatsu. Among the thirteen city banks, former Zaibatsu banks are still prominent, but even here non-Zaibatsu banks have made substantial inroads. Likewise, in trading, Mitsubishi Shoji and Mitsui Bussan, as powerful as they are, no longer enjoy their prewar eminence. Although prewar Zaibatsu groups have reemerged, they have done so in an altered form, and they are much reduced both in internal cohesiveness and in relative standing in the Japanese economy.

What is the outlook for the future? Will the postwar version of the Zaibatsu groups become more unified, will they stay as fluid and relatively unstructured as they are now, or will they fade away altogether? It is expected that increasing competitive pressure will force a number of Japan's key industries to try to restructure their highly fragmented firms, which, of course, will call for certain kinds of joint actions and mergers. One would think that a significant step toward this end would be the merging of firms *within* each group. Also, successful entry into new growth fields is likely to require joint efforts among a number of companies. In this connection, former Zaibatsu enterprises may be expected to show a greater inclination to cooperate with their sister firms than with outside ones.

Under pressure of the growing threat of international competition, prewar Zatibatsu groups, notably the Big Three, have been intensifying their efforts to further strengthen their group solidarity. Particularly notable in this effort is the Sumitomo group. In September 1967, it was estimated that the average cross-holding of stock among 15 nuclear Sumitomo firms reached 28 percent.[15]

Nevertheless, there are factors mitigating against all these developments actually taking place. The postwar corporate groups based on the prewar Zaibatsu ties will not necessarily become more closely united than they are now. Past efforts to bring about mergers among competing or related firms within the same group have encountered many difficulties. A number of possible mergers have been proposed, but the only significant one that has materialized, aside from the reunification of the trading companies, was the reemergence of Mitsubishi Heavy Industry Company, Ltd., brought about by the merger of the three firms into which the original firms was divided in the immediate aftermath of World War II. It has been particularly difficult to promote mergers in growth fields such as chemical and petrochemical industries. Despite persistent claims to the contrary, only limited progress has been made thus far in achieving them. The most important exception, however, is the agreement for an eventual merger reached between two Mitsui chemical firms — Toyō Koatsu and Mitsui Chemicals — in the summer of 1967.

It is very difficult for member firms to resolve their differences and conflicting interest and for executives to set aside their personal ambitions in order to achieve reunification. With the passage of time, traditional and personal ties will fade away. It will not be in the too distant future that top management positions in these enterprises will be occupied by men without any experience in the prewar Zaibatsu. Whatever cooperation or joint actions a member

[15] "Sumitomo Group Tightens Relations via Stocks," *The Japan Economic Journal*, September 26, 1967, p. 1.

firm will want to enter into with its sister firms will depend almost entirely on the business advantages that such collaboration will offer. While it is unlikely that the prewar Zaibatsu groupings will totally disappear from the Japanese business scene, the future pattern is likely to stay as fluid and loose as it is at present.

Bank-Centered Groups

The other important form of corporate grouping that has emerged in the postwar era is a loose cluster of large industrial firms organized around a major city bank. Although banks were important in the prewar Japanese industrial system, they have shown a marked gain in their relative influence vis-à-vis industrial firms in the postwar period. This is due to the fact that to finance postwar reconstruction and expansion, industrial firms have come to depend heavily on bank loans.

Because of the heavy destruction wrought by the war, and the dislocations of its immediate aftermath, reconstruction meant, to the great majority of Japanese industrial firms, almost total replacement of their physical assets. Such replacements required huge sums of capital. The rapid economic expansion of Japan's major corporations subsequent to the war also required heavy fund procurement (see Table 8).

During the decade ending in 1964, incorporated businesses, on the average, were able to meet only 40 percent of their total fund requirements from internal sources, that is, from retained earnings and depreciation; for the rest, they were compelled to rely on a variety of external sources, as can be seen from Table 9. During the decade under examination, approximately 50 percent of the funds obtained consisted of various forms of debts. Furthermore, it is worth noting that in spite of the remarkable progress made during the postwar period, the stock market provided, on the average, less than 10 percent of the total fund requirements. How heavily large Japanese corporations have depended on debt financing may be seen from the fact that the debt-to-net-worth ratio in the capital structure of the large Japanese corporation is, typically, about 3 to 1.

As shown in Table 9, over 50 percent of the fund requirements of all Japanese corporations during this period have been met by loans from financial institutions. The city banks have been particularly important in this respect, supplying, on the average, 14 percent of the total fund requirements of all incorporated businesses. These banks, numbering 13 at present, with their nationwide network of

TABLE 8

USES AND SOURCES OF FUNDS BY ALL INCORPORATED BUSINESS ESTABLISHMENTS BETWEEN 1954 AND 1965

(¥ in billions)

	Uses of Funds			*Sources of Funds*			
				Internal Sources			*External Sources*
Year	*Capital Investment*	*Working Capital*	*Total*	*Retained Earnings*	*Depreci-ation*	*Total*	
1954	733.8	126.7	860.5	297.6	329.1	626.7	233.8
1955	658.9	129.5	788.4	220.3	395.2	615.5	172.9
1956	1,115.8	416.7	1,532.5	270.0	487.9	757.9	774.6
1957	1,574.7	787.5	2,362.2	558.0	563.0	1,121.0	1,241.2
1958	1,407.4	66.1	1,473.5	466.1	619.2	1,085.3	388.2
1959	1,677.6	363.4	2,041.0	491.0	743.0	1,234.0	807.0
1960	2,539.7	400.9	2,940.6	974.1	960.4	1,934.5	1,006.1
1961	3,601.4	1,094.0	4,695.4	1,073.0	1,250.9	2,323.9	2,371.5
1962	3,475.0	443.3	3,918.3	992.4	1,464.3	2,456.7	1,461.6
1963	3,464.5	644.5	4,109.0	970.0	1,677.1	2,647.1	1,461.9
1964	4,301.0	1,277.1	5,578.1	1,225.8	2,368.2	3,594.0	1,984.1
1965	4,080.1	365.9	4,446.0	1,050.7	2,511.5	3,562.2	883.8

Source: *Keizai Hakusho: Showa 41 nen ban* [*White Paper on the Japanese Economy, 1966*] (Tokyo: Economic Planning Agency, 1966), p. 173.

TABLE 9

SOURCES OF FUNDS FOR ALL INCORPORATED BUSINESSES IN JAPAN, 1955–1964

(All Industries)

Source	*1955–1958* (%)		*1959–1961* (%)		*1962–1964* (%)		*1955–1964* (%)	
Private Financial Institutions								
City Banks	17.4		12.7		15.0		14.7	
Local Banks	6.6		7.2		7.3		7.1	
Long-Term Credit Banks	3.5		3.1		3.0		3.1	
Trust Banks	3.0		2.8		3.7		3.3	
Mutual Banks	5.2		6.9		7.4		6.8	
Others	7.5		6.7		9.1		8.1	
Subtotal		43.2		39.4		45.5		43.1
Government-Affiliated Financial Institutions	5.3		4.1		4.1		4.3	
Bonds	2.3		4.1		1.8		2.6	
Stocks	8.0		10.2		8.1		8.8	
Subtotal		15.6		18.4		14.0		15.7
Total External Sources		58.6*		58.5*		59.5		59.0*
Depreciation	25.6		23.1		26.6		25.3	
Retained Earnings	15.8		18.4		13.9		15.7	
Subtotal		41.4		41.5		40.5		41.0
GRAND TOTAL		100.0		100.0		100.0		100.0

* These figures do not total accurately in the original source.

Source: *Keizai Hakusho: Showa 41 nen ban* [*White Paper on the Japanese Economy, 1966*] (Tokyo: Economic Planning Agency, 1966), p. 175.

over two thousand branches, dominate Japan's private banking. Their preeminence may also be gauged from the fact that they claim over 50 percent of the total deposits in all private banks in Japan; nearly half of these deposits are concentrated in the four largest city banks, namely, Fuji, Mitsubishi, Sanwa, and Sumitomo.

The city banks have consistently favored large enterprises in their loan policy. During the exceptionally high growth period of 1955–1962, they channeled a yearly average of 75 percent of their total loans to large firms.[16] A recent survey reveals that, as of March 31, 1966, approximately 50 percent of the total outstanding loans extended by the city banks were committed to 671 firms (exclusive of financial institutions) listed in the first section of the Tokyo, Osaka, and Nagoya stock exchanges.[17]

Being fully aware of their strategic position, the city banks began, in the mid-1950's, to exert a persistent effort in forging close links with prominent industrial firms by pursuing a preferential loan policy, whose objective was to establish diversified industrial groups with the bank as the nucleus. By the late 1950's, there emerged clearly discernible patterns of corporate groupings based on banking ties.

Six major city banks — Fuji, Mitsubishi, Sumitomo, Mitsui, Sanwa, and Daiichi — have been particularly active in this effort. The importance of these six may be seen from the fact that the total capital of the firms linked to them has reached nearly 63 percent of the combined capital of all the firms listed in the first section of the Tokyo Stock Exchange.[18] In the case of the three Zaibatsu banks — Mitsubishi, Mitsui, and Sumitomo — the nucleus of each consists of its former sister firms, although each has made an effort to bring under its control prominent nonrelated firms as well. The Fuji group has developed somewhat differently, despite the fact that the Fuji Bank had been the main bank of the Yasuda Zaibatsu. This Zaibatsu had been essentially a financial combine lacking a broad industrial and commercial base, unlike the other three major

[16] Noriyoshi Imai, *et al.*, *Gendai Nihon no Dokusen Shihon: Shikin Chotatsu* [*Monopolistic Capital in Contemporary Japan: Financing*] (Tokyo: Shiseido, 1966), p. 124.

[17] "Zen Jojō Gaishi no Kinyu Keiretsu" ["Financial Affiliations of All the Firms Listed on Stock Exchanges"], *Tokei Geppo*, XXVI, No. 8 (August 1966), 1.

[18] "Rokudai Kigyō Shūdan no Genjō to Tenbō ["The Present Conditions and Future Outlook of the Six Major Enterprise Groups"], *Zaikai Tenbō*, XI, No. 2 (January 1967), 69.

prewar Zaibatsu. For this reason, the Fuji Bank has been particularly aggressive in the postwar period in building a strong industrial combine of its own to compete against the other major groups. The Sanwa and the Daiichi, non-Zaibatsu banks, have made special efforts to establish close links with firms that had belonged to lesser Zaibatsu and had never had their own banks.

The Fuji group, which consists of 25 major corporations, boasts a total paid-in capital of nearly ¥310 billion and combined sales of ¥1,685 billion, surpassing the Mitsubishi group. Comparably, the Sanwa group, which consists of a nucleus of 24 firms, reports a total paid-in capital of ¥345 billion and combined annual sales of ¥1,650 billion. Sixteen leading firms are believed to have a particularly close tie with the Daiichi bank, with a total paid-in capital of over ¥164 billion and combined annual sales of ¥728 billion.[19]

In all of these banks, Zaibatsu-linked and non-Zaibatsu-associated, 40 percent to 60 percent of their total loans are committed to the 30 to 50 large firms considered members of the group. The close relationship that exists between the major city banks and large industrial and commercial firms can further be seen from the following data: As of March 31, 1966, among 671 major corporations (exclusive of financial institutions) listed in the first section of the Tokyo, Osaka, and Nagoya stock exchanges, 22 percent obtained 20 percent or less of their total bank loans from a single bank, 50 percent obtained 20 percent to 40 percent, and 28 percent received over 40 percent of their total bank loans from a single city bank. Thus, over 50 percent of the 671 firms surveyed obtained at least 30 percent of their total bank loans from a single city bank. Given the average debt-to-net-worth ratio of 3 to 1 in the capital structure, the relative importance of its main bank to a typical industrial and commercial company can be readily appreciated. Of the enterprises surveyed, the Fuji Bank was the main source of loans to 55, the Mitsubishi Bank to 40, and Sanwa to 48; Sumitomo and Mitsui served as the main bank to 47 and 42 firms, respectively.[20]

When we consider the strength of the relationships between the various major banks and their respective major industrial and commercial firms, some interesting facts emerge. Of the 55 companies to which the Fuji has been the main bank, 17 obtained at least 40 percent of their total loans from this bank; in the case of Mitsubishi,

19 "Nihon no Kigyō Shūdan" ["Enterprise Groupings in Japan"], *Nihon Keizai Shinbun*, April 25, 1967, p. 11.
20 "Zen Jojō Gaisha no Kinyu Keiretsu," p. 3.

out of their 40 firms, 20 obtained at least 40 percent. But in contrast, among the Mitsui Bank's major clients, only 9 of the 42 firms obtained more than 40 percent of their total bank loans from Mitsui, again revealing the relatively weak position of the Mitsui Bank in postwar Japan.

As one would expect, each of the major city banks has sought to strengthen its own member firms by providing a great deal of the funds they have needed for expansion and diversification, and each has made concentrated efforts to encourage its member firms to enter into new growth fields, such as chemicals, automobiles, petrochemicals, synthetic fibres, and so forth. Although the relative strength of the banks varies in each major industrial field, the activities of each banking group are quite diversified.

The city banks have also encouraged their major client firms to cooperate with one another in diversifying into new fields and in establishing close ties among themselves. A number of industrial complexes have thus been established by firms with common banking ties. Invariably, in such cases, the main bank provides the bulk of the needed funds. To strengthen the competitive capacity of their client firms, and to increase their solidarity with one another, the banks have been promoting mergers and joint actions of various kinds among their member corporations.

Out of these practices has evolved what Giichi Miyazaki calls "one set policy," in which each major city bank sought, and largely succeeded for a time, to build a set of diversified industrial groups with itself as the nucleus.[21] This practice, as we shall see in the next chapter, had far-reaching implications in shaping Japan's postwar industrial structure.

The banks have also encouraged cross-holdings of stocks among their member firms. As a result, we find that the cross-holdings in the Fuji, Sanwa, and Daiichi groups were substantial — 11 percent, 9 percent, and 10 percent, respectively — at the end of the first half of the 1965 fiscal year.[22] And, in the three most prominent (former) Zaibatsu groups — Mitsui, Mitsubishi, and Sumitomo — the volume of interlocking of stocks is, as we have already seen, considerably larger than in the other three.

In addition to providing short- and long-term ordinary loans, the city banks have been major purchasers of corporate bonds. Because

[21] Giichi Miyazaki, *Sengo Nihon no Keizai Kikō* [*Economic Structure in Postwar Japan*] (Tokyo: Shin Hyōron, 1966), pp. 48–56.

[22] "Rokudai Kigyō Shūdan no Genjō to Tenbō," p. 72.

of the absence of an adequate bond market, it is estimated that the city banks own approximately 50 percent of the total corporate bonds outstanding.[23]

Moreover, the city banks have bought extensively into the equity of their major client firms. A study conducted among 200 large firms by the Fair Trade Commission, in 1960, reports that financial institutions were the largest stockholders among 131 firms. An examination of the identity of the three largest stockholders in each of these 200 firms reveals that out of a total of 600 stockholders, 434 were financial institutions.[24] According to the aforementioned report released in December 1966 by the Ministry of Finance, 21 percent of the total shares outstanding in 7,578 corporations with capitalization of ¥50 million or more, were owned by financial institutions, including the city banks.[25]

Moreover, this practice has become even more prevalent. It is reported that the total ownership of corporate stock by city banks reached ¥489 billion as of April 30, 1967, representing a 16 percent increase over the previous year. In addition to the determination of city banks to strengthen ties with selected corporations, this increase is partially a result of the corporations' desire to attract "stable" stockholders, in view of the impending liberalization of restrictions on entry of foreign capital.[26]

Another powerful means employed by the major city banks to enhance their control over their major client firms has been to *place* some of their executives on the boards of directors of client corporations. This practice is so prevalent that rarely does one find a board of directors of a major industrial corporation without at least one former executive of their main bank in its midst. Not infrequently, considerable pressure is exerted by the banks on their client firms by means of placing their men in key managerial positions. A survey made in 1956 reported that, among the 450 major firms studied, 311 top managerial positions were held by former executives of eight major city banks.[27] (The data are twelve years old, but they give a reliable impression of the close managerial ties

[23] *Keizai Hakusho: Showa 41 nen* [*White Paper on the Japanese Economy, 1966*] (Tokyo: The Economic Planning Agency, 1966), p. 180.

[24] Misonō, *Nihon no Dokusen*, p. 254.

[25] "Kabunushi no Sosū Heru" ["The Total Number of Shareholders Declines"], *Nihon Keizai Shinbun*, December 27, 1966, p. 3.

[26] "Banks Buying More Stocks of Companies," *The Japan Economic Journal*, July 11, 1967, p. 1.

[27] Misonō, *Nihon no Dokusen*, p. 255.

between the city banks and leading industrial and commercial corporations.) Again, there is no evidence to suggest that the situation has changed significantly in the past twelve years. In the great majority of these cases, the executives involved had officially resigned from their former positions with the bank to accept a full-time top managerial position with a client firm. Usually, these men are put in charge of the firm's financial operations and serve as the liaison officials between the firm and the bank.

We have noted earlier that the three dominant former Zaibatsu groups have a council of chief executives from member firms. The president of the group's bank usually has a strong voice in this council. Following the example of these three rival Zaibatsu groups, the chief executives of the firms belonging to the Fuji banking group began to meet regularly, and, early in 1967, the Sanwa Bank established a regular meeting of the presidents of 12 industrial and commercial firms closely related to it, to discuss problems of mutual interest.

There is no question that the city banks in Japan wield a considerably greater influence over their major client firms than do their American counterparts. Nevertheless, we should note that there is an inherent limit in the degree to which banks, however powerful, can dominate the major client firms, as long as the latter perform satisfactorily. These companies, we must remember, are large, independent corporations with an access to alternative sources for funds. They could, if necessary, obtain funds from other sources when they feel that the city bank's involvement in their managerial decisions is excessive. The keen competition among the city banks themselves for deposits and loans tends to work in their favor. As a result, the relationship between a major city bank and its client firms is rather flexible, and the bank's influence vis-à-vis a client corporation is often determined by such factors as the performance of the firm, the personalities involved, the past relationship of the company to the bank, and the firm's managerial competence.

There are recent developments indicating that the relationship between the city bank and its client firms is becoming more fluid. For one thing, the recent growth of many of the major client corporations has surpassed the capacity of city banks to supply the bulk of the funds they need. For example, although the Fuji Bank commits over 40 percent of its total loans to its member firms, it accounts for only 20 percent of their total debt. The Mitsui Bank has been able to supply only 13 percent of the total debt of its member corporations. This has compelled many industrial and commercial firms to seek additional funds from other sources. This fluidity can be seen from the fact that, according to a recent survey, as many as 148 out of 652 corporations listed in the first sections of the Tokyo, Osaka, and Nagoya stock exchanges changed their main bank during the two-year period ending May 30, 1967.[28]

Furthermore, the city banks have recently come under attack because, as is widely acknowledged, their strong inclination toward developing industrial groups of their own has contributed significantly to creating excessive competition, with its accompanying problems. Some prominent business leaders are becoming increasingly critical of the "one set policy" of the banks. We should also note that keen competition among the city banks for loans and deposits, as well as the pressure to support their member firms in the struggle against competitors tied to rival banks, has at times led to careless lending. Some major banks suffered a considerable loss of prestige when evidence of a number of carelessly made loans came to light during the recession of 1965.

Growing interest in the reorganization of the industrial structure to increase the competitive capacity of Japanese industries, in view of increasing foreign competition, is another factor that is likely to have a major impact in reshaping the relationship between the city banks and their client firms. Already, there have been mergers of corporations with different banking ties — for example, the recent merger of the two major automobile firms. Moreover, the possibilities of mergers among the city banks themselves, as a part of industrial reorganization, are currently being discussed. It is highly unlikely that they will occur within the foreseeable future; however, in the event that they do take place, the existing grouping patterns would be drastically affected.

Another very significant development, which may well lead to a basic change in the present structure of the bank-centered groupings, is the recent government decision to issue government bonds. This has created an additional source of funds for business enterprises. The traditional source from financial institutions, which has played so vital a role, is no longer so strategic. Reportedly, government bonds have already had a considerable impact on the fund

[28] "Yureugoku Daikigyō no Yūshikeiretsu" ["Changing Patterns of Financial Affiliated Relationship of Large Corporations"], *Tōkei Geppo,* XXVII, No. 9 (September 1967), 7.

supplies of major corporations. It is also important to note that the capacity of major corporations to finance their capital investment out of their internally generated funds — retained earnings and depreciation — has been increasing. All these factors are bound to alter significantly the future patterns of bank-centered groupings.

The Vertical Link Between Large Firms and Small- to Medium-Size Enterprises

Many large Japanese firms are industrial combines in their own right. They have under their control a network of subsidiaries, satellite or affiliated enterprises, and a pyramid of subcontractors. It is not unusual to find a large corporation effectively controlling as many as several hundred smaller firms. The latter depend to a varying degree on the major concern, not only for business, but for financial, technical, and managerial assistance, and their operations are, to a considerable degree, integrated with those of the major concern. In this section we shall examine the nature of the vertical link between the single large concern and its affiliated firms.

Although the satellite firms may be grouped in a number of different ways, we shall follow in our analysis what appears to be a common method of classification in Japan. Depending on the closeness of their ties to the main concern, these enterprises are grouped into two major categories: *Kankei Gaisha,* related firms, and *Keiretsu Gaisha,* affiliated firms.

The definition of *related* (firms) varies somewhat among the main companies. In some of them, only wholly owned subsidiaries are considered as related. However, in a great majority of cases, those subsidiaries in which the parent concern has the controlling interest are also considered related enterprises. For example, one leading corporation considers a firm related if it meets any one of the following three requirements: (1) the parent firm is the majority stockholder, (2) the parent firm is a minority stockholder but is in a position to select the top management personnel of the satellite enterprise, or (3) the parent company has a management contract. A similar definition of *related* is used by a number of other companies.

The *affiliated* firms (as contrasted to *related*) have a more remote relationship with the main concern, because their ownership tie to the parent concern is either weak or nonexistent. Affiliated firms are linked to the parent concern primarily through an ordinary business relationship. The majority of the enterprises in this category are subcontractors.

Relationships with Related Firms

When one examines the financial statement of a large Japanese corporation, he will readily notice that, typically, it has considerable financial commitment to other firms in the form of equity holdings and long-term loans. A recent survey conducted by the Mitsubishi Economic Research Institute reports that 632 leading companies had their total investments in corporate securities of other firms, in government and corporate bonds, and in long-term loans to other firms, the aggregate amounting to roughly ¥2,570 billion at the end of the first half of the 1965 fiscal year. This was approximately 70 percent of the total paid-in capital of these major firms, just less than 50 percent of their total net worth, and approximately 11 percent of their total capital. Among 463 manufacturing firms, the total amount committed to the three types of investment mentioned, for the same period, amounted to about ¥1,669 billion, or close to 65 percent of the total paid-in capital and 40 percent of the total net worth.[29] Among manufacturing concerns alone, there were as many as 9 major companies whose total commitment in investment in stocks and bonds of other firms exceeded ¥20 billion. If the companies with a total commitment to subsidiary firms of ¥10 billion and over were included, their aggregate number would be 36.

Although these sums include commitments to equally large firms, such as sister enterprises, major customers, major suppliers of raw materials, financial institutions, and security firms, the greater portion has gone to subsidiaries. Table 10 presents the degree of commitment that a selected list of large Japanese manufacturing corporations have in their subsidiaries.

These subsidiaries perform a wide variety of functions for the parent concern. Some are suppliers of raw materials; others perform subcontracting operations, feeding parts and components to the parent firms; and some perform marketing functions. Still others undertake different forms of auxiliary functions for the parent concern, such as maintenance, transportation, and janitorial services.

[29] *Kigyo Keiei no Bunseki: Tokei hen Showa 41 nen Jōkiban* [*Performance of Major Business Enterprises: Statistical Part*] (Tokyo: The Mitsubishi Economic Research Institute, 1966), p. 18.

TABLE 10

NUMBER OF SUBSIDIARIES AND AMOUNTS OF INVESTMENT IN SUBSIDIARIES BY SELECTED MAJOR JAPANESE CORPORATIONS

Name of Company	*Total Number of Subsidiaries*	*Total Amount of Investment in Subsidiaries (¥ in thousands)*
Hitachi, Ltd.	91	23,412,452
Yawata Iron and Steel Co., Ltd.	23	9,633,568
Tokyo Shibaura Electric Co., Ltd.	55	10,631,078
Toyota Motor Co., Ltd.	18	12,602,866
Toyo Rayon Co., Ltd.	23	3,689,573
Matsushita Electric Industrial Co., Ltd.	347*	18,949,002

* The figure includes sales dealerships.
Source: Company records.

Some subsidiaries are established or acquired with the express purpose of their carrying out diversification programs.

We shall now attempt to isolate the major reasons for the widespread existence of subsidiaries for major Japanese manufacturing firms. One important reason for this phenomenon is the ubiquitous presence of a substantial wage scale disparity between large and small enterprises, as noted earlier. Because of this difference in the wage structure, with the small enterprises paying a substantially lower wage, the large firms have found it advantageous to organize subsidiaries for the performance of labor-intensive operations. It has also been quite common in recent years for large firms to separate unprofitable phases of their operations, or supporting functions, from the main corporate entity by allocating them to independent subsidiaries established for that purpose. In addition to the lower wages, several other advantages are claimed for this approach. As consolidation of financial statements is not required by Japanese commercial law, the separation of unprofitable business from the main corporate entity can result in the improvement of the reported performance of the parent company. Moreover, it allows its management to focus attention on the specific ills of the severed operation in order to determine more effectively the indispensable reform measures needed. In the form of a separate company, its management benefits from greater flexibility and freedom of action.

One frequently cited advantage of incorporating supporting functions, such as transportation and maintenance, into a subsidiary is that such a subsidiary can be operated as an independent profit center allowing for tighter control over the operation. It is quite true that such a profit center may exist without its having a separate legal entity, but, given the wide diffusion of responsibilities that prevails in large Japanese corporations (see Chapters 7 and 9), the creation of a separate corporation makes it easier to assign more clear-cut responsibilities. Moreover, as an independent unit, it is possible for the separate firm to solicit profitable business from other enterprises, thereby reducing the burden of the parent company as the sole supporter of that operation.

A recent trend for the decentralization of authority has also contributed to the proliferation of subsidiaries. During the past several years, a number of large corporations have incorporated their key divisions into subsidiaries not only as a move toward greater clarification of profit responsibilities but also for the stake of decentralization of decision-making to lower levels. It is reported that such separation has significantly improved the performance in a number of firms, because, as separate firms, they acquired greater operating flexibility and can respond much more quickly to rapidly changing market conditions. For similar reasons, large corporations have used the subsidiary form of organization for entering new fields. This is particularly true when the new venture is not directly related to the operations of the parent concern, or when it involves a substantial risk. When a company acquires another firm for diversification (or for other reasons), it is quite common to maintain the acquired firm as a subsidiary. This is done for the same reasons that the similar practice is followed in the United States. Of course, when entry into new fields requires joint venture with other firms of equal rank, the new combine must be organized as an independent corporate unit.

Another factor in the proliferation of subsidiaries in Japan is the need for management to find suitable employment opportunities for retired personnel. The traditional practice of lifetime employment assures each regular worker a place in the corporation until he reaches the compulsory retirement age of fifty-five. (There is a recent trend for it to be extended by three or five years.) This relatively early compulsory retirement has been regarded as necessary, under the Japanese system of employment, to provide opportunities for younger men. Although retired personnel receive a substantial sum in retirement allowance, given the inadequacy of the social security system and the increasing life expectancy, the great majority of these men must find another source of income after retirement. But, in Japan's closed system, it would be impossible for these compulsorily retired men to seek employment with another firm. It has therefore been a common practice for management to find suitable employment for such men, particularly those in managerial ranks, in the corporation's subsidiaries.

As a consequence, the managerial and supervisory staff in most subsidiaries of major corporations is made up largely of employees retired from the parent concern. Similarly, since under the permanent employment system it is virtually impossible for firms to dismiss their employees for incompetence, some companies have followed the practice of transferring less competent personnel to their subsidiaries, where they will do less harm. Although it is not often openly admitted, the personnel considerations discussed above have exerted a strong pressure for the creation of new subsidiaries.

We have identified the major reasons why a large Japanese corporation typically has a number of related firms. Some, no doubt, have been acquired or established for bona fide strategic reasons. However, careful examination reveals that the reasons given by executives interviewed are frequently ambiguous, and in many instances they are cited as justification after the fact. Few firms studied had a clear-cut policy guideline for the formation of related firms. In almost all of the companies studied, each case is evaluated on its own merits, as it occurs. Nonbusiness considerations, such as personal ties and friendship of top management, have often been a major factor in acquiring subsidiaries.

In most cases, subsidiaries have been traditionally relegated to an inferior status in the corporate hierarchy. They have been commonly referred to as *Kogaisha*, or child company, and have been accorded a lower status in relation to the parent concern. The latter views its subsidiaries with a condescending and patronizing attitude. The subsidiaries, for the reasons noted earlier, have often lacked dynamic leadership and have been content to assume a secondary role.

Recently, however, a gradual change has become noticeable in the traditional relationship between the parent company and its *Kogaisha*. There are two interdependent reasons for this. One is the growing competitive pressures; the other is that during the past decade, the number of subsidiaries has significantly increased in most large firms, and with the increase grew the commitment of resources of the parent concern to its subsidiaries. A view has gradually emerged among the managements of a number of progressive concerns that subsidiaries could and should be much more than a haven for retired personnel. By assisting their subsidiaries to develop their potential capabilities and by integrating their activities effectively with those of the parent concerns, the performance of the entire group could be substantially improved. The top managements of a number of large corporations have come to realize that what they were managing was not just one major corporation but an industrial combine consisting of a large number of firms, with the parent concern as the nucleus.

To give continuing attention to the problems of the related companies, a number of leading corporations recently established a staff unit in the corporate headquarters to serve as a liaison between the parent company and its related firms. This section or department seeks to assure a steady flow of useful information to the subsidiaries from the parent company and to integrate their activities with those of the parent concern. A change is also notable in personnel practices: Some firms have begun to send capable managers to their subsidiaries on a "loan" basis. In the past, those in the parent company were hesitant to move to subsidiaries, not only because of a negative connotation attached to such moves but because, once they left the parent company, their chances for returning to it were almost nil. This is gradually changing, however. Some firms even go so far as to view assignments to subsidiaries as part of their executive development program, because in a smaller company it is possible to give younger men broader managerial responsibilities. Of course, this infusion of competent managerial talents has also benefited the subsidiaries.

A few firms have a gone a step further and have undertaken a thorough evaluation of each subsidiary and its functions with the hope of ultimately consolidating them. Gradually, marginal ones will be phased out or merged with other subsidiaries. Some large corporations have been actively promoting mergers among smaller subsidiaries to attain greater efficiency. Others are also attempting to encourage joint actions and coordination of activities among the subsidiaries themselves in order to avoid costly duplication of capital investment, to encourage use of common facilities, and so on.

Thus, though slowly, signs are appearing that the classical relationship between the parent concern and its subsidiaries is changing Although the parent companies' attitudes toward their subsidiaries are gradually becoming more positive, few have definite and meaningful criteria for establishing new subsidiaries or related firms, which appears to be just as critical as improving the parent company's relationship with the existing related firms.

Relationships with Affiliated Firms

Since the great majority of affiliated firms are, in reality, subcontractors, we shall confine the following analysis to the parent company's relationship with its subcontractors. Large Japanese manufacturing firms in most industries have made rather extensive use of subcontractors, who have thus become an important and indispensable element in the total production process. In the automobile, machine tools, and electric home appliance industries, the role of subcontractors has been particularly important. In many cases, large firms confine their activities merely to assembly operations. In fact, in these industries, it is not unusual to find that payments to their subcontractors represent over 50 percent of the cost of goods sold by major manufacturers.

For example, in 1966 a leading automobile manufacturer had 124 primary subcontractors — those with whom the firm dealt directly. Most of these subcontractors were small- to medium-size firms. In this case, the typical subcontractor had annual sales of roughly ¥80 million and a labor force of approximately 300. Some subcontractors have a considerably smaller operation, with annual sales of less than ¥10 million and with no more than 50 employees. The great majority of these smaller subcontractors are located in the immediate vicinity of the large company's major plants. About 30 of these affiliated firms sold their output exclusively to this company, and the rest sold at least one-third of their total output to it.

Use of subcontractors is not limited only to the manufacturing of parts or components. In some industries, subcontractors perform various phases of a given production process, or they manufacture finished products for the large concern. For example, manufacturers of synthetic filaments and staples use subcontractors extensively in their spinning, dyeing, and weaving processes. An executive of a leading manufacturer of staples and filaments reported in 1966 that 70 percent of his firm's spinning and nearly 90 percent of its weaving and dyeing were performed by subcontractors. Such an extensive use of subcontractors is quite typical in this industry. Moreover, it is a common practice in this industry to engage subcontractors to manufacture a wide variety of finished products ultimately to be sold to consumers under a main firm's trademark. Such enterprises rely in this manner on subcontractors to achieve downward vertical integration.

A noteworthy feature in the use of affiliated firms is that beyond primary subcontractors, there are a host of secondary subcontractors who are only indirectly tied to the large firm via the primary ones. It is not unusual to find several "layers" of hierarchically organized subcontractors in a pyramid-like pattern, with each performing subcontracting operations for those at a higher level in the pyramid. Most commonly, the lower its stratum, the smaller the establishment. In the automobile firm mentioned earlier, the executive we interviewed estimated that if all the secondary subcontractors affiliated with his firm were counted, the total would reach as high as several hundred establishments, some no bigger than shops with only several employees. In fact, many of these small subcontracting workshops were started by former employees of the parent company.

A noteworthy development during the past decade with regard to subcontracting operations is the pronounced trend for large firms to make concentrated efforts toward establishing close ties with their subcontractors and to integrate them into a total operation. This relationship is often referred to as *shitauke keiretsu*, or subcontracting affiliated relationship. We shall examine it in some detail in the section that follows.

It is relevant to indicate in this connection the reasons why large Japanese enterprises have relied so heavily on subcontractors. Some of these reasons are similar to those that have prompted their use of related firms. The presence of a substantial disparity in wage scales, according to size of enterprise, has, of course, been an overriding factor (Table 5). Although the lower wage scale in smaller enterprises is partially offset by lower productivity, large manufacturers have been able to realize substantial savings in production costs by having smaller subcontractors perform the labor-intensive phases of their manufacturing operations. Subcontracting has also served as an effective buffer against economic fluctuations; this has been particularly important to large Japanese enterprises weighed down by the high degree of inflexibility resulting from the permanent employment practice. A common strategy of a large Japanese firm has been, therefore, to limit the number of permanent employees to a cyclically justifiable minimum and to rely on subcontractors and temporary workers to handle the additional volume of work.

The extensive use of subcontractors has also resulted in a substantial reduction of risks for the large firm. Much of the burden associated with capital investment, inventory storage, and so on, has been traditionally assumed by the affiliated firms. This feature has been particularly attractive to manufacturers of products characterized by frequent model changes, producers of items such as electric home appliances and automobiles. It has been common for subcontractors to bear certain financial burdens for the large firm. Though the specific terms vary somewhat among the industries, as well as according to prevailing economic conditions, subcontractors customarily extend 60- or 90-day credit to their customers. Subcontracting has also made it possible for large companies in certain industries to achieve downward vertical integration with a minimum of risk and investment, as already illustrated in the synthetic fibre industry.

Until recently, large manufacturing concerns had only been interested in maximizing their short-run gains from extensive use of subcontractors. It has been quite common for them to exploit the relatively weak bargaining position of small subcontractors. A series of recent developments, however, has forced these concerns to depart from a relationship of exploitation and to move gradually toward one of cooperation with the subcontractors by extending them financial, managerial, and technical assistance. This, of course, increased the degree of control exercised by the parent concern over these subcontracting firms.

What factors have been responsible for this gradual change in the attitude of large enterprises toward their subcontractors? The first signs of this change became noticeable in the late 1950's, when most large businesses greatly expanded their capacities to meet the rising demand for their products. Because many of these businesses had relied extensively on subcontractors, it was impractical for them to expand their own productive capacity without a simultaneous growth in the capacity of their subcontractors. The smaller firms, however, lacked sufficient financial, managerial, and technical resources for such expansion, necessary for keeping up with their major customers. Consequently, the large companies were compelled to extend assistance to their subcontractors.

The growing competition and the resulting interest in rationalization have been other important factors. Most large firms undertook extensive rationalization measures to achieve greater efficiency. As rationalization programs progressed, it soon became apparent to the management that because of the heavy dependence on subcontractors, rationalization in the main concern alone was not sufficient and that such efforts should include subcontractors. Moreover, because of the traditional inefficiency of small subcontractors, there was much room for improvement. The need for improving their operating efficiency has been further heightened by the fact that the growing labor shortage has substantially narrowed the disparity in wage scales between large and small establishments.

As part of their rationalization measures, some parent companies have closely integrated the operations of their subcontractors with their own. For example, leading automobile manufacturers have integrated the operations of their subcontractors to the point where the production plans of each subcontractor are completely synchronized with the master production plan of the parent factory, so that the subcontractors can feed, on demand, the assembly lines of the parent concern. Such a degree of integration in production planning requires considerable direction and assistance from the parent concern in the areas of technical know-how, quality control, purchasing of raw materials, and production scheduling. There must also be a constant flow of information concerning changes in production plans. The parent firm must notify its subcontractors well in advance of model changes and often has to help them make needed adjustments.

Competition among large concerns for the services of subcontractors has been another important factor promoting the establishment of closer ties between the parent firm and its affiliates. In such industries as synthetic fibres and plastics, the extent to which large manufacturers of raw materials have been able to control the market for finished products has depended, to an important degree, on their ability to establish and maintain firm control over their subcontractors. Thus, large firms have competed vigorously to bring selected, well-managed subcontracing firms under their exclusive control. The ties, once established, have often been strengthened to prevent "pirating" by competitors. Competition for subcontractors has become particularly keen when new entrants into an industry have attempted to induce subcontractors of their major competitors to come under their control.

The rapid introduction of new technology and products has been another impetus causing large enterprises to forge closer ties with their subcontractors. A parent firm's decision to add new products, or to change its production processes to cope with technical changes, has often required some important changes in operating methods of subcontractors as well. The large concern has often found it necessary to assist its subcontractors in making those changes. For example, when manufacturers of rayon filament began to market other types of synthetic filaments and staples after World War II, it required considerable effort on their part to persuade small subcontractors performing spinning, dyeing, and weaving operations to take on the new, unfamiliar products. To induce subcontractors to do so, the manufacturers had to provide them not only with extensive technical assistance, but also with liberal financial aid for purchasing the new equipment and changing production methods. It is also likely that by changing the equipment and operating methods to meet the requirements of one large firm, the subcontractor loses his flexibility in serving other customers, which of course increases his dependency on a particular parent firm. Moreover, in order to protect its technical know-how, the parent firm may well insist that subcontractors serve the firm on an exclusive basis.

Subcontractors themselves have found certain advantages in affiliating themselves with a leading concern, and a large number of them have actively sought opportunities to do so. There are two main advantages in this for the subcontractors: (1) the possibility of attaining greater operating stability and (2) the opportunities to receive financial, technical, and managerial aid. Because subcontractors have borne the brunt of economic fluctuations, they have welcomed opportunities to attain greater degrees of stability in their operations. Most of the subcontractors were undercapitalized, did not possess superior technical expertise, and were unable to attract competent managers; they therefore welcomed the assistance from large firms. It was out of these considerations and conditions that closer links between parent concerns and a selected number of their subcontractors were forged.

Some large manufacturing firms have attempted to formalize this closer relationship by organizing associations of their subcontractors. The automobile industry provides a good example of this; each major automobile manufacturer has organized an association for its subcontractors. For example, Toyota Motors has an organization called *Kyohōkai*, consisting of some 190 subsidiaries and subcontractors. Such associations promote not only a close relationship between the large firm and its affiliates, but also the cooperation among the parent firm's group of subcontractors themselves. The management of the parent firm meets regularly with the members of the association to inform them of its plans and to exchange views. The association also sponsors educational activities, such as seminars for management and technical training, and provides opportunities for the exchange of technical information among the subcontractors. It is also through the association that the parent firm extends financial, technical, and managerial aid. It also serves a useful function in coordinating the activities of various subcontractors, thus establishing a sense of solidarity and loyalty to the parent firm and to the group. Some large concerns are actively seeking to bring about mergers and joint actions among subcontractors to increase their productivity. Similar organizational efforts are being made by manufacturers of synthetic fibres and electric home appliances.

Thus a number of large companies in various industries have been making a considerable effort to create a sense of mutuality of interest and close identification with the parent company among, particularly, their primary subcontractors. The traditional relationship characterized by one-sided domination and exploitation has been gradually giving way to a more cooperative type of relationship characterized by mutual trust.

The emergence of this close link between the parent firm and its subcontractors has not, however, been without problems. From the point of view of the large firms, the closer relationship has imposed on them substantial burdens, particularly in the form of financial commitment. It has also tended to reduce the flexibility they had enjoyed in their former use of subcontractors. Tied to a certain number of subcontractors, the large concern is often prevented from evaluating make-or-buy decisions on an objective basis. Also, being tied to the affiliated firms tends to impede the use of other, nonaffiliated subcontractors, even though it would be economically advantageous to do so. Moreover, the closer relationship has had a serious long-term ramification in that it has discouraged the development of large-scale independent suppliers of parts and components, with its accompanying advantages of economy of scale, and has forced the large firm to deal with many small inefficient enterprises. This has posed serious problems in the face of growing international competition and narrowing disparity in the wage levels between large and small enterprises.

From the subcontractors' point of view, the strengthening of their vertical links with the parent firm has tended to weaken cooperative activities among the subcontractors themselves, in spite of active encouragement for such cooperation on the part of the government during the last decade. Moreover, entering into a close relationship with a particular large firm has not always resulted in the desired advantages. This became particularly evident in the recession of 1965, when many subcontractors found, to their great disappointment, that in times of economic stress and real need, the close affiliation did not really bring about the stability they anticipated. In fact, in many cases, it created new problems, offsetting the advantages gained by such a relationship. A high degree of dependence upon a single parent firm has often resulted in the loss of the subcontractor's bargaining power and in his inability to obtain business from other, larger firms. Many of these subcontractors have had no choice but to accept the terms prescribed by the main concern. In a recent study of nearly 1,000 subcontractors closely tied to large enterprises, over 80 percent of those surveyed reported that terms were almost totally dictated by the parent firms.[30] Some also find the burden of modernization or expansion excessive, for frequently the cost is not totally covered by the large concern. Moreover, the parent firm often expects its subcontractors to reflect all of the cost reduction achieved through the assistance given in lower prices and/or better services. Thus, modernization and rationalization carried out by means of financial, technical, or managerial assistance from the large concern have not invariably benefited the subcontractors.

The disadvantages in the closely affiliated relationship became particularly apparent during the recession of 1965. As a result, the conviction grew among both large firms and subcontractors that they might have gone too far in their interdependence upon one another. In the past year or two, therefore, the pendulum has been gradually swinging in the other direction. A number of large firms are carefully evaluating each of their subcontractors. They are now attempting to eliminate the weaker ones from the group, and, in selecting new ones, they are being more discriminating. A number of parent firms are encouraging their subcontractors to seek out other customers, so that they will not be exclusively or even primarily dependent on one large firm.

The subcontractors themselves have been actively seeking means

[30] *Chūsho Kigyō Hakusho* [*White Paper on Small- to Medium-Size Enterprises*] (Tokyo: Ministry of International Trade and Industry, 1966), p. 306.

of reducing their dependence on a particular large concern, looking to find other outlets. They have become more interested in joining their own cooperative associations. In fact, in some cases subcontractors who deal with a particular parent firm have formed a cooperative association of their own to bargain collectively with the firm, in an effort to overcome their weak bargaining position as individual enterprises. The *keiretsu kankei,* or affiliate relationship, forged between parent companies and their subcontractors, continues to exist, but because of the developments discussed above, it is likely to remain fluid and flexible.

6

Challenges of International Competition

The very success of Japan's postwar industrial growth brought about steadily increasing international pressure for liberalization of her very stringent restrictions on entry of foreign goods and capital. By 1964, import restrictions on all but a few products had been lifted. In 1967, the Japanese government took the first step toward the relaxation of stringent restrictions on entry of foreign capital as well. Thus, Japanese industries will now be exposed to the full challenge of foreign competition, in both the domestic and the international markets. Japan's key industries, in spite of their very rapid postwar growth, were, and still are, too small and too uneconomically fragmented to compete effectively against American and European giant firms. To overcome this competition gap, it is imperative that Japan's key industries reorganize along a more efficient line.

Looming in the background of this situation is the issue of the relationship between government and business. As we have already noted, Japan has developed a rather unique system of mixed economy, which combines an extensive reliance on private initiative and a market mechanism with pervasive government guidance. Because of the overriding role the government assumes in the entire economy, it has also taken a very active interest in guiding Japan's key industries in the task of reorganization to meet the exigencies of industrial competition from abroad.

The government, with the conservative Liberal Democratic Party in power and supported by the state bureaucracy, is sympathetic and responsive to big business interests. The latter are, in turn, firmly committed to the perpetuation of the existing political system. Beyond this basic consensus, there is, however, considerable disagreement, not only between the government and big business, but even within each group. Thus, examination of the issues of reorganization will also serve to reveal the close and intricate but dynamic relationship that has evolved in Japan between the government and big business. Before examining and evaluating the various issues relating to the reorganization of key industries, we should first consider the competitive behavior of large Japanese firms, during the last two postwar decades, which has brought about the fragmentation of Japan's key industries.

Competitive Behavior of Large-Scale Firms

The competitive pattern that has emerged in most large oligopolistic industries in postwar Japan has been rather fluid, characterized by keen rivalry on the one hand and by various types of collusive actions on the other. In spite of the prevalence of oligopoly, a number of the significant characteristics usually associated with it have been missing in many of Japan's key industries. Interdependence, such as price leadership among leading firms within an industry, a common feature of oligopoly, has not existed nearly to the degree observable in other industrialized nations. Interfirm rivalry has been rather keen in almost every industry. Many key industries have experienced considerable difficulty in establishing, let alone holding, price leadership. Nor have the established firms been able to keep out new entrants even in capital-intensive and highly technically-oriented industries. In spite of easy access to various forms of collusive actions, interfirm agreements to restrict output, to stabilize market shares, or to harmonize investment plans have been typically difficult to enforce. In short, the postwar competitive pattern in Japan's key industries has been very fluid.

This fluidity in the structure may be seen from the fact that the degree of concentration in the top *three* firms, measured in terms of value of output, has steadily declined during the high-growth period in all major industries but food processing. In the twelve-year period ending in 1962, the index-of-concentration ratio in the top three firms in textile, paper, and pulp, combined, declined from 100 (in 1950) to 66.5; in the petroleum and chemical industries, the rate went down from 100 to 83.8, and in the metals and machinery industries, from 100 to 91.8 and 82.6, respectively.[1] Even

[1] Shūichiro Nakamura, *et al.*, *Nihon Sangyō to Kasen Taisei* [*Japanese In-*

the index-of-concentration ratio among the ten largest firms showed a decline in all but the food processing industry. The index in the textile, paper, and pulp industries, combined, declined from 100 in 1950 to 70.3 in 1962. In the chemical and petrochemical industries, it declined to 91.7. In metal and machinery industries, the rate declined to 99.5 and 90.6, respectively.[2] The details are presented in Tables 1 and 2.

TABLE 1

CHANGES IN THE INDEX-OF-CONCENTRATION RATIOS IN THE THREE LARGEST FIRMS IN SELECTED INDUSTRIES, 1950–1962

(1950 = 100)

Year	*Food Processing*	*Textiles, Paper, and Pulp*	*Chemicals, Petroleum, and Ceramics*	*Metals*	*Machinery*	*Average*
1950	100.0	100.0	100.0	100.0	100.0	100.0
1951	95.9	88.8	99.2	95.1	95.1	94.0
1952	101.9	79.9	95.6	95.3	90.7	91.8
1953	101.1	74.7	95.6	95.2	85.1	90.4
1954	101.7	76.3	94.7	95.3	85.3	90.5
1955	102.0	70.5	94.0	96.4	89.5	90.2
1956	101.0	69.0	94.5	94.6	84.2	88.9
1957	103.7	66.3	90.0	94.4	82.0	87.4
1958	103.8	64.8	87.1	94.7	81.9	86.1
1959	108.7	65.7	85.4	93.5	79.4	86.2
1960	112.3	64.5	85.2	92.6	80.1	86.6
1961	112.9	65.0	85.5	92.3	80.5	86.9
1962	112.8	66.5	83.8	91.8	82.6	86.7

Source: Shūichiro Nakamura, *et al.*, *Nihon Sangyō to Kasen Taisei* [*Japanese Industry and Oligopolistic Structure*] (Tokyo: Toyo Keizai Shinposha, 1966), p. 17.

Another study reports that between 1956 and 1964, in 41 major products, the index-of-concentration ratio among the three largest firms declined in all but 9 items. Included among the 32 products in which the index showed a decline were such items as synthetic fibres, petroleum products, cement, crude steel, passenger cars, trucks, television sets, sheet glass, steel pipes, and electrolytic copper. Equally significant is the fact that out of the 9 products in which the concentration rate among the three largest firms remained

dustry and Oligopolistic Structure] (Tokyo: Toyo Keizai Shinposha, 1966), p. 21.

[2] *Ibid.*

unchanged or increased, in 7 of them the composition of the three leading firms changed during the period surveyed. In another product, the ranking among the three firms was altered.[3]

Another significant indicator of fluidity is that downward price rigidity, an important characteristic normally associated with oligop-

TABLE 2

CHANGES IN THE INDEX-OF-CONCENTRATION RATIOS IN THE TEN LARGEST FIRMS IN SELECTED INDUSTRIES, 1950–1962

(1950 = 100)

Year	*Food Processing*	*Textiles, Paper, and Pulp*	*Chemicals, Petroleum, and Ceramics*	*Metals*	*Machinery*	*Average*
1950	100.0	100.0	100.0	100.0	100.0	100.0
1951	97.2	93.9	100.2	98.0	96.6	98.8
1952	102.6	86.5	99.8	97.8	93.1	97.6
1953	104.3	80.4	99.9	96.6	91.7	96.9
1954	104.0	79.7	98.9	97.8	90.2	96.3
1955	104.8	76.2	98.4	99.4	94.4	96.5
1956	104.2	75.2	97.8	99.0	93.3	95.7
1957	107.0	72.7	95.7	98.6	92.6	95.5
1958	108.1	72.2	93.7	99.6	90.6	95.0
1959	111.2	70.9	93.2	99.2	90.0	95.1
1960	115.1	70.4	92.2	98.8	87.7	95.4
1961	117.1	70.0	92.0	99.3	88.2	96.1
1962	117.8	70.3	91.7	99.5	90.6	96.8

Source: Shūichiro Nakamura, *et al., Nihon Sangyō to Kasen Taisei* [*Japanese Industry and Oligopolistic Structure*] (Tokyo: Tokyo Keizai Shinposha, 1966), p. 17.

oly, did not follow in a number of Japan's major industries. Even in industries where the concentration ratio was very high, the price showed a substantial decline during the high growth period. For example, among the six very highly concentrated industries (whisky, beer, nylon filaments, polyethelene, sheet glass, and aluminum ingots), prices declined, on the average, from the level of 100 in 1960–1961 to 93.7 in 1963–1964. In six moderately concentrated industries (urea, wire rod, ordinary steel pipe, bearings, electric motors, and cold-rolled black sheets), prices declined, on the average, from the level of 100 in 1960–1961 to 88.7 in 1963–1964.[4] This

[3] *Ibid.*, p. 20.
[4] *Ibid.*, p. 21.

absence of downward price rigidity is particularly remarkable in view of the easy access to formal or informal cartels.

The absence of interdependence among firms, in the best tradition of oligopoly, is often referred to in Japan as *kato kyōsō*, or excessive competition. It is an apt description of the conditions found in a number of Japan's major industries in the postwar period. One may well wonder, however, how the decrease of market share by the largest firms, and the price decline, could occur during a period of very rapid growth. Under these circumstances, one would normally expect the supply not to meet the demand, thereby generating a price increase. What factors, then, have been responsible for this excessive competition? One factor was the immediate postwar dislocation and the subsequent deconcentration measures of the Occupation, which weakened considerably the monopolistic power of the prewar giant firms, thus creating opportunities for new entrants. Perhaps the single most important cause was the very rapid growth of the postwar Japanese economy. The phenomenal expansion of demand for all types of goods and services encouraged numerous firms, both large and small, to push forward in each field to obtain a greater share of the rapidly growing market. This was, indeed, a very normal reaction on the part of dynamic entrepreneurs lured by the tremendous growth opportunities. Starting about the mid-1950's, under the encouragement and protection of the government, which was heavily committed to rapid economic growth, large firms began to engage in a most vigorous investment race to out-rationalize and out-invest their competitors.

This extremely aggressive investment behavior further accelerated the pace of growth. In addition, the rapid rate of technological development in the postwar period created a number of new growth industries. Firms aggressively sought to establish their foothold in these industries. The fact that the market was rapidly growing for most types of products reduced considerably the barriers that are associated with entry into new fields.

In this postwar period, entry into new growth industries was further facilitated by the utilization of already-developed foreign technology. No long lead time or huge investment in uncertain research and development projects were necessary. This also meant that it was difficult for any one firm to establish a clear-cut monopoly over a given technology or to gain a substantial technical lead over potential competitors. Alternate sources of like technology were vigorously sought by potential competitors, and in most instances, such sources were available. Although keen competition for foreign technical know-how tended to raise the cost of imported technology, once the technology was obtained, and given the rapidly growing market situation, new entrants could quickly erode the dominant position of established enterprises.

The postwar dissolution of the Zaibatsu, resulting in the loss of central control and coordination, was another factor contributing to excessive competition. We noted in the last chapter that considerable intragroup rivalry is now found within each of the reestablished major Zaibatsu groups, particularly in growth fields.

Relatively easy access to credit from financial institutions, especially from the large city banks, and the willingness of the banks to carry their major clients in times of economic recession have also been responsible for excessive competition. We noted earlier that the city banks, anxious to create industrial combines of their own, vied vigorously with one another in attempts to forge close financial links with promising enterprises. The preferential loan policies pursued by these large banks, in turn, stimulated an expansionary mood among executives of leading industrial corporations. We should also note that most of the new growth industries in which competition has been particularly keen have been capital-intensive, with the economy of scale being a very significant factor. As a result, management has been under constant pressure to expand capacity and to make full utilization of existing facilities, which of course has tended to intensify competitive pressure.

Immobility of the labor force is also a factor in excessive competition. Firms unable, because of the traditional paternalistic employer-employee relationship, to dismiss their excess employees, were forced to diversify into new fields in order to absorb this superfluous labor force, thus increasing their competition.

Though government officials have often blamed "irresponsible" expansionary investment behavior of the private sector for creating excessive competition, they, themselves, have not been totally faultless in this regard. The government's approval is required for the importation of new equipment and machinery as well as for the purchase of new foreign technology. Because high stakes are generally involved in these matters, large industrial firms have exerted considerable pressure on government officials, who have found it difficult to be selective in granting approval.

Excessive competition has also thrived on the very orientation of executives that emerged in postwar Japan. As a result of the separation of management and ownership, which progressed so markedly in the immediate aftermath of the war, real control in most large firms has since shifted into the hands of professional executives. Freed from the tight control of the holding company and from government restrictions, the new type of management has, indeed, been anxious to prove its worth. Long-pent-up energies found fresh outlets in a rapidly growing economy. Given a very fast growth situation, it is readily understandable that growth and diversification have become management's dominant concern, with the majority following aggressive and bold expansionary policies. The initial success of such policies served as a stimulus to intensify them. A company's performance has been rated, more often than not, in terms of total sales, market share, growth rate, or the number of new products introduced, rather than in terms of profit measurements, such as the rate of return on investment.[5] Caught up in a highly expansionary mood, which has been further encouraged by the government's active policy to promote economic growth, some executives have disregarded inherent market limitations in their expansion programs, making serious miscalculations in their capacity planning, thus contributing further to the intensification of competitive pressure.

Finally, we should note that relatively easy access to various means for collusive actions among firms has tended to keep marginal firms in existence. Many of them would be squeezed out — or prevented from entry in the first place — were it not for the availability of such protective measures. Knowing that they could resort to collusive actions under pressure of a recession, many executives have been less cautious in their expansionary programs. Moreover, in many of these collusive actions to restrict output, the prevailing market share or the existing capacity has been used as a basis to determine the quota for each firm. In either case, firms have been anxious to expand their market share or capacity in good times, to insure against the deterioration of their relative positions within their industry in the next recession.

All of these factors combined not only prompted but made it possible for large Japanese firms to pursue dynamic expansionary programs. In fact, their strongly aggressive investment behavior soon caught up with even the exceptionally rapid rate of economic growth. By the late 1950's, a number of key industries began to

[5] This is not unique to Japanese executives. See William J. Baumol, *Business Behavior, Value and Growth* (New York: The Macmillan Co., 1959), pp. 45–53.

show excess capacity. The demand for many products, which was once thought to be almost insatiable, was quickly filled and then reached a point of saturation. For the reasons noted, most major firms, nevertheless, persisted in their expansionary practices despite the apparent fact that their capacity was exceeding the existing demand.

We have briefly examined the major underlying factors contributing to the excessive competition characteristic of the Japanese postwar economy. Having noted at the outset that the behavior of Japanese industries in the market has been a strange blend of keen competition and various collusive actions, we shall now examine the patterns of collusive actions.

We pointed out earlier that Japan's Anti-Monopoly Act, enacted in the immediate postwar era, was substantially weakened through its two successive revisions. Cartels are now officially permitted for government-regulated industries, for small businesses, and for those engaged in foreign trade. Cartels may also be organized to promote rationalization and to protect industries seriously affected by depressions. Moreover, special laws were enacted to exempt a number of industries from the Anti-Monopoly Act. Relaxation of restrictions has led to a great increase in the number of cartels. By 1958, the number of cartel agreements reached over 400; by 1963 it exceeded 1,000. It was reported in 1963 that 28 percent of the total output of manufacturing industries had come under the influence of cartelization in one way or another.[6] The great majority of these cartels were formed by small- and medium-size firms, and among the cartels legally sanctioned by the Fair Trade Commission there were only a few linking large firms before the mid-1960's. For reasons to be noted later, the recession of 1965 stimulated a flood of applications from large firms for permission to form legal depression cartels. At the height of the recession of 1965, there were 18 such legally approved depression cartels, a record number among large enterprises. Among these 18 depression cartels were such industries as cotton spinning, automobile tires, sugar, corrugated cardboard, structural steel, cameras, and ferro-alloys.

Even more significant than the legally sanctioned cartel as a means for collusive actions among large firms has been the *advice* cartel, formed under the administrative guidance of the Ministry of International Trade and Industry (MITI), with the reluctant

[6] Hitoshi Misonō, *Nihon no Dokusen* [*Monopoly in Japan*] (Tokyo: Shiseido, 1965), p. 290.

acquiescence of the Fair Trade Commission (FTC). Although the MITI lacks a firm legal power for enforcement, for all practical purposes, the advice cartel differs little from the legally sanctioned cartels.

The history of the advice cartels goes back to the immediate aftermath of the Korean war. The end of the conflict brought a severe readjustment problem adversely affecting a number of Japanese industries. The MITI advised these industries to restrict their output in order to bring supply down to the level consistent with peacetime demand. A classic case was the cotton spinning industry: The chief of the Textile Bureau (of the MITI) advised the industry to restrict output according to a suggested formula. To enforce this administrative guidance, the chosen instrument of the MITI was its authority over the allocation of foreign exchange needed for raw cotton imports. Similar advice was issued to manufacturers of synthetic fibres and automobile tires.[7] In the case of these manufacturers, the MITI went only so far as to recommend the output quota for the entire industry, leaving it up to the industry itself to work out allocations of the quota to individual companies.

The FTC was unable to prohibit advice cartels of the first type because they were presumably based on the MITI's administrative guidance to each individual firm within an industry and enforced by its legally constituted control over foreign exchange allocations. The FTC reluctantly acknowledged that it had jurisdiction only over collusive actions *among* firms and was powerless to move against MITI's power to advise each firm separately, as long as there were no overt collusive actions among the firms it advised, even though such MITI action resulted in a cartel-like arrangement. Thus, the participation of the MITI established legal immunity and greatly weakened Japan's antimonopoly policy. With this precedent, subsequent recessions saw the emergence of a number of advice cartels, and they became one of the important instruments of the MITI to exert its influence over industry. So, the advice cartel under this ministerial guidance was extended to cover price setting as well as to restrict or harmonize new investments in several industries. The best example of price-setting practices with the sanctions of the MITI is found in the "open price system" in the steel industry, introduced in 1958. The system, in effect, enabled the leading steel producers to cooperate in setting prices of six major steel products

[7] *Ibid.*, p. 66.

and to restrict their output when the market prices were unduly depressed.

By the early 1960's, the advice cartels were extended to restrict and harmonize new capital investment plans for productive facilities on an industry-wide basis, when excess capacity began to plague the Japanese industry and the prospect for trade liberalization became imminent. They were also promoted because of the realization by MITI officials and business executives that output restrictions provided only temporary relief, and that a more basic solution was needed to overcome the condition of excessive competition. As noted previously, aggressive investment programs pursued by Japan's leading firms soon resulted in excess capacity, with such imbalance becoming apparent in a number of key industries by the late 1950's.

Through the guidance of the MITI, a number of industries agreed to cooperate in coordinating their future plans for capacity expansion. Included among these were such key industries as paper, petrochemicals, synthetic fibres, cement, and steel. The advice cartels in these industries were usually administered through a committee consisting of representatives from the MITI, industry, and the public. The committee prepared target plans, set criteria for screening, and acted on applications submitted by individual firms.

Aside from legal immunity, the advice cartel offered several other advantages to business. One of its chief advantages was flexibility. It enabled business firms to enjoy essentially the same benefits associated with the legally sanctioned depression cartels without having to comply with the time-consuming and complicated formal application procedures. Moreover, formation of depression cartels, purely on a voluntary basis, was often very difficult because of conflicting interests among the various firms in the industry. Business tended to be more responsive to the guidance from the prestigious MITI. The involvement of the MITI was also viewed by industrial groups as advantageous from the point of view of public relations. The MITI's participation somehow gave an official sanction to cartel-like arrangements and helped to shield the industry from public criticism for monopolistic practices.

By the early 1960's, however, advice cartels came under increasing attack from various quarters. The FTC, though reluctant to take direct action against the powerful MITI, expressed its disapproval of advice cartels from time to time. Severe criticism came from interests representing agriculture, small business, and the consumers, as well as from unions and the socialist parties. These groups violently opposed advice cartels and the MITI's involvement for diverse reasons. Some opposed them primarily on economic grounds. Others claimed that advice cartels were a violation of the Anti-Monopoly Act, certainly in spirit, if not technically. These critics pointed out that advice cartels enabled firms to enjoy essentially the same benefits as those associated with formal depression cartels without receiving the close supervision of the FTC. They contended that no government agency, however powerful, had the right to supersede a statute law by its administrative actions; and they noted that, in many cases, advice cartels had been formed at the initiative of industry groups — the MITI simply went along by giving them its official approval — meaning that there were collusive actions among those firms.

Still others opposed advice cartels on the grounds that the ease with which they were allowed to be formed was an important factor contributing to excessive competition, and in the long run, they were therefore detrimental to the healthy development of Japanese industry. There were those who expressed concern that the very informal nature of advice cartels, characterized by frequent behind-the-scenes arrangements, was likely to give rise to an undesirable fusion of business and bureaucratic interests at the expense of the public. And, in fact, the history of modern Japan is replete with such precedents.

Though the business community on the whole saw certain advantages in advice cartels, its reactions were not invariably favorable. Some felt that advice cartels resulted in the loss of freedom of action and in the increase of government intervention, reminiscent of the prewar situation. Others saw that the MITI was using the advice cartel as a means to enhance its already pervasive influence over the country's economy.

Sensitive to these pressures, the MITI did away with advice cartels as a device for restricting output by the spring of 1964, although it continued to advise selected industries to restrict and/or coordinate new investment plans. The latter type of advice was justified as a way to promote a reorganization of the industrial structure. During the recession of 1965, the MITI was extremely reluctant, despite much pressure from a number of industrial groups, to direct the formation of advice cartels. Instead, it encouraged industries in serious trouble to form depression cartels with the official sanction of the FTC.

Anxious to take the initiative away from the MITI, the FTC simplified the application procedures for depression cartels and speeded up the screening process. This was the chief reason that the latest recession, as noted earlier, witnessed a sudden surge of depression cartels among large firms. There is irony in the fact that the FTC could avoid the creation of advice cartels only by facilitating the formation of depression cartels.

Although, in the great majority of industries, the MITI lacks statutory power to enforce its administrative guidance, in some it is legally empowered, either through permanent industrial laws or through temporary legal measures, to participate in key operating decisions. Typical of this is the case of the petroleum refining industry. Because of its importance to the national economy and because of Japan's almost total reliance on foreign sources for crude oil, the Petroleum Industry Law was enacted in 1962. This law was to serve, after the liberalization of import restrictions on crude oil, as the chief instrument of the MITI in its efforts to guide the development of Japan's petroleum refining industry and to restrain foreign incursions.

The primary objective of the law is stated as that of maintaining the supply of petroleum on a stable and low-cost basis, thereby contributing to the progress of the national economy and to the improvement of the country's standard of living. The Petroleum Industry Law empowers the MITI, among other things, to regulate output, screen capacity expansion, and scrutinize new entrants and mergers whenever such actions are deemed necessary. Temporary relief laws, primarily geared to depressed industries such as coal and textiles, give the MITI similar powers.

Despite their prevalence, enforcement of cartels or cartel-like arrangements has been very difficult. Significantly, this has been equally true of formal depression cartels as well as of the advice cartels formed under the guidance of the MITI. Examples of sabotage, evasion, and even open defiance have been many. This has been true even in the case of the steel industry, dominated by half a dozen major producers and traditionally having close government ties. Output restrictions and agreements on price fixing have been repeatedly violated.

A recent case involving the Sumitomo Metal Company, the country's fifth-ranking steel producer, dramatized the difficulty of enforcing the regulations for an advice cartel. In the recession of 1965, the major steel manufacturers brought considerable pressure on the

MITI to intervene on their behalf by reviving the advice cartel. The MITI, still sensitive to criticism of the recent past against this type of cartel, only reluctantly agreed to advise the industry to curtail its output. The MITI directed the industry to set the total output of crude steel for the second quarter of fiscal year 1965 at 10 percent lower than that of the last quarter of 1964, and this was to be prorated among the various firms on the basis of the 1964 output. Sumitomo Metal, which had been aggressively expanding its productive capacity to challenge the more established firms in the industry, expressed its dissatisfaction with the suggested formula. Heated controversy between the MITI and the company ensued. The upshot of the whole matter was that Sumitomo boycotted the advice cartel and sought to pursue an independent course of action, whereupon the MITI immediately took the retaliatory action of withholding a license for foreign exchange to pay for crude coal imports needed for the production of extra crude steel. This, of course, only hardened Sumitomo's attitude. The strong retaliatory action taken by the MITI also created much controversy within the business community. Only after considerable pressure from the MITI, from other steel producers, and from financial institutions, as well as from prominent and well-respected business leaders, was a compromise reached.

Even a closely regulated industry such as petroleum refining, where the MITI is *legally* authorized to advise restriction of output and capacity expansion, has not always been responsive to MITI guidance. The enforcement of formal or advice cartels, as can be expected, has been even more difficult in industries where entry has been easier and where the MITI's guidance has been less effective. For example, the cotton spinning industry has experienced chronic difficulties during the past decade and a half. A cartel had restricted output and capacity intermittently for some decades even prior to World War II. It was also one of the first industries to enter an advice cartel arrangement under the guidance of the MITI in the postwar era. Because, in this case, the advice cartel was enforced by the MITI's control over raw cotton imports, it helped considerably to stabilize the market. However, because the restrictions did not apply to smaller firms, they continued to expand their output; the result was a considerable erosion of the relative share of the number of spindles of major firms in the industry. With the worsening of market conditions, the output restrictions became progressively tighter, reaching the high level of 50 percent. The cartel also resorted to buying excess inventory.

As a more effective means, a law was passed in 1956 requiring, among other things, the registration of spindles and encouraging mothballing of excess equipment. This law became the chief instrument of MITI control after restrictions of raw cotton imports were liberalized. Ironically, anticipating that the output quota would be set on the basis of the existing capacity, many firms vigorously expanded their capacity just prior to the enactment of the law. Even after the law's enactment, the expansionary mood continued to dominate the industry, giving rise to numerous unregistered or "black market" spindles. Thus, the enactment of the law did not result in an appreciable improvement of market conditions.

After a series of unsuccessful attempts to enforce cartels or cartel-like arrangements, the industry finally came to realize, with considerable prodding from the MITI, that the basic problems would not be solved by means of cartels. In fact, as past experience had shown, they would only worsen the situation. From this realization came the feeling among leaders of the textile industry that a more basic remedy was necessary to remove its structural weaknesses and to increase its competitive capacity. To achieve these ambitious goals, a new law, modeled after Britain's Cotton Industry Act, was enacted in 1964. It was to restrict capacity expansion until 1968; during this period it was to rid the industry of excess spindles and eventually to return it to a freer competitive basis. The new law stipulated that output restrictions would no longer be employed to adjust to short-run market fluctuations. It also required the industry to mothball nearly 1.4 million of the total 12.8 million officially registered spindles in existence, and to limit the acquisition of new spindles to a two to one "scrap and build" basis. At the same time, the law allowed the recognition of hitherto unregistered or black market spindles.

To the amazement of the MITI officials and industry leaders, over one million unregistered spindles surfaced. The total number of spindles registered reached nearly 14 million units. In the face of these developments, the new law was virtually ineffective. The market became increasingly glutted with the continuing pressure for price decline. The depressed market dealt a particularly harsh blow to the smaller firms. Just a year after the enactment of the new law (that is, in 1965), the MITI, under strong pressure from numerous small firms, rescinded the ambitious reform measures embodied in the law and reverted to the cartel. This was done despite strong opposition from the large firms. The cartel arrangement, like the cartels of the past, was also difficult to enforce. Noncompliance was rampant. It was estimated that within a year, nearly half a million new black market spindles were in operation. Not only did the MITI action fail to solve the immediate problem, but, on the contrary, it intensified the conflicts of interest that existed between the large firms and the smaller ones, making future cooperation all the more difficult.

These are but a few examples of the difficulties of enforcing output or capacity restrictions. Similar instances are found in nearly every industry that entered cartel arrangements at one time or another. Thus, mere listings of cartels tend to exaggerate their economic impact.

Some efforts have been made to measure the effect of cartels or cartel-like arrangements on the prices of products,[8] but as Misonō notes, the very fluidity and dynamic expansion that have characterized the Japanese economy during the past decade and a half tend to make accurate measurement extremely difficult, if not impossible. Recognizing these limitations, available evidence seems to support the view that prices of products affected by cartels have largely failed to demonstrate a downward rigidity. Particularly significant has been the trend for prices of products affected by cartels to show a marked decline in recessions. Insofar as generalization is warranted, it is safe to conclude that cartels, despite their prevalence, did not result in a widespread growth of restrictive practices. Notwithstanding some isolated cases of success, postwar cartels have been, on the whole, short-lived and even less effective than the prewar variety. As Misonō observes, in the face of a heavy excess of inventory or chronic overcapacity, even the most stringent cartels cannot be expected to be markedly successful.

It is interesting to note that the MITI has been rather hesitant to resort to outright retaliatory actions against recalcitrants. Of course, in the case of advice cartels, the MITI lacks statutory power of enforcement. But even in those cases where the MITI is legally empowered to penalize violators, it takes formal action against them only on rare occasions. Several factors account for this reluc-

[8] For example, see Noriyoshi Imai (ed.), *Gendai Nihon no Shihonshugi to Bukka Mondai* [*Price Problems in Contemporary Capitalism in Japan*] (Tokyo: Shiseido, 1964).

tance. For one thing, MITI officials are anxious to overcome the traditional authoritarian image associated with the state bureaucracy and are willing to exercise great restraint to avoid giving the impression that they are unduly encroaching on managerial prerogatives. Their desire is partially influenced by their pragmatic assessment that, given the sensitivity of management to bureaucratic control, they can achieve their goals more effectively by avoiding direct confrontation with the private sector. Another important reason is the very tradition of the Japanese bureaucracy. It has always preferred to resort to informal pressure and bargaining in dealing with interest groups. In this respect, the bureaucracy has demonstrated a considerable degree of flexibility.

It must be noted that the bureaucratic elite and professional executives of large corporations have essentially similar social and academic backgrounds and are basically committed to the existing power structure; this tends to facilitate informal communication and understanding between the two groups. Channels of communication for informal guidance and consultation are readily available. Japan's indigenous social arrangements and customs provide ample opportunities for the exchange of views through other than formal channels. By means of ready access to trade associations, to other firms in the industry, and to prominent leaders of the business community, MITI officials, if they so desire, are capable of mobilizing everyone concerned to bring considerable pressure on recalcitrants. This was well illustrated in the aforementioned Sumitomo case.

Reorganization of the Industrial Structure

In April 1964, Japan joined the Organization for Economic Cooperation and Development, accepted Article 8 of the International Monetary Fund obligations, and liberalized trade restrictions on all but a few products. Steps are also being taken, though slowly, for the liberalization of restrictions on foreign capital entry. These developments mean that Japanese industries can no longer operate within the protected environment and that they will now be exposed to the full rigor of international competition. There is a great concern among business leaders, as well as among key MITI officials, over the capacity of the Japanese industries to compete effectively against American and European giant firms. The most serious source of competitive vulnerability lies in the fact that excessive competition has led to uneconomical fragmentation of

Japan's key industries and underutilization of their productive capacities, resulting in a high unit production cost. The concern of Japanese business leaders and government officials is further heightened by the fact that key industries, both in the United States and Western Europe, are currently undertaking major expansion programs. A growing trend for mergers and tie-ups among major European firms adds to this concern.

One striking example of a market divided among small competing firms is found in Japan in the automobile industry. In terms of total output, the performance of the Japanese automobile industry is quite impressive. In 1966, Japan outranked Great Britain and became the third largest automobile manufacturer in the world. The total output reached 2,286,399, as compared with 10,371,141 and 3,050,708 for the United States and West Germany, respectively. In 1967, Japan overtook West Germany and became the second largest automobile manufacturer in the world. Although the Japanese output has been growing rapidly, the industry is highly fragmented. As may be seen in Table 3, in late 1966, as many as nine firms were competing with numerous models at a production cost substantially higher than that in the United States and Western Europe.

TABLE 3

OUTPUT SHARES IN THE JAPANESE AUTOMOBILE INDUSTRY, AS MEASURED BY VALUE OF OUTPUT

Firms	*Share of Output* (%)
Toyota Group*	28.15
Nissan Group†	24.10
Toyo Kogyo	12.88
Mitsubishi Heavy Industry	10.49
Daibatsu Kogyo	7.52
Fuji Heavy Industry‡	6.25
Isuzu‡	4.75
Suzuki	3.03
Honda	2.83

* Included in the Toyota group is Hino Motors (2.09%), which established close operating ties with Toyota in late 1966.

† Included in the Nissan group are Nissan Diesel (0.32%) and Aiichi Machine Industries (1.67%).

‡ These two firms established close operating ties late in 1966, with the combined output share reaching 11%.

Source: "Reorganization Trend Given Fresh Impetus by Isuzu-Fuji Move," *The Japan Economic Journal*, December 27, 1966, p. 12.

As of the end of 1966, the Toyota group, the largest manufacturer, accounted for only 28.2 percent, with the Nissan group and Toyo Kogyo responsible for about 22 percent and 13 percent of the total output, respectively. Together, the Big Three accounted for only 63 percent of the total output. This was considerably less than the ratio of concentration in the three largest firms of each of the other two major automobile manufacturing countries.[9] The total ratio of concentration for the three largest firms in the United States in late 1966 was 92.1 percent; for West Germany, 82.5 percent; for Great Britain, 83.2 percent; for France, 78.6 percent; and for Italy, 87.9 percent. The largest manufacturer in each of these countries accounted for the following proportion of the total output: 49.3 percent (General Motors, United States); 45.3 percent (Volkswagen, West Germany); 40.1 percent (British Motor Corporation, Great Britain); 32.6 percent (Renault, France); and 87.9 percent (Fiat, Italy) — against Japan's 28 percent for Toyota.[10]

The Japanese automobile industry is particularly vulnerable in passenger car production. In 1966, the total output of passenger cars was only about 878,000 units; although the output increased to over 1,375,000 units in 1967, this value was still only a fraction of the output of American manufacturers and considerably smaller than that of a number of European producers. The output of passenger cars by Toyota Motors — Japan's largest automobile manufacturer — in the first half of 1967 stood at less than one-fifth of the output of General Motors, about a third of that of the Ford Motor Company, and roughly 60 percent of Fiat's output during the same period.[11]

The degree of fragmentation just described is not unique in Japan to the automotive industry. Petrochemicals represent another example of a highly fragmented industry. The industry has experienced a tremendous growth since its inception in 1957. The total output of all petrochemical products was initially less than $5 million, but only a decade later its output reached nearly $1.2 billion. The country's ethylene production capacity is now second only to that of the United States. Nevertheless, Japan's petrochemical industry is highly atomized. In 1967, there were eleven complexes,

[9] "Reorganization Trend Given Fresh Impetus by Isuzu-Fuji Move," *The Japan Economic Journal*, December 27, 1966, p. 12.

[10] *Ibid.*

[11] "Japan Holds 2nd Spot in Global Production of Autos in 1st Half," *The Japan Economic Journal*, August 15, 1967, p. 6.

with two more in the development stage. In the summer of 1967, the annual capacity for the production of ethylene of the largest single complex stood around 200,000 tons, with the others ranging between 100,000 and 200,000 tons.[12]

The Japanese also perceive that the competitive vulnerability of the country's industries is further heightened by two additional factors. One is the high degree of reliance on debt financing. Typically, 75 to 80 percent of the total capital in large Japanese corporations consists of some sort of debt. This has saddled Japanese corporations with a high fixed financial charge. A semiannual study (from April to September 1966) of the performance of leading corporations by the Bank of Japan reports that, among 387 manufacturing firms included in the study, the financial charge, on the average, was as high as 17.7 percent of the gross value added.[13] A similar semiannual survey by the Mitsubishi Economic Research Institute reports that the percentage of average financial charge incurred by 478 leading manufacturing firms for the six-month period ending March 1965 came to be over 5 percent of total sales.[14] This is much higher than the rate commonly found in leading American and European firms.

The other source of concern lies in inadequate research and development capabilities of most Japanese firms, compared with their major foreign competitors. As we have previously noted, Japanese industrial firms, particularly those in growth fields, have relied heavily on foreign technology. Although Japanese firms have not neglected their own research and development activities, it is evident that a rather wide gap exists between Japan and other industrial nations in research and development capabilities. This is evidenced by the difference in the level of expenditures for this purpose.

For the fiscal year ending March 1967, Japan spent a total of roughly $1.35 billion for research and development. Of this, private corporations were responsible for about 60 percent. While the expenditures have been steadily increasing during the last decade,

[12] "Petrochemical Industry Facing Fresh Trials After Sound Growth," *The Japan Economic Journal,* June 6, 1967, p. 10.

[13] *Shuyō Kigyō Keei Bunseki, Showa 41 nen do Jōki* [*Analysis of Performance of Leading Corporations, the First Half,* 1966] (Tokyo: The Bank of Japan, 1967), p. 15.

[14] *Kigyo Keiei no Bunseki: Showa 41 nen Jōki ban* [*Performance of Major Business Enterprises, 1966 Edition*] (Tokyo: The Mitsubishi Economic Research Institute, 1966), p. 8.

the amount spent represents only 1.7 percent of the country's gross national product as contrasted to 4.3 percent in the United States. On a per capita basis, Japan's expenditures are only 8 percent of those of the United States and a third of the amount spent by France.[15] In electronics, for example, where research and development is critical, it is reported that the amount spent for this purpose by the entire industry, in Japan, is less than half of that spent by IBM alone.

To dramatize the competitive vulnerabilities of Japanese industries, the MITI has for some time annually rated leading Japanese firms in selected industries on the basis of a number of indices related to their counterparts in the United States and Western Europe. In this connection, a partial result of the most recent study available at the time of this writing is presented in Table 4. Although some caution is necessary in interpreting these comparative data, they do illustrate significant differences between major Japanese and foreign firms.

There has been a critical need, then, for measures to overcome the various competitive vulnerabilities of key Japanese industries. The measures proposed call for achieving greater concentration and specialization of production, attaining joint actions in the areas of capital investment and research and development, strengthening equity capital, rationalizing subcontracting, standardizing models and parts, and improving managerial practices. Among these measures, the reorganization of industrial structure, that is, the increase of productive efficiency through mergers and joint actions of highly fragmented firms, has received the utmost priority. Beyond the basic agreement that these actions are needed, bureaucrats and business leaders have differed in their opinions as to how they are to be implemented and, more importantly, as to who should take the initiative. When it comes to specific action, rivalry and working at cross-purposes are evident on all sides.

We shall first examine the basic approach offered by the MITI. The MITI has long been concerned over the vulnerability of Japan's key industries to growing international competition. In fact, until very recently, the greatest initiative for improving the competitive capacity of major Japanese industries had come from the MITI. Its officials have for some time been attempting to spark a sense of urgency among complacent or reluctant business leaders of the

[15] "Gijitsu Haku Sho no Naiyō" ["The Content of White Paper on Technology"] *Nihon Keizai Shinbun*, November 24, 1967, p. 2.

need for taking drastic actions to overcome competitive weaknesses. The keen interest of the MITI in this matter is due to a variety of factors. The MITI is the chief architect of the government's industrial policy, and as such, it is charged with the primary responsibility of guiding the sound development of Japanese industries. It is therefore understandable that the competitive capacity of Japan's key industries is a vital concern to MITI officials. It must also be noted that high-ranking MITI officials represent the very elite of the Japanese bureaucracy. In the best tradition of this bureaucracy, they are deeply imbued with a sense of mission to guide and direct the development of Japan's industries for the good of the nation. They view themselves as guardians of Japan's national interests (as defined by themselves) and are determined to guide and direct business leaders who are, in their opinion, prone to be preoccupied with the pursuit of their own interests. The MITI officials feel that the business community will not achieve this overriding goal if left to its own devices.

But the involvement of the MITI does not solely stem from these patriotic, altruistic motives. Its stringent regulations over foreign imports and capital and foreign technology had given the MITI considerable power vis-à-vis the business community. By the early 1960's, however, this power had been considerably weakened through successive measures for trade liberalization. Anticipating these developments, MITI officials felt that by carving a leading role for themselves in the promotion of industrial reorganization, they could continue to exert their powerful voice vis-à-vis the business community.

By the early 1960's, therefore, the MITI had begun to take a series of active steps, the most important of which was the establishment of a Council on Industrial Structure, to serve as chief advisory body in formulating a viable policy and program to guide the reorganization of Japanese industries. The Council membership consisted of business leaders, high-ranking MITI officials, and representatives of the public. Within the Council, a subcommittee was organized for each key industry. In the fall of 1963, the Council made the first of a series of recommendations. Subsequently, the various industry bureaus of the MITI, working closely with respective subcommittees of the Council as well as with industry representatives, issued numerous plans, goals, and guidelines.

Although details have differed for each industry, the MITI's basic formula has been unambiguous. It has sought to circumvent

TABLE 4

INTERNATIONAL COMPARISON OF CORPORATE SIZES AS MEASURED BY TOTAL SALES AND TOTAL ASSETS*

Industry and Enterprise	*Country*	*Total Sales Ratio*†	*Gross Value Added per Worker (¥ 1,000)*	*Gross Value Added, Fixed Assets (¥ 1,000)*	*Percent of Equity in the Capital Structure*
Steel					
Yawata Iron and Steel Co.	Japan	1.00	2,287	24.36	29.0
U. S. Steel Corp.	United States	5.41	5,236	40.98	68.0
August Thyssen Hutte A.G.	West Germany	2.12	(1,976)	(33.3)	—
Electric Equipment and Machinery					
Hitachi, Ltd.	Japan	1.00	1,943	45.08	29.1
General Electric Co.	United States	7.83	4,672	154.84	48.5
Associated Electric Ind., Ltd.	Great Britain	0.90	(928)	(74.7)	—
Siemens (Group)	West Germany	2.43	—	—	—
Automobiles					
Toyota Motors Co., Ltd.	Japan	1.00	2,617	51.60	47.3
General Motors Corp.	United States	30.16	4,738	111.42	71.8
Ford Motor Co.	United States	16.78	5,263	102.03	—
Volkswagenwerke A.G.	West Germany	2.71	—	—	51.9
Chemicals					
Mitsubishi Kasei Co.	Japan	1.00	3,202	28.05	21.5
E. I. duPont de Nemours	United States	12.45	6,498	60.96	84.7
Imperial Chemical Ind.	Great Britain	9.41	(2,392)	39.62	65.2
Communications Equipment					
Nippon Electric Co.	Japan	1.00	1,222	74.28	25.5
IBM Corp.	United States	15.02	—	—	68.8
Phillips	Holland	14.00	1,581	75.18	49.2

* 1965 figures.
† Sales of Japanese company = 1.00.
Source: "Sekai Kigyō Tono Keiei Hikaku" ["International Comparison of Major World Enterprises"], *Nihon Keizai Shinbun*, June 24, 1967, p. 3

the Anti-Monopoly Act in order to bring about greater concentration and specialization through mergers and joint actions and to overcome the ills of excessive competition. After a series of studies and deliberations, a view gradually emerged within the MITI as to how this overall goal was to be realized, who was to participate, and what role each party was to play. The plan, articulated by a group of high-ranking MITI bureaucrats, became known as *Kyōchō Hōshiki* (the Cooperative Formula). The formula, not unexpectedly, called for an active participation by MITI officials in the entire process of reorganization, and as the name implies, it emphasized cooperation among three groups: the industrial firms, the MITI, and the major financial institutions. It suggested that these three groups jointly set goals for the reorganization to be achieved by each industry. We should note here that, because financial institutions are traditionally closely regulated by the Ministry of Finance, and because the latter has the same vested interest in them as the MITI has in industrial firms, the participation of financial institutions has meant an active involvement of the Ministry of Finance in carrying out the Cooperative Formula.

MITI officials professed to recognize the efficacy of voluntary action by the industry groups in most matters. They were, however, quick to point out that the reorganization of the industrial structure was of such vital and critical importance to the whole economy that the participation of the MITI as the representative of the government was essential. As a further justification for their participation, MITI officials observed that since reorganization of the industrial structure was likely to raise issues that would deeply affect the very basic interests of individual firms, the conflicts of interest among the various firms within a given industry might well inhibit any meaningful voluntary actions. The MITI officials were quick to point out the difficulties experienced by most industries even in enforcing temporary cutbacks of output. They noted that the MITI would perform a useful guiding role as well as that of arbitrator of conflicts of interest as an interested but objective third party. MITI officials advocated the inclusion of financial institutions in this formula for two major reasons. One was that because of the strong tie between major city banks and industrial firms, it would be inconceivable to implement structural reorganization without cooperation from the banks. The other reason was that if reorganization of the industrial structure was to be carried out effectively, enormous funds would be required, an important share of which would have to be supplied by financial institutions.

The formula emphasized that once the three groups agreed on specific goals for a given industry, implementation of programs to achieve these goals would be left primarily to voluntary actions of the industry group. The MITI would offer a series of incentives to facilitate achievement of the goals, and simultaneously, the financial institutions would render their support to cooperating firms.

This view culminated in the early 1960's in the proposed Bill for the Promotion of Specific Industries, in which the above triparty corporate formula was incorporated. The bill further called for (1) designating strategic industries that needed special attention to help them increase their international competitiveness, (2) exempting these industries for a five-year period from the provisions of the Anti-Monopoly Act, and (3) extending various forms of incentives, such as special tax privileges and long-term, low-interest loans, to the designated firms. It is extremely interesting to note that even in the drafting stage, both the Ministry of Finance and major city banks vigorously opposed the version of the Bill for the Promotion of Specific Industries proposed by the MITI. Though not averse to the basic goals of the bill, the Ministry of Finance objected to it on the grounds that the formula would unduly commit it, and the financial institutions operating under its guidance, to the industrial policy of the MITI, resulting in the loss of its own independence and freedom. This reaction of the Ministry of Finance was in part due to the rather strong interministerial rivalry that existed between the two powerful government agencies. Major financial institutions, echoing the objections of the Ministry of Finance, expressed their concern that the formula would be too restrictive; that, if implemented, it would obligate financial institutions to channel a substantial portion of their funds to firms undergoing reorganization under this formula, regardless of their past banking ties. This, of course, would result in the weakening of bank-centered corporate groups. After prolonged negotiations and bargaining, a compromise was reached to the effect that representatives of the Ministry of Finance and of financial institutions would confine themselves to entering the preliminary discussion stage but would not participate in the final decisions, thus making it clear that they had no obligation to abide by the ultimate decision.

When the Bill for the Promotion of Specific Industries was finally presented to the Diet, it encountered strong opposition from a coalition of the socialists and from representatives of small- and medium-size businesses, farmers, and unions. The legislators opposed the bill on the grounds that it would result in an excessive concentration of economic power and monopolistic practices. They also feared further fusion of interests of high-ranking bureaucrats and executives of large corporations. After much heated debate, the bill was defeated, despite strong promotion by the MITI. Only after three abortive attempts did the MITI finally decide to shelve the bill permanently.

The failure of this bill was, of course, a major setback for the MITI, and dramatized the difficulty of achieving meaningful cooperation among various elements essential to bringing about industrial reorganization. It also demonstrated to both the MITI and the business community the strength of the countervailing powers.

How did the business community respond to the MITI's proposal? Although it saw certain advantages in the bill, it was far from enthusiastic. Although there were some very influential business leaders who strongly denounced any form of government participation in the private business sector, the great majority did recognize and accept the inevitability of MITI involvement in the key issue of industrial reorganization. But these more accepting elements were anxious to keep MITI's participation to a very minimum; they advocated that the initiative rest with the business community and that the MITI confine itself to a facilitating role. By facilitating role, the business community meant creating a climate favorable to industrial reorganization through further relaxation of the Anti-Monopoly Act, extension of special tax privileges, provision of low-interest, long-term loans, and so forth.

The desire of the business community to keep government participation to a minimum stemmed from several factors. For one thing, business leaders felt that extensive MITI participation would tend to blur the division of responsibilities between the public and the private sectors. The voluntary approach they favored had the advantage of clearly establishing a division of responsibilities. Although the MITI formula carefully stipulated that the ultimate decision on reorganization would be arrived at jointly through discussions in a cooperative atmosphere among the three parties, the business community was fearful that once this plan was implemented, the MITI might well emerge as the dominant partner. Given the highly authoritarian orientation of the Japanese state bureaucracy, this possibility posed a real and serious threat to the private sector. Management was also disturbed over the nature of the goals to be established jointly, being fully aware that the goals under consideration were specific ones (such as the optimum number of firms within a given industry, the optimum scale of production, capital investment plans, etc.) relating to a particular industry, often to a particular firm. These objectives represented, in the opinion of business leaders, the very essence of managerial decisions.

Involvement of the MITI and the financial institutions in such decisions would mean a substantial encroachment upon managerial prerogatives and freedom. Business executives were generally willing to concede that MITI bureaucrats were highly competent in routine affairs, but they were also quick to note that bureaucrats did not typically understand entrepreneurial dynamism and were often unwilling to experiment and innovate. Thus, participation by MITI officials in these key entrepreneurial decisions, they believed, might be detrimental to the economy in the long run.

Management also questioned the validity of a frequent claim by bureaucrats that their participation in key business decisions could bring about the convergence of the interest of a single firm or industry with that of the economy as a whole. Business leaders countered this claim by contending that the bureaucrats' susceptibility to political pressure and their bureaucratic instinct for self-preservation were likely to weaken their impartiality.

Beyond these specific objections, there were deep-rooted suspicions, nurtured since the prewar days, against government intervention. Memories of excessive government control and bureaucratic intervention were still too vivid in the minds of most business leaders for them to accept the MITI plan without strong reservations. Even in more recent years, management has been less than pleased about the time-consuming, tedious discussions and arrangements with MITI officials in obtaining licenses for the importing of foreign products and technology. Those businesses that have been affected by the advice cartel under MITI guidance and those that have operated under special industry laws have also experienced considerable loss of independence. Furthermore, many executives have found distasteful the condescending and patronizing attitudes toward them on the part of bureaucrats. For these and other reasons, the business community resisted the MITI formula.

However, management's chief dilemma has been that the voluntary approach to reorganization has been notoriously difficult. It has witnessed the difficulties of achieving even temporary restriction of output through voluntary actions. Thus, the difficulties of bringing about reorganization of an entire industry through voluntary actions have been readily appreciated. High-sounding pleas for voluntary remedies and for the independence of business from government intervention have tended to lose their conviction quickly in the face of cold reality. Another basic problem has been the fact that management has not been able to come up with concrete and effective policies or specific recommendations for the inevitable industrial reorganization — policies and recommendations that might be considered as alternatives to those suggested by the MITI.

More Recent Developments

The defeat of the Bill for the Promotion of Specific Industries by no means spelled an end to the desire of the MITI to participate in, if not to direct, the reorganization of the Japanese industrial structure. Its officials have become more sensitive than ever to the voices of management and other opposing elements. Consequently, they have become more conciliatory in their dealings, particularly with the business community, but their basic goal has remained unchanged. Through the Council on Industrial Structure, the MITI has continued to propose various reform measures. Each MITI industry bureau, working closely with a respective subcommittee of the Council, has continued to conduct a variety of studies in a number of key industries and has suggested targets and plans for their structural reorganization.

The severe recession of the mid-1960's not only opened a wedge for greater MITI involvement in the reorganization of the industrial structure, but it also convinced the business community that there was an urgent need to take concrete action. At this time, the MITI encouraged the formation of advice cartels to limit, coordinate, and screen new capital investment plans in a number of key industries. The MITI was anxious to use these advice cartels as an instrument for structural reorganization.

Beginning early in 1966, with improving business conditions and increasing pressure for capital liberalization, the MITI began to press for structural reforms with more zeal than ever. In the face of impending liberalization of restriction of foreign capital entry, business leaders themselves became aware of the urgent need for Japanese industries to overcome competitive weaknesses. By early

1967, their efforts began to bear fruit in the form of tangible achievements.

Several important mergers have been achieved since 1964. In that year, three Mitsubishi heavy industry firms, which were separated at the end of the war through deconcentration measures, remerged to form Mitsubishi Heavy Industries. Another significant recent merger was the one between Nissan Motors, Japan's second largest automobile manufacturer, and Prince Motors, the fourth-ranking firm. This merger was primarily brought about by the strong insistence of the MITI. In late 1962, MITI officials had undertaken a detailed study of the Japanese automobile industry to evaluate its competitive capacity. On the basis of this study, they concluded that Japan could support no more than three or four automobile manufacturers; they then began to explore various merger possibilities. They discretely sounded out the opinions of various firms in the industry. Despite the initial unenthusiastic response from the industry, MITI officials persisted in their efforts, which culminated in the merger of Nissan Motors and Prince Motors in 1965. The MITI immediately made available a substantial sum of low-interest loans to facilitate the rapid integration and rationalization of the merged corporation. This merger was considered particularly significant because both firms had had different banking ties.

The next year also witnessed a rapid increase in various forms of corporate tie-ups and joint actions. In the fall of 1966, Toyota Motors, the largest automobile manufacturer in Japan, entered into a cooperative agreement with Hino Motors, a major manufacturer of trucks and utility vehicles. The two firms agreed to cooperate closely in almost every operational aspect, including production, marketing, export, purchasing, and product planning. It is expected that, barring unexpected developments, Toyota will eventually absorb Hino. Late in 1966, a similar arrangement was made between two relatively minor automobile firms — Isuzu and Fuji. In late 1967, Toyota Motors and Daibatsu Motors agreed to establish a cooperative relationship. As a result of this arrangement, the market share of the Toyota group increased to 33 percent, surpassing Nissan Motors, the second largest manufacturer, whose market share was only about 23.7 percent at the end of 1967. Three major firms in the synthetic fibre industry — Teijin, Kanegafuchi Spinning, and Nippon Rayon — agreed to establish a close cooperative relationship through cross-holding of stocks, interlocking of directorates, and joint planning in production and marketing. The three firms combined will have 44 percent and 42 percent of productive capacities for polyester and nylon, respectively. In the chemical and petrochemical industries, a number of joint ventures have been formed, not only to avoid expensive duplication of investments, but to take advantage of each other's comparative advantages as well. A number of joint actions for vertical integration were under serious consideration early in 1967. In fact, some of these joint ventures cut across banking ties and enterprise groupings. Particularly interesting is a gradual move toward establishing integrated operations between chemical firms, as suppliers of raw materials, and manufacturers of synthetic fibres.

The MITI has intensified its efforts to increase the productive capacity of key industries. For example, at the beginning of 1967, it increased the minimum prescribed annual capacity of every ethylene plant to 300,000 tons, tripling the minimum prescribed capacity of the previous year.

The pace has been stepping up since late 1967, and in early 1968 a number of very significant merger plans were announced. The three leading members of the Kawasaki group have announced a merger. In the machine industry, Sumitomo Machinery and Uraga Heavy Industries have tentatively agreed to merge in the near future. In the automobile industry, in the summer of 1968, the automobile division of Mitsubishi Heavy Industries Co., Ltd., and Isuzu Motors Co., Ltd., agreed to enter into a cooperative arrangement, which may lead to a merger sometime in the future.

Also, in the spring of 1968, three leading paper mills, Ōji, Honshū, and Jujō, announced a plan for reunification. They once constituted a powerful paper interest of the Mitsui Zaibatsu, but they were split into three firms immediately after World War II. If consummated, the combined firm would have over 50 percent of the market share of key paper products, and the sales of the merged firm would be three times that of the next largest competitor.

Most dramatic, however, is the contemplated merger of Yawata Iron and Steel and Fuji Iron and Steel, the two leading steel manufacturers in Japan. The merger is expected to take place in early 1969. These two firms constituted the government-owned steel monopoly until the end of World War II. In the immediate aftermath of the war, the monopoly was broken up into two major private corporations. The new firm will have the combined annual capacity of over 22.3 million tons and will be the second largest steel mill in the world.

Another significant development relates to the cooperative efforts in research and development for the sake of greater economy and efficiency. Although this is still in a very early stage, one or two research institutes, financed and staffed jointly by several independent firms, have been formed.

To encourage these trends of Japan's key industries, the MITI now offers a series of inducements and plans to increase them in the future. These incentives include special tax privileges and long-term, low-interest-rate loans. To encourage rationalization in three key industries — petrochemicals, special steel, and automobiles, the government established a loan program in 1963. And beginning in fiscal year 1967, it expanded this program by creating a rationalization fund in the Japan Development Bank, under which the bank can extend a loan as large as ¥18 billion at an interest rate of 8.2 percent to an eligible firm undergoing a rationalization program. The coverage has now been extended to ten industries.

The MITI, long concerned about the heavy dependence of Japanese industries on foreign technology, also announced the development of a five-year plan, beginning in fiscal year 1968, to bolster indigenous technological development in Japan. The plan calls for the following measures:[16]

1. Significant increase in government expenditure for research and development;
2. Provision of direct government subsidies to selected basic research projects;
3. Further tax concessions to encourage research and development;
4. The establishment of a joint industrial research fund ($138 million), with government participation; and
5. The establishment of a government-sponsored clearing house of technological information.

With the progress of industrial reorganization, disagreement between the MITI and the FTC became intensified. The MITI and the business community now considered the attitude of the FTC and the provisions of the Anti-Monopoly Act major stumbling blocks in industrial reorganization. Although management had believed that the FTC would look with disfavor upon mergers of firms whose combined market share exceeds 30 percent of the total market, the

[16] "MITI Plans to Bolster Technology," *The Japan Economic Journal,* June 20, 1967, pp. 1, 4.

position of the FTC toward mergers and joint actions for the purpose of industrial reorganization was not clearly articulated, which resulted in considerable uncertainties and uneasiness within the business community. Because of the several past abortive attempts, the MITI officials were understandably reluctant to wage a frontal attack on the Anti-Monopoly Act. Instead, they attempted to reach an informal understanding with the FTC to refrain temporarily from applying the Anti-Monopoly Act to industries undergoing reorganization.

At the end of 1966, the MITI and the FTC reached an understanding that was to resolve many of the uncertainties that had plagued the whole issue. In an agreement specified in a memorandum of understanding between the two government agencies, the FTC was to take a more lenient posture toward interfirm arrangements and joint actions, as well as toward mergers designed for the express purpose of strengthening the competitive capacities of Japanese industries. Implicit in the understanding was the MITI commitment not to subvert the Anti-Monopoly Law, but to pursue its policy for industrial reorganization within its framework.

Characteristically, the details were not spelled out in this agreement, but the memorandum established the following points: The FTC agreed to give its tacit approval to voluntary adjustment and coordination of capital investment through interfirm consultations, as long as this did not significantly affect the current, or the future, supply-and-demand relationship. The FTC also agreed to modulate its criteria for evaluating the legality of mergers. It has also reaffirmed its willingness to engage in preliminary consultations with industry groups on matters concerning the legality of various joint actions.

It is, of course, too early at the time of this writing to estimate the effect of this agreement. The memorandum is stated only in very general terms, which may well lead to new disagreements when specific cases are considered. Nevertheless, the agreement has helped to resolve many of the uncertainties and apprehensions of the business community over the legality of various forms of joint actions necessary for industrial reorganization.

As we have seen, some progress has been made, but both Japanese management and the MITI officials agree that it has not come about fast enough. Joint actions, particularly mergers, are inherently difficult to achieve. Many potential mergers and joint actions have been blocked by a number of factors, such as conflicting personal aspirations of key executives, objections from the unions, and so forth. The immobility of the labor force, seniority-based particularistic patterns of wage determination, a well-entrenched system of subcontracting, and a deeply entrenched system of distribution tend to make cooperative actions difficult.

Strong but often narrow identification of employees with one enterprise also tends to create difficulties in promoting mergers and cooperative efforts. There is a fear, particularly among employees of lesser firms, that joint action or mergers with larger enterprises may place them at a clear disadvantage. Actually, in a number of past instances, there were incidents connected with mergers in which employees of the lesser firms were given an inferior status. Although a similar anxiety is not entirely absent among employees of United States companies contemplating mergers, the strong collectivity orientation prevailing among the Japanese and the permanent employment practice tend to exaggerate this fear.

Although their attitude is changing somewhat, major city banks still resist mergers that cut across banking ties. A few cases of abortive merger negotiations or unsuccessful mergers have resulted largely from the lack of careful preplanning and investigation. All these factors have made the management of firms contemplating cooperative and concentrative actions proceed with delaying caution.

To overcome these problems the MITI proposed, early in 1967, the holding company as a means of facilitating mergers. Because the holding company is still prohibited by the Anti-Monopoly Act, the proposal, even though it is only in its preliminary stage, has already stirred up much controversy.

In conclusion, we shall summarize the major existing problems. First, both business executives and MITI officials should guard against an illusion that greater concentration through mergers and joint actions will automatically result in greater efficiency of operation. There is a danger in simply equating size with efficiency. True, size is important, particularly in capital-intensive industries, but it represents only one of a number of dimensions.

Also important is the vital role of management in reaping the full benefits accruing to a merger. Managing a large, conglomerate, capital-intensive, and technically-oriented firm requires very sophisticated, high-level managerial competence. In the final analysis, managerial competence is the single most important determinant of productive efficiency. The issue of managerial competence is sometimes overshadowed by the discussion of the form the reorganization of industrial structure is to take, but its importance cannot be overemphasized.

Second, given Japanese tradition and the historical record, it is unlikely that the reorganization of industrial structure would be achieved only by voluntary action and without some government participation. However, in the final analysis, the very critical decision for or against mergers and joint actions rests with the private sector; more specifically, it rests with each industry and with each firm. Really significant progress in industrial reorganization will not be achieved until the business community itself realizes that it has the ultimate responsibility for industrial reorganization. It must also not be overlooked that, by its own actions and attitude, the business community can determine, to a large degree, the character and the extent of MITI involvement in this matter. Although business leaders deplore excessive government intervention and stress voluntary action and self-determination, it is questionable if they have completely overcome their traditional tendency for dependence on the government in solving their problems.

Finally, there are three important public policy issues. First, once greater concentration of economic power is achieved, Japan will eventually face the age-old problem of how to keep oligopoly efficient. In the process of reorganization, this factor needs to be carefully weighed, so that the pattern that emerges will be, at the same time, large enough to obtain full benefits of scale and competitive enough to innovate and respond quickly and effectively to the changing needs of the market.

Second, there is a critical issue involved: At what stage of development in a given industry should the MITI phase out its guidance and preferential treatment or protection? MITI officials claim that government intervention is only a temporary measure, meant to increase the international competitive capacity of Japan's strategic industries. However, it is difficult to find evidence to support this contention. The steel industry provides a good example: Through a series or rationalization measures, the Japanese steel industry has certainly attained a high degree of efficiency. In fact, in many respects it now surpasses the production efficiency of its American and European counterparts. Despite this, the MITI is still continuing the policy it adopted earlier, before Japan's steel industry realized its present competitive superiority. The MITI's participation in this instance has thus been far from temporary, and there is every indication that it has become firmly entrenched with the apparent acquiescence of the industry itself. There are a number of similar examples.

The third issue is that a certain degree of MITI participation is inevitable; therefore, the criteria that it employs in its industrial policy become extremely important. In the past, MITI policies have been largely based on the protection and development of Japan's strategic industries. This, of course, is consistent with the tradition from the early Meiji era. MITI policy is not difficult to justify as it applies to the past, but given the present stage of Japan's industrial development and the present political climate, it is questionable whether its exclusive application to strategic industries will be compatible with the long-range national interest.

Amidst all these problems and controversies, the exigent pressure of international competition will force Japanese industries to evolve an internationally viable and internally acceptable industrial order. This is more likely to be achieved not according to consistent blueprint, but by means of a series of groping experiments.

7

Organizational Structures and Practices

Having examined the broad setting of corporate environment and the dominant ideologies of Japanese management, we shall now turn our attention to the examination of key aspects of the internal management of large business enterprises. As we proceed with this analysis, it soon becomes evident that Japanese managerial practices are, indeed, different in a number of significant ways from their American counterparts, bearing the distinct social and cultural imprints of Japanese society.

Many of the peculiar characteristics of Japanese managerial practices have been identified by other authors.[1] We must note at the outset, however, that Japanese managerial practices, like their counterparts in other industrially advanced nations, have by no means remained static. A sufficient number of significant changes have taken place in recent years to warrant the present inquiry.

These changes have been accelerated by the growing realization on the part of progressive Japanese firms that the corporate environment is in great flux. As we have shown in former chapters, new developments in the industrial environment have included growing international competition in both the domestic and the international markets, the country's progress to a new level of industrialization, a rapid rate of technological advance, an erosion of traditional values, a growing shortage of labor, and an ever-increasing complexity in the size and operation of firms.

[1] See, for example, James C. Abegglen, *The Japanese Factory: Aspects of Its Social Organization* (Glencoe, Illinois: The Free Press, 1958); and Frederick Harbison and Charles A. Myers, *Management in the Industrial World: An International Analysis* (New York: McGraw-Hill Book Co., Inc., 1959), pp. 249–264.

There is, consequently, a widespread feeling in Japan that these developments have reduced the effectiveness of the traditional managerial practices and that in order to prosper or even survive in an increasingly complex and demanding corporate environment, management must adapt itself to meet the new needs of the economy. (As we pointed out in Chapter 4, the recent public declarations made by such management associations as the Doyukai emphasize this point.)

With the growing awareness of the changed situation, managements of progressive Japanese firms are making gradual but deliberate efforts to alter their traditional managerial practices. Against this background, it should be useful to review here, and in the ensuing chapters, the key aspects of past managerial methods and the significant modernizing changes that have taken place. Of course, as one may well expect, the process and content of change have brought about new problems and imbalances, which we shall also examine.

In this chapter and the two that follow, we shall analyze organization, personnel practices, and, finally, organizational processes and behavior, with special focus on the decision-making process in large corporations.

Organizational Structure

At the top of the corporate organization is the board of directors, in which rests the ultimate collective responsibility for the management of the corporation. Legally, directors are elected at a general meeting of shareholders. In most publicly held Japanese corporations, however, the wide diffusion of stock ownership has made it difficult for shareholders to exercise this right in a meaningful way. Moreover, the Occupation-directed revision of the Japanese Commercial Code increased significantly the legal power of the boards of directors and reduced control by stockholders. In most cases, the directors are elected by proxies, which means — except in highly unusual circumstances — that they are nominated and elected upon the recommendation of management.

The size of the board of directors in a large Japanese corporation is typically somewhat larger than that of its American prototype. A recent survey of 1,112 leading Japanese corporations (by the Toyo Keizai Publishing Company) reveals that the average number of directors among the firms surveyed is 14, the size of the boards ranging from 5 to 37; nearly half of the firms have 14 to 20 members on their boards.[2]

The Japanese Commercial Code, as revised by the Occupation, stipulates certain legal functions to be performed by the board, but its managerial functions are defined only in a very general way. The Code merely states that "the administration of the affairs of the company shall be decided by the board of directors."[3] Consequently, most firms have developed a set of rules of their own, defining the functions of their board of directors. The managerial functions of the board are commonly stated in these rules in terms of what decisions must be made or approved by it. For example, in the case of one corporation, its board of directors rules on the following:

1. Important policies relating to production and sales;
2. Matters relating to the acquisition and disposal of important property;
3. Matters relating to entry into important contracts;
4. Matters relating to important litigation;
5. Matters relating to important organizational and personnel affairs;
6. Matters on which the board has been authorized by a general meeting of the shareholders to make decisions; and
7. Other matters of the company's functioning that are comparable in significance to those just mentioned.

Characteristically, the decision-making functions of boards of directors, as seen from the above example, are stated in vague terms, leaving much to the discretion of the chairman of the board, or the president, in determining what role the board will actually play in the management of the corporation.

A unique instrument of directorship in Japanese corporations is the "representative directorship." The Commercial Code requires that the corporation have one or more directors with legal power to represent the corporation. A "representative director" is to be appointed by a resolution of the board of directors, and he is authorized to perform "all judicial and extra-judicial acts relating to the business of the company."[4] Commonly, representative directorship is held by two or three of the highest ranking corporate officers.

[2] "Gendai Shacho no Shinjō Chōsa" ["A Study of Personal Backgrounds of Presidents of Major Corporations"], *Business*, July 1966, p. 10.
[3] Commercial Code, Article 260.
[4] Comercial Code, Article 78.

In addition to the general meeting of shareholders and the board of directors, the Commercial Code prescribes another corporate organ, the office of *Kansayaku,* or auditors. Every corporation must have at least one auditor. The Code requires that the auditor be elected by the shareholders for a term of one year and that he may be reelected for consecutive terms. He may not concurrently serve as a director, manager, or other employee of the company, but he may be a shareholder.[5] The auditor's chief duties, according to the Code, are to examine the corporate accounts that the board must submit to the general meeting of shareholders, and to report his opinion of the state of these accounts to the meeting.

We shall now go on to examine the organization and functions of operating top management. According to common definition in Japan, only members of the board of directors are considered members of top management. Except for directors, representative and otherwise, and auditors, there are no statutory requirements of special titles or positions for company officers. The titles and executive duties of various corporate officers may be designated in the articles of incorporation, by resolution of the board, or they may even be established internally by usage. Top management positions are divided into several hierarchical levels. Top management offices commonly found in large Japanese corporations include chairman of the board, president of the corporation, executive vice-president, senior managing director, managing director, and ordinary director. While these titles are not legally prescribed, they are used with a high degree of consistency in Japanese corporations.

To illustrate the common pattern in top management organization of the firms studied, we shall cite the example of one large diversified manufacturer of electrical machinery and equipment. In this firm, top management consists of 26 executives. The office of chairman of the board, as is common in large Japanese firms, is occupied by a retired president. (We should note here that according to the aforementioned study of 1,112 leading firms by the Toyo Keizai Publishing Company, the office of board chairman was found in 36 percent of the firms studied.)[6] The role of board chairman varies widely among firms. In some, the chairman of the board is the chief executive officer of the corporation, who is actively involved in its management, whereas in others, his functions are only of a ceremonial nature. In our particular firm, the incumbent chairman is not actively involved in the direction of the firm. A good

[5] Commercial Code, Article 273.
[6] "Gendai Shacho no Shinjō Chōsa," p. 30.

measure of the status of the board chairman in a given corporation, and of how actively he participates in management, is whether or not he is a representative director. If he is a representative director, it is quite likely that he retains an important voice in management.

In the firm cited, it is the president of the corporation who functions as the chief executive officer. In prewar Zaibatsu firms, the office of president was frequently not an operating office, and day-to-day operations were entrusted to managing directors. Today, however, in almost all firms, the most important operating office is that of the president. In our sample firm, three executive vice-presidents report to the president. One of these executive vice-presidents does not have any operating responsibilities, but the other two serve in functions similar to those of group executives in a large American corporation, having a number of division heads reporting to them.

Immediately below the executive vice-presidents in the top management hierarchy are two senior managing directors; one of them serves as the head of a division, and the other has under his supervision three staff departments — finance, accounting, and purchasing. Next in line are seven managing directors; one is the head of an engineering division, two are responsible for a number of corporate staff departments, one is head of the Tokyo sales office, and each of the remaining three serves as the head of a division. The lowest position in the top management hierarchy is that of ordinary director. Among the twelve ordinary directors in this sample firm, one is president of a large associated firm. He is the only outside director, in the sense that he is not a full-time operating executive of the parent firm. Six of the remaining eleven ordinary directors are superintendents of major plants; one is the head of the international division; and the other four serve as deputy heads of operating divisions.

In addition to the positions already mentioned, we find in this corporation, as in most firms, several executives, known as advisors, who hold peripheral top management positions. The advisor is usually a retired senior executive, and his position is largely honorary. Advisors are seldom given operating responsibilities, and they are not members of the board of directors.

In our firm, typically, there is an executive committee, consisting of upper-echelon top management, managing directors, and on up, which meets once a week. This committee discusses key policy matters and handles the broad administrative functions of general management. A similar committee, known under various names, such as council of managing directors or operating committee, is commonly found in large Japanese corporations. Although the executive committee is not a legal corporate organ in operational terms, its importance surpasses that of the board of directors.

There are various subordinate operating and staff groups under top management. Most large Japanese corporations are geographically decentralized. The corporate headquarters containing the main administrative units are usually located in Tokyo or in Osaka. However, plants, sales offices, and research laboratories are likely to be scattered throughout the country, and some are located abroad.

Inside the corporate headquarters of a typical large corporation there are a number of staff departments, including planning, personnel, finance, accounting, public relations, the office of subsidiaries, and so on. Line organization may be departmentalized either according to functional demarcations or on the basis of major product categories.

As may be expected, functional departmentalization is found in firms with limited product lines. Rapid growth in size and expansion of product lines in the last decade has caused a substantial number of large firms to adopt divisional forms of organization along major product lines. Among the twenty firms studied, nine were organized in this manner.

In both functional and divisional forms of organization, departmentalization within a given function or product division follows a similar line. A division is typically broken into three or four departments, and each department is, in turn, divided into several sections. A section in a department consists of a staff of about a dozen to twenty, and about half to two-thirds of this number are management personnel; the rest are clerical assistants, the majority of whom are female employees. In some firms, even a section is further divided into two or three subsections, each consisting of no more than half a dozen members. The organization of factories and sales offices is virtually a microcosm of the organization of corporate headquarters, with comparable staff units having functional reporting relationships to their counterparts in the corporate headquarters.

In the brief sketch we have given of the organizational structure of large Japanese corporations, the reader may have discerned that there are a number of important aspects in which the organizational structure of a large Japanese corporation bears some resemblance to that of a large American firm. This is not a coincidence, because most Japanese firms have closely followed organizational developments in leading American corporations and have, in many cases, adopted their organizational practices. However, there are some clear differences, which we shall now explore.

One of the distinct features of the Japanese corporate organization is that it is structured in collective organizational units rather than in terms of individual positions. This is very evident in the organization chart, in which the corporate organization is depicted in terms of divisions, departments, and sections, rather than individual positions; only one or two of the highest top management positions — usually those of the chairman of the board and the president — are identified. These two positions are explicitly recognized because of the importance that the Japanese have traditionally attached to the formal leadership position of the collectivity (see Chapter 1). It must be noted that even though these two positions are indicated on the chart, they are not identified by the names of the incumbents, as is frequently done in the organization chart of an American firm. Beyond the one or two top-most positions, however, none of the other top management positions is shown on the chart individually — they are merely indicated collectively as the board of directors or as the executive committee. As a result, from the organization chart alone, there is no way of telling how many top management positions exist in a firm. Likewise, reporting relationships between various levels are indicated not in terms of individual positions, but in terms of collective units. Similarly, the organizational manual, which is now commonly found in almost all large Japanese corporations, describes assignments and responsibilities in terms of a division, a department, or a section, rather than as individual positions.

Although this may appear somewhat strange to American students of management, both the organization chart and the organizational manual of Japanese corporations accurately reflect management's view of the organizational structure. Because of a high degree of collectivity orientation, the Japanese management does, in fact, view a corporate organization in terms of hierarchically related collective units, rather than individual positions. To the Japanese, a task is performed by a group, not by individuals, and responsibilities are consequently shared by the entire group. True, each group has a formal leader with appropriate status and title, but the task is assigned not to him but to the group of which he happens to be the head. It is the group's performance that matters, rather than that of the individual or the formal leader. The basic unit in the organization is a collectivity, not an individual. Herein lies one of the fundamental differences between American and Japanese management.

A closely related feature of the collectivity orientation is that the responsibilities of each organizational unit are defined only in very general terms. Detailed job descriptions, as typically specified in large American corporations, do not exist in Japanese firms. For example, the functions of the export department in one firm are described in its manual as follows: "The Export Department shall take charge of exportation and the necessary investigations and negotiations (connected with it)." Descriptions found in other companies studied are equally brief and general. Even in those rare cases in which a job description of an individual position is found, it is stated only in very broad terms. For example, the description of the position of section chief is stated by one firm as: "A chief shall be assigned to a section [note that even here, the emphasis is on a section, a collectivity]. The chief of the section takes charge of and is responsible for its administration to his immediate superior."

This characteristic also stems from the traditional Japanese view that a task is to be performed through *cooperative* efforts among individual members of an organization. Thus, Japanese managers are much less concerned about who performs a task and where the responsibility lies than about how individuals within the organization work together harmoniously toward the accomplishment of the goals of the collectivity. The importance that Japanese managers place on group harmony cannot be overemphasized. One impressive evidence of this is the frequency with which group harmony, teamwork, and cooperative spirit are mentioned in company mottos or slogans.

Nurtured in the traditional collectivity orientation, it is readily understandable that Japanese management would emphasize loyalty and duty to the group, harmony and cooperation among group members, rather than individual functions and responsibilities. Permanently committed to the interest of the collectivity, each member is expected to do whatever is deemed most important in the fulfillment of the goals of the collectivity at a given moment in time. It has been commonly held by Japanese managers that each employee is strongly identified with the enterprise, even to the point that the interests of the individual employee and the enterprise are the same and inseparable. Some rudimentary division in the performance of a task is obviously necessary, but under the Japanese philosophy of corporate organization, a precise definition of individual functions and responsibilities is deemed unnecessary, and it is believed that it may even disrupt the harmonious cooperative relationships between various groups. Other aspects of traditional Japanese management practices, such as permanent employment and the *ringi* system of decision-making, as we shall see later, have also lessened the need for clear-cut definitions of individual responsibilities and functions.

Another distinct feature commonly observed in the organizational structure of large Japanese corporations is the strong emphasis on hierarchy. The relative status of each organizational unit is distinctly defined in relation to others, and much emphasis is placed on the *vertical* relationship between units; little concern is shown for the horizontal relationship between functionally related units. In fact, Japanese organization is typically structured on the basis of a number of vertically linked "layers" that fan out from the pivotal positions of the leader. This point is incisively made by Chie Nakane in her recent book offering an analysis of the salient features of Japanese group structure, which she illustrates in the following manner.[7]

Assuming that a group consists of three members, A, B, and C, a likely structure this group will take in the Japanese setting is shown in the following diagram:

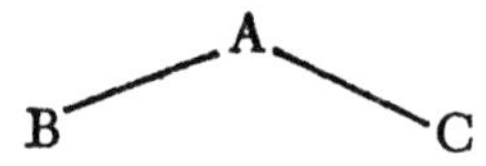

In other words, both B and C are related in a hierarchical and particularistic manner to A, but no direct relationship exists between B and C; they are related only through the leader, A. When the group increases in size, it is likely to take the following pattern:[8]

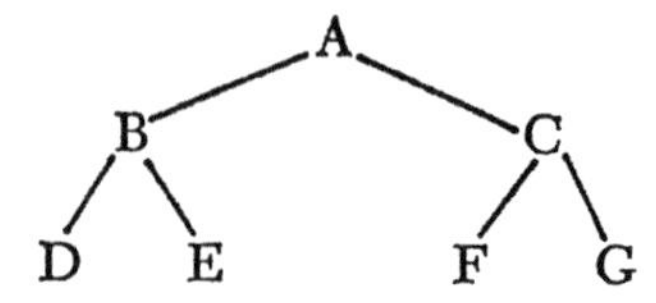

The hierarchical relationship is the primary or the only formal relationship that exists in this type of group. A new member can join

[7] Chie Nakane, *Tate Shakai no Ningen Kankei* [*Human Relations in a Vertically Related Society*] (Tokyo: Kodansha, 1966), pp. 114–115.

[8] *Ibid.*

the group only by establishing a particularistic relationship with one of the present members, and it is likely that he must begin at the lowest status in the hierarchy.[9] Nakane points out another distinct feature of what she calls vertically linked group structures — the fact that the leader, A, controls D only through B, since D is tied to A indirectly through B. Thus, if the relationships between A and B and C are severed, the entire group is likely to disintegrate.[10]

The relationship patterns discussed above are very apparent in the organizational structure of large Japanese corporations, where the formal status of every member, in relation to other members in the hierarchy, is defined in the most meticulous and particularistic manner.

The two major determinants of relative hierarchical status have been the level of education and seniority. Each member has his place in the organization, and he must behave in a manner congruous with his status. One finds, therefore, a very interesting situation in a typical Japanese corporate organization, where the relative status of each individual is rigidly defined and observed, *but where his functions and responsibilities are not.* This peculiar emphasis on hierarchy is quite consistent with traditional Japanese cultural values, with their emphasis on hierarchical status, as we have seen in Chapter 1.

The peculiarities of the Japanese corporate organizational structure have important implications with regard to the leadership function. Given the tremendous emphasis placed on collectivity as a basis for task performance, the primary function of a leader is to facilitate group performance, that is, to maximize the output of the entire group by avoiding friction within it and by developing a stronger sense of group identity and solidarity. Moreover, since assignments and responsibilities are not determined on an individual basis, the leader must see to it that those who are capable but do not have an appropriate status are given the opportunity to demonstrate their full ability without disrupting group harmony. In other words, more often than not, the leader, in the Japanese context, is not a strong individual directing and inspiring the group to achieve objectives that he himself has set for the group. Rather, his main function is to create a proper atmosphere for the group's achieving *its* objectives. Thus, a commonly accepted approach in Japan is to assign only a limited range of functions to leadership

[9] *Ibid.*, p. 116.
[10] *Ibid.*, pp. 120–121.

and a rather passive role. In fact, the great majority of executives interviewed — though there were some significant exceptions — viewed the role of leader in this manner.

The primary requisite for leadership, then, is the skill needed to build harmonious interpersonal relationships and to develop group solidarity; technical competence is far less important. In fact, an exceptional technical competence in a leader may even be a hindrance, for he may have difficulty in eliciting group cooperation.[11] Repeated assertions were made by executives interviewed throughout this study as to the importance of "human relations" skills in leadership.

Another noteworthy characteristic of leadership in Japanese organizations is that the leader's power is relatively uncertain. As Nakane observes, because there is no clear-cut delineation of individual authority and function, there is a tendency for the power of a leader to be determined according to his relative strength vis-à-vis the group.[12] In other words, if a leader is extremely strong, the vertically- and hierarchically-oriented organizational structure yields to his authoritarian and autocratic control. But if he is not strong, the indirect nature of his control over the group tends to weaken his power and constrain his freedom. In extreme cases, the control of the group rests almost entirely with key subordinates, thus making the leader a mere figurehead. In Japanese organizations — including large corporations — a leader's ability to maintain his position is frequently determined to an important degree by his skill in achieving a subtle balance of power by means of cleverly manipulating certain key subordinates. For all these reasons, it is often difficult, if not impossible, to judge the quality and competence of a Japanese organization in terms of the caliber of its formal leader.[13]

Another noteworthy feature of the organizational structure of the major Japanese corporation is the fact that it is elaborately and minutely divided into separate and quite distinct organizational units. The span of control is typically quite narrow, as only a limited range of functions is assigned to each unit. It is not uncommon to find that a department head, a ranking upper-middle-management executive with several deputies, has no more than two or

[11] *Ibid.*, p. 146.
[12] *Ibid.*, p. 142.
[13] *Ibid.*, pp. 141–144.

three sections. Though somewhat uncommon, cases exist in which a department has only one section.

Several factors are responsible for this organizational fragmentation. One important reason is the traditional reluctance of top management to delegate authority to lower levels. Another is that the very rapid postwar growth of most Japanese firms rendered a systematic approach to organizational development very difficult. New organizational units were created, or the existing units were divided, purely on an expedient and piecemeal basis. Contributing further to this trend is the fact that the importance of organizational planning and development, as a continuing process, is not always appreciated by the top management of even some of the leading corporations. Many senior executives feel that organizational planning and development are not important enough to warrant their personal attention. Some executives consider it unnecessary, on the basis that it is people who make up an organization, and as long as the firm has capable and hard working personnel, organizational structures per se make little difference. Some executives, though they are definitely in the minority, actively resist systematic efforts for organizational planning, fearing that it may lead to the weakening or even the destruction of their informal power structure. For these reasons, and others, organizational planning and development are often neglected or relegated to lower echelons of management and, as a result, do not receive adequate attention. Third, although Japanese executives are, on the whole, well educated and highly intelligent, they often lack specialized managerial training and administrative competence, and thus require close supervision.

The traditional personnel practices of lifetime employment and the seniority-based reward system have also been important factors contributing to the fragmentation of the corporate organization. The seniority-based reward system insists on giving status recognition to managers appropriate to their chronological age. Consequently, new sections and departments are at times created merely to add managerial posts to accommodate those eligible for promotion on the basis of seniority. Thus, personnel considerations, rather than the optimum division of tasks, frequently become the overriding criteria for the creation of new organizational units.

Closely related to the foregoing is the bestowing of numerous formal titles — particularly widespread are such titles as "deputy" and "assistant to." The chief of a section with no more than a dozen subordinates may have as many as two or three deputies. Again, these titles are primarily created as the formal recognition of special status in the organization. Because it is simpler to create new titles than to add new sections or departments, this practice has been carried to extremes in a number of firms. The titles fulfill another important function. They facilitate communication with customers, suppliers, government officials, and so forth, in the highly status-conscious Japanese society.

Up to this point we confined our analysis to the formal organizational structure. However, an analysis of Japanese corporate organization is incomplete without an examination of its informal components. Particularly important in the Japanese scheme of things is the existence of the unique informal group commonly known as the *habatsu* (the clique).[14] The *habatsu* is commonly found in Japan in almost every form of large bureaucratic organization, including corporations, government ministries, and universities. It often wields considerable power in the formal organization. In contrast to informal groups in American organizations, *habatsu* have several distinct features, which we shall now proceed to consider briefly.[15]

First, because the traditional culture of Japan does not provide any notions of or experience in large, impersonal, bureaucratic organizations, the Japanese tend to feel isolated and uncomfortable in such organizations. They seek to relieve this feeling in the comfort of narrow social groupings, offering particularistic and emotional ties within the impersonal formal organization. The *habatsu* owes its origin to this factor. Second, the *habatsu* is highly goal-oriented. The overriding objective of the *habatsu* is to enhance its power and influence in the formal organization. The *habatsu* seeks to protect and promote the interest of its members through vigorously competing against other *habatsu* in the control of hegemony in the formal organization. Third, the membership of the *habatsu* is based on the common *unchangeable* tie, such as a common birthplace or school. Such common and unchangeable ties often automatically establish a mutual bond of trust and dependence even among almost total strangers. Thus, membership in *habatsu* is not based on the extension of personal relations, as is true in the case

[14] The subsequent analysis of *habatsu* relies heavily on Tohru Matsumoto, "The Role of Informal Organization in Japanese Business Enterprises" (unpublished Master's thesis, School of Industrial Management, Massachusetts Institute of Technology, 1963). The author is grateful to Dr. James C. Abegglen for calling this study to his attention.

[15] *Ibid.*, pp. 92–93.

of informal groups in the United States. Also, unlike American informal groups, membership in *habatsu* is nonoverlapping. In American organizations, it is quite possible for an individual to belong to more than one informal group without jeopardizing his standing in any particular one. In Japan, however, one can belong only to one *habatsu* — the *habatsu* demands of its members permanent and total commitment. Fourth, *habatsu* membership is drawn from various hierarchical levels within the formal organization, and the *habatsu* itself is hierarchically organized. One's status within a particular *habatsu* is, therefore, likely to be determined by his standing in the formal organization. Moreover, the relationship between the leader and his subordinates is characterized by highly personal and emotional ties akin to the traditional *Oyabun-Kobun,*[16] or patron-client relationship. The *habatsu* leader is generally one with a high status in the formal organization, and he patronizes his followers who, in turn, submit to him. He is likely to wield considerable power over the *habatsu* members and is also in a position to reward them.

Matsumoto cites two key conditions leading to *habatsu* in large bureaucratic organizations.[17] One of them is the absence of high competence or ability among participants. The other is that certain conditions exist that make it difficult for members of the formal organization to demonstrate competence when they do have it.

Habatsu can affect the functioning of formal organizations in several ways. First, they have their own networks of communication. Because of their very structure and the loyalty they command from their members, their networks of communication are highly effective. Although this can be highly beneficial to the goal-attainment of the formal organization, it may, on the contrary, have an extremely adverse effect in this regard.

Second, *habatsu,* because of their strong determination to enhance their influence in the formal organization, can create strains and conflicts. Intense internal *habatsu* rivalry is not uncommon in the Japanese bureaucratic organization. Particularly important is the fact that because of the very nature of the *habatsu* grouping, intra-*habatsu* struggles are not only likely to pit leaders of one *habatsu* against those of another, but they are also likely to involve men in

[16] For details of the *Oyabun-Kobun* relationship see John W. Bennett and Iwao Ishino (eds.), *Paternalism in the Japanese Economy: Anthropological Studies of Oyabun-Kobun Patterns* (Minneapolis: University of Minnesota Press, 1963), pp. 25–247.

[17] Matsumoto, "Role of Informal Organization," p. 90.

the lower levels of the organization. Closely related to this point is that because of common ties, one may be automatically identified with a particular *habatsu,* thereby becoming enmeshed, involuntarily, in inter-*habatsu* struggles.

Third, *habatsu* often create serious morale problems. When a dominant *habatsu* emerges, members of other *habatsu* and those who do not belong to any are placed at a disadvantage, and as a result, their morale is likely to suffer.

Fourth, *habatsu* can adversely affect the goal-attainment of formal organizations. Their goals and those of the formal organization may not harmonize; when this occurs, because of the strong particularistic ties and the ability of *habatsu* to reward or punish their members, they are likely to emerge as the dominant reference groups for their members, and the interest of the organization as a whole is subordinated to that of the *habatsu.*

Finally, the presence of *habatsu* also complicates decision-making. In extreme cases, no major decisions can be made without the approval of the influential *habatsu.* Dominant *habatsu* can veto almost any decision if they perceive a threat to themselves in such a decision. This tends to slow down decision-making, because seeking the support of the dominant *habatsu* can be quite time-consuming. Moreover, it is sometimes necessary to reshape a particular decision to make it acceptable to the *habatsu.*

Problem Areas and Recent Developments

In the past few years, concomitant with the rapid postwar industrial growth and the increasingly demanding business environment, matters relating to corporate organization have received much attention within a number of leading Japanese firms. There is a growing awareness that some of the distinct aspects of the traditional organizational structure have become increasingly incongruent with the realities of a demanding business environment. In this section, we shall attempt to identify major problems and the corrective actions that are being taken by some leading corporations.

We shall begin with top management organization. A most serious shortcoming in the top management organization of Japanese corporations is the absence of an effectively functioning board of directors. This stems from the fact that boards of directors in large Japanese corporations are predominantly, if not exclusively, staffed by full-time operating executives. In 17 of the 20 firms studied, the boards of directors consisted solely of such full-time executives. In each of the remaining three firms, there was but one "outside" director. In all of these three cases, however, the outside director was the president of one of the company's associated firms, and in two of the three, the outside member had been an executive of the parent firm prior to assuming the current assignment. In none of the three cases, therefore, can the term "outside" be regarded as justified in the strict sense of the term.

The practice of staffing the board with full-time operating executives is largely a postwar phenomenon. In the prewar era, boards of directors of major corporations did include a substantial number of outside directors who were representatives of large stockholders, of the holding company, or of the Zaibatsu families; these directors served without having day-to-day managerial responsibilities. The postwar economic reforms, including the dissolution of Zaibatsu, the steps for deconcentration of corporate power, and the purge of key executives, created a large number of vacancies on boards of directors of leading firms; these were quickly filled by full-time operating executives. Once this pattern was established, there was every incentive for these excutives to perpetuate the practice. The wide diffusion of stock ownership in the postwar era further facilitated the continuance of this practice.

The problems associated with a board dominated by operating executives are well known and do not need detailed elaboration here. But we should note that several factors that are somewhat peculiar to the Japanese situation tend to further reduce the effectiveness of boards so constituted.

Because of the widespread diffusion of stock ownership in most publicly held Japanese corporations, the power to select directors is vested in one or two senior directors, usually the chairman of the board and/or the president. They may occasionally consult with large stockholders, upper echelons of top management, or the firm's main bank. Under ordinary circumstances, however, such senior officers control the appointment of new directors. Once selected, junior directors serve at the pleasure of their seniors. Thus, as far as the highest ranking executives are concerned, the board of directors consists exclusively of their subordinates. Understandably, such a board cannot be sufficiently independent or effective.

Since the directorship is a highly coveted position, there is every incentive for junior directors to remain in this post as long as possible. This motivation tends to make junior directors very cautious in their relationships with their superiors on the board. The fear of being removed from the board of directors to a ceremonial post with little real prestige, or to the board of an obscure subsidiary, is constantly present in the minds of many junior directors; this fear tends to encourage conservatism and conformity among them. It would, indeed, take much courage on the part of a junior board member to express an unpopular view or to criticize the decisions of his superiors, even if such actions were deemed to be in the best interest of the company.

Some junior members also feel that they owe their very appointment to the board to the senior directors, and they are guided by a personal sense of obligation and loyalty to their superiors. This loyalty often takes the form of absolute obedience and a self-effacing attitude toward their sponsors. Moreover, the Japanese typically find it extremely difficult to participate in discussions without being conscious of their own relative status in the hierarchy; this inhibits the free exchange of opinion between individuals of different ranks. There is a strong tendency on the part of subordinates not to express views that may conflict with those of their superiors.[18] Directors are also affected this way. Hierarchy tends to determine not only one's overt behavior but one's thought patterns as well. As a result, junior directors feel very much constrained in expressing their views in the presence of their seniors, and their superiors find it equally difficult to accept the free expression of opinion by the younger directors.

Furthermore, it must be remembered that the directors, with few exceptions, have spent their entire careers in the same organization; the superior-subordinate pattern of relationship nurtured over a 25- to 30-year period naturally persists, even after one is appointed to the board of directors. As one senior director put it, a junior director is no more independent in his relationship to his senior director than a section chief is to his department manager. Moreover,

[18] On this point, R. P. Dore presents the following point made by Takeyoshi Kawashima in summary form: "The subordinates should always give way to the superior when there is objectively a potential conflict of interest. When there is a conflict of opinion within a group where such relationships prevail, the subordinate should never be seen to win an argument. Skill lies in giving the superior an escape route, and allowing it to appear that the final solution was what the superior first proposed. This is the sort of skill on which success depends in Japanese society." R. P. Dore, *City Life in Japan: A Study of a Tokyo Ward* (Berkeley: Univerity of California Press, 1958), pp. 208–209.

directorship is often viewed by senior directors as a reward for outstanding past services. This selection criterion tends to limit the value of the board to the corporation and to increase the turnover among junior members of the board.

For the foregoing reasons, the power within a corporation is highly concentrated in two or three of its high-ranking executives, and there is no separate and independent body to check on their performance. This problem is further compounded by the fact that the functions of the auditors are, in practice, also extremely limited. There is no requirement in the Commercial Code that auditors be independent; nor are they required to have professional accounting backgrounds. Auditors, as is the case with directors, are, in reality, appointed by ranking corporate officers. The office of auditor is usually occupied by a retired executive or is used as a training ground for executives being groomed for directorship. Auditors are frequently given managerial responsibilities that are of little direct relevance to their legally prescribed functions. Although in theory auditors are supposed to be independent of the board of directors, in practice they are considered subordinate to it.

Although most senior executives are discreet in the use of their power, there have been a number of cases in which wrong judgment or miscalculation on the part of senior executives went unrecognized or unchallenged by the board of directors, eventually leading to grave consequences.

One common problem that deserves special attention in this connection is the fact that the tenure of the highest ranking executives — the chairman of the board and the president, in particular — in large Japanese corporations is left almost entirely to their own discretion, provided, of course, that their performance is not glaringly unsatisfactory. Although retirement is compulsory for those below the rank of director, few firms have established a formal compulsory retirement age for directors. Some boards have an informal understanding among their members as to the age at which they will be expected to retire. Even then, highest ranking officers are often exempted from such an informal agreement. While there has been a rather frequent turnover among lower-level top management — to make room for younger men — senior directors have at times remained at their posts for excessively long periods. Although managerial competence at the highest level of top management does not necessarily decline with increasing age — in fact, some of the most capable senior executives in Japan's leading corporations are in their seventies — nevertheless, there is an inherent danger in such a system.

Moreover, the absence of a formal procedure to assure the necessary turnover of top management often makes the orderly replacement of leadership difficult, encouraging power struggles within the ranks of top management. As a result, frequently, the only way to assure a change in senior executive cadres is for those aspiring to such positions to force the incumbents out by less than honorable means.

Most of the senior executives interviewed expressed an awareness of the problems just mentioned, but few, if any, significant corrective actions have been taken. It is readily understandable why management is reluctant to include outside directors on the board; this would tend to curtail the power of the incumbent members. Two objections are often cited against the inclusion of outside directors: (1) qualified directors are difficult to find and (2) the value of outside directors is limited because of their lack of familiarity with the company's operations. The first point is hardly disputable, but the validity of the second point is highly questionable. Outside directors are not likely to possess intimate knowledge of the firm's operations, but if they are chosen properly, this limitation is compensated for by their broad and relatively independent and objective views and their ability to bring fresh ideas to the organization. The latter point is particularly important in view of the fact that because of the permanent employment system, Japanese managers, even when highly knowledgeable about their own operations, are not often broadly gauged enough in their viewpoint.

Despite the advantages, inclusion of outsiders on boards of directors is likely to be resisted, not only because it would tend to restrict the power of top management, but because it would also reduce opportunities for men within the organization to be promoted to a directorship. It is likely, therefore, that the present pattern will continue despite the fact that the need for independent and effectively functioning boards of directors will undoubtedly increase in the future.

Although no significant actions have been taken to change the composition of boards of directors, a few firms have recently established a compulsory retirement age for all top management, including the chairman of the board and the president of the company, to assure infusion of fresh talent in top management ranks. This practice is limited to only a few firms, and as may be expected, it is a highly controversial matter among Japanese executives. The compulsory retirement age, where specified, usually varies according to the position. In one firm, for example, it is set for ordinary directors at sixty, for managing directors at sixty-three, for senior managing directors and executive vice-presidents at sixty-five, and for the president at sixty-seven.

Another basic difficulty observed in the top management organization of a typical Japanese corporation is that virtually every member of top management has direct responsibility over certain aspects of the company's operations, and he is deeply immersed in day-to-day operating problems in his area. As we shall show later, the particular manner of decision-making in Japanese corporations involves top management in rather routine types of decisions. Thus, the three distinct levels of top management — the board of directors, the general management, and the divisional or departmental management — are virtually indistinguishable, because all three levels are occupied practically by the same executives, despite the obvious differences in their respective functions. This has created some baffling problems.

The close identification of senior executives with day-to-day operations tends to limit their outlook. For example, it is frequently noticed, even in the executive committees, that members consider themselves representatives of a particular area rather than members of the top management responsible for the welfare of the entire corporation. Faced with a conflict of interest, there is always the possibility that they will place their departmental or functional interest above that of the entire corporation. Their lack of familiarity with other areas severely limits their ability to deliberate each key decision from the company-wide point of view. Moreover, because of their heavy workload in the performance of particular operating responsibilities, directors scarcely have time to study proposals relating to other than their own areas prior to general meetings. A number of executives interviewed candidly admitted that they often do not even have time to read the agenda of the forthcoming executive committee meeting, let alone to carefully study the content of each proposal to be discussed.

There is also a danger that even the most carefully prepared proposal may be rejected because of ill-considered comments made by ranking members of the committee who are not adequately familiar with a particular area, or who feel that the proposal, if approved, may be disadvantageous to the particular area they represent.

Also, given the very strict status differentiation among top management, areas represented by higher ranking directors tend to be favored over those represented by junior members. There is, too, an unhealthy tendency for members to refrain from raising objections to proposals from other areas for fear of reprisal, even when it is felt that such proposals are not in the best interest of the company. This tendency also sometimes encourages imprudent programs through logrolling.

In almost every firm, the chairman of the board, the president, and/or the executive vice-president are free from operating responsibilities. It is observed, however, that even these executives are often preoccupied with problems of some aspects of day-to-day operations. This may stem from their personal interest in a particular area or from a feeling that a given area, for some reason, needs special top management attention. In addition, these executives must concern themselves with political and social relations and with representing the firm to outside organizations and persons, including government agencies, trade associations, financial institutions, and major customers. As important as these activities are, they do divert attention and time from the overall direction of the firm. In fact, some senior executives prefer to spend their time performing duties that are immediately rewarding rather than trying to grapple with complex and often frustrating problems of general management. As a result, there is frequently no one in the entire corporation who gives continuing, full-time attention to such matters.

Few of the problems cited in this section are peculiar to Japan. Nevertheless, the Japanese situation is particularly serious because of the absence of reasonably independent and effectively functioning boards of directors.

These problems have not gone unrecognized by the top management of progressive Japanese corporations, and a number of steps have been taken to solve them, but with limited success. One solution is found in relieving ranking executives of operating responsibilities, so that they may have adequate time to devote to general management activities. Another approach is to make a formal provision in the organization chart and manual emphasizing the general management responsibilities of senior executives. For example, a few large firms place the president, executive vice-presidents, and senior managing directors in the same box on the organization chart to emphasize that as a group, they share general management responsibilities.

Another popular method is periodically to devote the full session of the executive committee to a discussion of matters relating to the entire corporation. In addition to these formal provisions, some senior executives are exerting considerable efforts to train their junior colleagues to develop a general management point of view.

All these efforts, although highly laudable, have thus far enjoyed only a limited success. A major retarding factor is the traditional promotion pattern of senior executives. In most large Japanese corporations, it has been common for executives to advance within a particular functional area. Moreover, many of them have been promoted to their present position on the basis of their technical competence in a given area (within the overriding range of seniority, of course) and not necessarily on the basis of their potential ability as general managers. There are frequent cases in which marketing executives have been chosen largely on the basis of their sales ability, or executives in charge of research and development have been promoted to their present position as a reward for their outstanding research performance. Although American corporations are by no means innocent of such practices, negative results appear to be more pronounced in Japanese enterprises.

Despite the narrow functional orientation that has characterized much of their careers, some senior executives do, in fact, develop a general management point of view as they advance to top management ranks. But many, quite naturally, experience considerable difficulty in making this transition. They feel much more comfortable supervising day-to-day operations in their own functional specialty than tackling unfamiliar general management problems.

This difficulty is further compounded by a particular method of decision-making commonly found in Japanese corporations. The traditional system of decision-making, as we shall see later, severely restricts top management's ability to exercise its initiative and leadership in directing the affairs of the firm. Unfortunately, the changes in top management organization have not always been accompanied by corresponding changes in the traditional decision-making process. As a result, when executives are relieved of operating responsibilities, they cannot readily and effectively assume general management functions. Executives who are separated from their operating responsibilities become detached from the mainstream of corporate activities, and as a result, they often suffer a considerable loss of personal influence and prestige in the organization. This loss has happened frequently enough in a number of corporations for many executives to be reluctant to give up their operating responsibilities.

Thus, the mere act of relieving executives of day-to-day operating responsibilities or placing them in the same box in the organization chart has not always overcome the difficulties of assuring the functioning of top management for the good of the *entire* corporation.

Let us now go on to evaluate the strengths and weaknesses of the Japanese corporate organization. To Western observers it may appear to suffer from all sorts of limitations, but in the Japanese context, this is more apparent than real. One of the notable strengths of Japanese organization lies in the ease with which, because of clear-cut vertical and hierarchical relationships, a leader can quickly and effectively mobilize the group when the need arises. The line of communication from the leader to the lowest member, even in a complex organization, is vertically defined and unequivocal, so that not only can communication be easily and speedily achieved down through the line, but the hierarchical structure also lends itself to the kind of authoritarian and autocratic control that allows a very rapid and total group mobilization.[19] The strong collectivity orientation, and the high degree of emotional commitment of each member to the group that it generates, constitutes another potential strength of Japanese organization — group unity and cooperation can easily be achieved because of strong organizational loyalty and group solidarity.

These two potential strengths of Japanese organization especially manifest themselves in crises. Faced with an emergency situation, the leader can quickly and successfully mobilize the group and direct its efforts toward the solution of the threatening problem at hand. When the group perceives a danger to its security, its strong collectivity orientation can generate enormous collective energy. Individual members then are ready to sacrifice self-interest for the protection and security of the collectivity.

Japanese organization is, indeed, extremely effective and efficient in meeting crisis situations. There were repeated manifestations of this in modern Japanese history, when the authoritarian elite exploited the crisis psychology almost to its limit to mobilize the

[19] Nakane, *Tate Shakai no Ningen Kankei*, p. 128.

masses for the ultimate collectivity — the nation-state. At the enterprise level, perhaps the best illustration is found in the immediate aftermath of World War II, when virtually every leading corporation faced the test of survival. Examination of the histories of a number of corporations in this period reveals tremendous self-sacrifice and devotion on the part of a hard core of employees at all levels toward the rebuilding of the enterprises. This was undoubtedly an important factor in the rapid postwar recovery and phenomenal subsequent growth of the Japanese economy.

Another one of the Japanese organization's strengths lies in the fact that, outward impressions to the contrary, it does have considerable flexibility. As we noted earlier, individual responsibilities and assignments are not clearly defined; this vagueness, notwithstanding its limitations, does make it possible for capable individuals to assume greater responsibilities than those prescribed by their status in the hierarchy.[20] Thus, despite the marked rigidity of the seniority-determined status, there is sufficient built-in flexibility to allow competent and ambitious individuals lacking the appropriate status to demonstrate their ability with considerable freedom, as long as these men are tactful and do not disrupt the formal status hierarchy but maintain harmonious interpersonal relationships. It is even possible for a capable subordinate to exercise actual leadership, provided that he recognizes and pays appropriate deference to his superiors in the formal hierarchy.

On the other hand, what are the potential weaknesses in the Japanese organizational structure? For the reasons we have just noted, Japanese organization is very effective in crises, but it is highly questionable whether the same effectiveness obtains or can be sustained in normal times. In fact, under normal circumstances, considerable difficulties are experienced in maintaining group solidarity. Intragroup conflicts that erode solidarity are likely to occur, or complacency will set in. In the absence of clear-cut individual responsibilities and a performance-oriented reward system, each person has a wide range of discretion in deciding how much he will contribute to the group. In other words, one could get by with a minimal personal contribution of effort without jeopardizing one's membership in the collectivity. There is, therefore, a serious danger that the group will drift along or stagnate complacently.

Another potential weakness of the Japanese organization is the

[20] *Ibid.*, p. 152.

extreme sensitivity of the Japanese to their relative standing in the hierarchy (this applies both to individuals within a group and to whole groups), frequently making it necessary for the collectivity to set its goals in terms of competing groups in order to achieve effective solidarity. In other words, group mobilization within a company becomes much easier when the goals of the company are determined in terms of its chief competitors and when its performance is measured against that of its rival firms. Under these circumstances, determination of goals in terms of its own needs, interests, and distinct competence becomes extremely difficult. This is very much evident in the strategy formulation of leading Japanese corporations.

Still another potential limitation of the organizational structure of Japanese corporations lies in the fact that because of the particular group configuration, the formal leader's position can be rather insecure and can depend, to too great a degree, on the support he can command from his key subordinates. This tends to encourage internal struggles and power manipulation among top echelons of the organization. Moreover, given the strong vertical orientation of the organizational structure, power struggles at top management levels can and frequently do involve those in the lower echelons. To assure the security of his position, the leader may well become excessively involved in the manipulation of his key subordinates to establish and sustain an intricate power balance within the organization.

To the aforementioned weaknesses of the traditional corporate organization in Japan may be added the one caused by the great emphasis placed on maintenance of harmony, which may well constrain the organization's ability to innovate. It is true that harmony is generally sought only as a means to goal-achievement, since conflicts between members would disrupt the smooth attainment of collective goals. But not infrequently, the maintenance of harmony gains precedence over goal-attainment. This tendency is particularly evident in an organization with a weak leader who feels that his tenure may be threatened by disrupting the status quo.

We have noted earlier that the organizational structure of a large Japanese corporation tends to be elaborately and minutely divided into separate, formally distinct units, with a large proportion of the personnel holding formal titles. Although many of these titles are created largely for the purpose of status recognition, in the absence of a clear definition of the functions and responsibilities of each position, there is a definite adverse tendency for holders of such titles to assume line authority. Both of these organizational flaws have contributed to the lessening of organizational efficiency.

Specifically, these flaws duplicate effort, overlap authority, and unnecessarily complicate and confuse reporting relationships; they have introduced a considerable degree of rigidity into the organizational structure, which sharply limits the corporation's ability to respond to the rapidly changing economic environment. They have slowed down decision-making and have complicated communication within the organization. They have also had an adverse effect on personnel and have seriously limited the effective use of manpower, for assignments are often too narrow to be challenging to capable individuals, leading to poor morale and limited opportunities for their personal growth and development.

Fragmentation of the corporate organization into a large cluster of small but discrete units has had still another adverse effect. Because of the strong collectivity orientation, there is a marked tendency among the personnel of a corporate organization to develop close identity with and loyalty to the immediate formal organizational unit to which they belong. The very close group solidarity tends to give rise to its own subgoals, which may be in conflict with the goals of the whole organization. As may be expected, this tendency was observed to be particularly pronounced in those firms in which the corporate goals were not clearly articulated. This very intense group solidarity encourages each group to protect and promote its own interests against other groups, resulting in strong intergroup rivalry and conflicts of interest. In a collectivity-oriented society such as Japan, with the basic unit of organization being a group, conflicts within a corporate organization often take the form of struggles between groups rather than between individuals. This tendency is further aggravated in Japanese corporations where the functions and responsibilities of each unit or position are not well defined, thus giving each group greater room to maneuver for higher status and more authority within the larger organization.

We have noted earlier that the managerial functions and authorities in Japanese corporate organizations are not clearly defined. The clear-cut definition of functions and individual responsibilities has been deemed unnecessary because of the traditional collectivity orientation. However, recent developments have cast serious doubts on the continued effectiveness of this basic premise.

An important factor mitigating against the continued acceptability of this basic premise is the phenomenal postwar growth experienced by most large Japanese firms, resulting in a rapid growth of organization, both in size and complexity. There is growing concern on the part of management that the classical Japanese concept of organization, though effective in a small and relatively simple setup, cannot be applied with the same effectiveness to extremely large and complex enterprises. The absence of a clear-cut definition of functions and positions has led to considerable confusion, duplication of effort, and overlapping authority, resulting, in turn, in the deterioration of organizational morale. Moreover, the rapid growth of firms, both in size and complexity, has made it increasingly difficult to solicit close identification of the individual's interest with that of the enterprise.

Another significant factor is that there are indications (noted in Chapter 2) that the traditional collectivity orientation itself is gradually weakening. It is still premature to determine, as indicated earlier, whether the new trends will result in the emergence of an individualistic orientation or of other forms of collectivity orientation. But any modification in the traditional collectivity orientation will tend to reduce the effectiveness of the organizational structure based on the classical premises.

We should also note that there is growing doubt whether or not Japanese management can continue to expect from its employees undivided loyalty and total commitment to the enterprise. This is particularly apparent among the younger generations. A number of junior management personnel interviewed in this study were critical of the concept of total allegiance to the company. They are surely willing to perform their assigned task adequately, but they are not willing to place company loyalty over everything else. No longer are they solely committed to the company nor to the achievement of their professional success at any cost.

A number of senior executives interviewed in this study were highly critical of these developments. In their view, too many of their younger managers have learned to compromise their ambitions to their realistic prospects and are content with mediocre achievement. They deplore the privatized pettiness of their younger subordinates, "who have lowered their sights to a cozy little house in the suburbs, a pretty wife, a couple of kids and the occasional game of golf."[21]

These trends of "apathy," "privatization," and "consumer orientation" may well be characteristics common to all highly industrialized

[21] R. P. Dore, "Mobility, Equality and Individuality," in R. P. Dore (ed.), *Aspects of Social Change in Modern Japan* (Princeton: Princeton University Press, 1967), p. 141.

societies. While it is impossible to ascertain how prevalent these trends are, it is true that these attitude changes are eroding the basic premises upon which Japanese corporate organization has been structured.

Recognizing the growing incongruities between the classical pattern of corporate organization and the contemporary industrial environment, a growing number of Japanese firms have begun to take steps to overcome them, though their efforts have not always been successful. Some commonly used approaches in these efforts to lessen the discrepancies that retard the optimum functioning of modern Japanese corporate organization have been the following:

1. To define functions and responsibilities for each key position by preparing detailed job classifications and descriptions. While some progress has been made in this direction among production workers, similar efforts for managerial personnel have thus far realized only a very limited success, largely because they have not been accompanied by changes in the managerial process itself, particularly in the decision-making process.
2. To introduce the divisional system of management. *Jigyobusei,* or the independent divisional system, had received much attention during the boom years of the late 1950's and early 1960's. The success of this system in the United States was well publicized and stirred much interest among Japanese executives. Anxious to emulate this success, a number of firms rushed to adopt it without a careful prior examination of its applicability to Japanese needs. The result, as might have been expected, has been disappointing. In many cases, the American divisional system only worsened the very conditions in Japan it was meant to remedy; that is, it only contributed to the overlapping of authority and the duplication of functions, creating further overhead burdens and organizational fragmentation.

This has, in part, been due to the fact that the adoption of the divisional management system has seldom gone beyond changes in the organizational structure and in the titles of executives. Rarely has it been accompanied by a parallel adoption of management concepts and techniques essential to the successful functioning of the division system itself, including the profit-center concept and appropriate techniques of managerial control. In many cases, the divisional organization structure has been superimposed on the existing pattern of management. True, in some firms, the current pattern is considered only as a transitory state, and their eventual plan calls for the instituting of a full-fledged division system. However, the incomplete adoption of this system too frequently stems from an inadequate understanding of the way it works and from an illusion that the structural changes alone are sufficient to attain the full complement of the benefits from the division system of management.

Managements of progressive firms have gradually come around to recognizing problems associated with organizational fragmentation and have begun to take corrective measures. This effort has been intensified since the recession of the mid-1960's. One step has been to carefully evaluate the rationale for departmentalization, with the ultimate goal of consolidating highly fragmented sections or departments with larger organizational units on the basis of a more meaningful and logical set of criteria. Greater attention is now being paid to the task to be performed as a key criterion for departmentalization. In a number of firms, this approach has considerably simplified the organizational structure and reporting relationships, resulting in a better utilization of personnel.

Another corrective measure has been the elimination of sections or subsections as independent organizational units and the organization of personnel on a task force or a project basis. Although this approach can be applied only to certain staff functions, it has been successfully adopted by a number of firms. For example, one large firm has recently reduced the number of sections in corporate staff groups from 54 to 26 by eliminating some sections altogether and consolidating others. Using this approach, the firm was able to reduce personnel requirements for the reorganized groups by 10 percent. Elimination of sections has not only helped to break down organizational rigidity and sectional barriers, but it has also made it possible for the department manager to deploy his personnel much more efficiently and flexibly, and has relieved a number of men from quasi-administrative responsibilities.

In this chapter, we have examined the salient features of Japanese corporate organization and the changes that are currently taking place in a number of progressive Japanese firms. The process of change has not been easy, nor has it avoided creating new problems. But there is no doubt that Japanese managements, at least of progressive firms, are now aware of the shortcomings of the traditional form of corporate organization and are making deliberate efforts to introduce improvements congruous with the contemporary business environment.

8

Personnel Practices and Policies

A decade ago, James C. Abegglen, in his excellent study of Japanese factory organizations, identified a number of distinct features of personnel practices in Japanese corporations. These features included the permanent employment system, the seniority-based reward system, and the heavy involvement of management with the personal life of each employee and his family.[1]

In the past ten years, however, the Japanese economy has achieved a phenomenal growth and has reached a new level of industrial development. Simultaneously, the past decade has witnessed quite significant changes in the corporate environment. To meet these new challenges, progressive Japanese corporations have been attempting to introduce innovations in their personnel practices. These changes call for an examination of more recent and current personnel practices in large Japanese corporations, which is the goal of the present chapter. We shall focus the ensuing analysis on personnel policies and practices for managerial personnel.

Among factors affecting personnel practices and policies, the following are particularly important: Japan has begun to experience labor shortages for the first time in her industrial history; there has been a particularly pronounced shortage of younger workers. Also, the growing competitive pressure has been for some time, and is now, demanding greater flexibility in operations. The permanent employment pattern, the seniority-oriented reward system, and the extensive provision of fringe benefits have imposed considerable rigidities on the operations of Japanese firms. To soften these rigidi-

[1] James C. Abegglen, *The Japanese Factory: Aspects of Its Social Organization* (Glencoe, Ill.: The Free Press, 1958), pp. 11–109.

ties, large Japanese corporations have relied extensively on two devices—the extensive employment of temporary workers and the widespread reliance on subcontractors. The growing labor shortage, however, is making it increasingly difficult for large Japanese enterprises to avail themselves of both of these ingenious devices at the very time when competitive pressure is demanding greater flexibility. Competitive pressures have also made the liberal provision of fringe benefits increasingly burdensome.

Traditional personnel practices are not compatible with Japan's rapid rate of technological innovation, which also demands greater operating flexibility. The momentum of technological progress has virtually made meaningless a key justification for traditional personnel practices. As noted in Chapter 3, one of the important *raisons d'être* claimed for the seniority-based reward system was that an employee's level of contribution to the firm increased with seniority. Clearly, however, the nature of today's rapid technological change has largely eliminated the close relationship that formerly existed between the employee's length of service and his competence. In fact, the younger employee with up-to-date training and greater adaptability is more valuable than the older employee whose accumulated skills and experiences may be sadly obsolete.

The guarantee against dismissal and the seniority-based reward system have tended to breed a feeling of complacency among employees; this is totally incongruous in a situation such as the present one, where the need for competent personnel at all levels of management is indeed acute. Along with the gradual erosion of traditional values, this incongruity becomes especially pronounced as the organization grows in size. The larger the organization is, the greater is the tendency for impersonalization of the relationship between the company and its employees. It is true that throughout this study we observed many hardworking and highly motivated persons at all levels of management, but we also found that there were a substantial number who could be considered as complacent and indifferent. There is also little doubt that the traditional personnel practices have tended to encourage conformity and conservatism. Observant senior executives in a number of firms candidly admitted that many highly capable and motivated young men lost their initial enthusiasm as they became affected by what one executive described as the "tepid" environment.

There is a growing conviction among concerned government officials and progressive executives that the traditional personnel practices, particularly the system of lifetime employment, limit the effective utilization of manpower, not only within the limited scope of individual firms, but also in the larger context of the national economy. Although this loss may be compensated for, in part, by strong employee loyalty to the enterprise—which is likely to result in greater productivity—the problem will become increasingly serious with mounting labor shortages. Moreover, a certain waste of human resources is unavoidable in the permanent employment system, since those who, for some reason, do not fit in a particular type of organization, or who lack the aptitude for a certain kind of business, are prevented by the system for seeking career opportunities elsewhere. This is a loss not only to the individual and to the company, but to the whole economy.

Although a number of the basic characteristics of the traditional personnel practices seem to have remained unaltered during the last decade, a closer examination reveals that subtle but highly significant changes have taken place. In this chapter, we shall first examine the changes in two key aspects of Japanese personnel practices —the system of permanent employment and the seniority-reward system—particularly as they relate to managerial personnel. Then we shall discuss the growing interest in advancing a systematic approach to management development, one of the most significant developments in the postwar Japanese industrial scene.

The Managerial Career

We should note at the outset that a managerial career with a large corporation is highly valued in contemporary Japan for several reasons. Employment with a large private corporation offers one of the most attractive (if not *the* most attractive) opportunities for upward social mobility in contemporary Japanese society. A managerial career with a large firm is also desirable from the point of view of the lifelong security it can provide for an individual and his family. Such a career also carries with it high social prestige, for in Japan, the place of one's employment is a key determinant of one's social status.

Consequently, entry into a managerial career with a large corporation is highly competitive. A university education constitutes, with few exceptions, the single most important prerequisite to qualifying for managerial rank. Not only is a university education required, but a very strong preference traditionally has been shown for graduates of a limited number of leading universities. Because of the highly particularistic pattern of recruitment established by a group of large corporations and selected leading universities, graduates of less prestigious schools have been largely excluded from consideration for employment by leading firms. The clear preference given graduates of certain leading universities is well reflected in the fact that the top management positions of leading corporations are predominantly filled by graduates of these universities (see Chapter 4). Since the type of university one graduates from virtually determines one's lifetime career, a high premium is placed on entry into the "right" school.[2]

Furthermore, because entry into these top-ranking universities is based strictly on rigorous entrance examinations, virtually any youth, regardless of his family background, can enter these institutions, provided that he passes the entrance examination. Thus, a young man with a degree from the "right" school can gain access to major corporations with little regard to his father's occupation or social status. Nepotism and family connections can be important in assuring entry into large corporations, but those without them are not usually placed at undue disadvantage. However, family connections or a father's influence may be used to compensate for an aspiring candidate's deficiency in his educational background. For example, a high-ranking executive in a major corporation can use his influence to arrange for his son, who holds a degree from a second-rate university, to enter one of the corporation's related firms. But this practice is neither common nor well accepted.

There is a gradual tendency for large Japanese corporations to broaden the range of universities whose graduates they will consider for employment. This is particularly noticeable in technical areas because of the increasing demand for technically trained personnel, but still, graduates of the better universities are definitely preferred. The reason cited most frequently for this practice by Japanese management is that graduates of the leading universities, by virtue of the schools' high standards, are better material than graduates of less prestigious schools. It is difficult to deny the validity of this assessment. However, it appears that there are other, less-articulated reasons as well. Great importance is attached to group

[2] Not infrequently, preparation for entry into the "right" university begins with the parent's choice of the child's kindergarten — attending the "right" kindergarten will enable the child to be admitted to the "right" grade school, and so on.

solidarity in Japanese enterprises; as noted in Chapter 7, a large Japanese enterprise is a closed and narrow social nexus. Those with a common bond or with similar experiences and backgrounds are preferred, inasmuch as they can be more easily integrated into the existing group, and their common ties will tend to strengthen group solidarity. Especially if the top management is dominated by graduates of a certain university, there is a natural tendency for that school to be preferred in recruiting new trainees.

Moreover, because school ties are particularly strong in Japan (group solidarity and a close sense of identification stemming from the shared membership in the same collectivity), there is a practical advantage in recruiting from prestigious universities. It is likely to facilitate communication with customers, financial institutions, or government agencies that also recruit from these same schools. In view of the extraordinary importance given to personal relationships and contacts, this practice has its undeniable advantages.

Abegglen observed in his study that one of the most distinct characteristics of personnel practices in Japanese factories is the permanent employment system. An employee commits his entire working career upon accepting employment with a company.[3] The permanent employment system has had many ramifications, of which the following have been particularly important:

1. All managerial employees are recruited directly from universities. Only at the time of college graduation can one choose his lifelong career without undue disadvantage. At the time of entry into the firm, both the firm and the employee make a permanent and irrevocable commitment to one another. Permanent employees can be dismissed only under very dire circumstances, such as a serious moral offense. Neither incompetence nor the changing need of the corporation constitutes a justifiable ground for the dismissal of an employee. It is not a contractual relationship in which each party agrees to an employer-employee relationship, bearing certain conditions and terms, which can be terminated at the option of the parties involved. The Japanese employment relationship is an unconditional one, requiring *total* commitment on the part of employer and employee.[4]

[3] Abegglen, *The Japanese Factory*, p. 11.

[4] The absence of the concept of a contractual relationship in Japanese society is discussed in detail in Hajime Nakamura, *Ways of Thinking of Eastern Peoples: India, China, Tibet, Japan* (Honolulu: East-West Center Press, 1964), pp. 449–467.

2. Under the permanent employment system, managerial personnel are recruited not to fill specific positions, but to become members of the organization who will be given a wide variety of assignments in the course of their working careers. All prospective managerial personnel enter the corporation as management trainees, presumably aspiring for top management positions. As a result, occupational specialty is much less of a concern to Japanese management personnel than to their counterparts in the United States. One's security and identity depend largely on permanent membership in the firm, rather than on occupational specialty. Under this system, criteria for recruitment and selection must be, of necessity, quite general and are largely based on one's personal qualifications, such as intellectual capacity, congenial personality, emotional stability, and family background. Specialized professional competence and training are relatively unimportant. This is particularly true among nontechnical management personnel.

We should also note that under this system, it is difficult for firms to base their recruitment on a careful assessment of their current and projected personnel needs. Although a growing number of enterprises are attempting to move in this direction, the number of trainees to be recruited each year is often decided upon arbitrarily by such factors as the *current* economic conditions, ignoring the fact that firms are bound to the commitment made at the time of recruitment for nearly 40 years into the future.

3. Retirement comes at a relatively early age, and for those under the directorship level, retirement is most strictly enforced. Under the permanent employment system, early retirement is thought necessary to insure the infusion of fresh talents to managerial ranks and to provide opportunities for younger employees.

The permanent employment practice has remained basically unchanged throughout the past decade, but there have been at least two noteworthy developments. One is that in very recent years, there has been some degree of interfirm mobility of personnel. Although recruitment from sources other than the universities is still considered as irregular by most firms, some large firms have, from time to time, recruited experienced personnel from other companies and from government agencies. The boom years of the late 1950's and early 1960's spurred this practice. As a consequence, some leading firms have engaged in *Choto Saiyo,* or mid-career recruitment—a newly coined term to describe recruitment from sources other than the traditional one of the university. Even after the rate of growth has tapered off, some large firms occasionally have continued to resort to this practice when there has been a clear need for it. Those recruited in this manner have usually been technical personnel—engineers, computer specialists, those trained in operations research, and research scientists. Perhaps the most frequent occasions for this "irregular" manner of recruiting occurred when, in the early 1960's, a number of large firms sought to strengthen their own research and development capabilities by establishing or expanding their research laboratories. To staff the newly created or expanded research facilities, the shortage of qualified research and development specialists within their own organizations forced these firms to seek them elsewhere. Furthermore, in diversifying into new fields of activity, some large firms recruited a small number of trained engineers in a similar manner. (In addition to the circumstances just described, in a few cases former Zaibatsu firms took over a small number of management personnel from their sister firms in declining industries with an excess of personnel. But this was largely done out of their sense of obligation to aid their sister firms in difficulty, rather than out of their own need for these employees.)

It should be noted, however, that wherever "irregular" recruitment took place, it was only a last resort. Firms first explored possibilities of training their own personnel in the needed skills. Moreover, it is interesting to note that these men were sought among junior members of university faculties, employees of government agencies, and personnel of smaller firms. Very seldom were they recruited from competing firms in the same industry. This reluctance stemmed partly from a feeling on the part of some executives that it is unethical to raid trained personnel from a competing firm, but more importantly, it stemmed from the fear of reprisal by competitors. In addition, the greater salary differential that has existed between private industries on the one hand and educational institutions, government agencies, or smaller firms on the other has made it easier for the larger corporations to entice qualified personnel from these sources rather than from other large corporations. Another interesting feature of mid-career recruiting practices of the well-established older Japanese firms has been to seek prospective candidates through informal means, such as through school and professional ties or personal friendships.

Significantly, in placing these mid-career recruits in an organization, it is customary for the firm to take the utmost care to protect the interests of its "own" personnel. Mid-career recruits are somewhat discriminated against in terms of both salary and rank, in comparison to those with a comparable education and of comparable age who joined the company directly from their universities. It is quite common for mid-career recruits, regardless of their excellent qualifications, to be placed in a salary scale a year or two behind that of an average university-recruited employee with an equivalent background. Of course, due to the salary differentials that are likely to exist between their new employer and their former place of employment, mid-career recruits usually substantially improve their salaries by transferring to the large corporation. In addition to formal differentiations, mid-career recruits frequently encounter informal discrimination of various sorts. A Japanese corporation is a tightly knit, closed collectivity. One of the striking characteristics of the Japanese collectivity orientation, as noted in Chapter 1, is the strong suspicion that the group feels toward outsiders. Implicit in the collectivity orientation is the feeling that one's loyalty and commitment to the group are commensurate with the length of his affiliation with it. This tendency is clearly observable even in the modern corporation. Mid-career recruits tend to be looked upon as "quasi outsiders," and they are frequently treated with a certain amount of suspicion.

A number of personnel directors expressed their apprehension that mid-career recruits, having first been exposed to another company, may not be molded to fit into the *shafu,* or climate, of the one that they have later joined. There is a common belief among Japanese managers that new school graduates are pristine and untainted, and not indoctrinated, and that they can be trained to fit the company mold. On the other hand, there is a widely shared conviction that the mid-career recruit is likely to experience some difficulties in adapting himself to a new organization. Some mid-career recruits interviewed in this study expressed the opinion that it would take them several years to be allowed to become completely integrated with the new organization. A few expressed doubt that they could ever completely overcome the stigma of being mid-career transferees. What is in question is not one's technical competence, but his organizational loyalty and commitment. Moreover, in a highly collectivity-oriented organization, characterized by particularistic interpersonal relationships, the extent to which one can demonstrate his technical competence depends, to an important degree, on his knowledge of the firm's complex web of interpersonal relationships as well as on the group's willingness to accept and trust him. It may well take several years for mid-career recruits to meet these two conditions. There was a general consensus among them that these apprehensions were the single most serious factor in their consideration of whether or not to change their place of employment.

Although the great majority of firms have kept their mid-career recruitment to a minimum, a small number that have undergone an exceptionally rapid growth in the postwar years — and some that were established in the postwar years — have been forced to recruit mid-career experienced personnel, both technical and managerial, to staff their rapidly growing organizations. (Though it is a highly exceptional case, in one firm, which has achieved a phenomenal growth in recent years, nearly a fourth of its more than 8,000 employees are reportedly mid-career recruits.) Such firms, unlike the more established ones, have developed a formal procedure for mid-career recruiting and they do it at regular intervals. It is noteworthy that on the whole, these successful growth companies have been able to attract a large number of qualified applicants. For example, when one well-known growth firm advertised in the newspapers to fill 40 openings for management personnel, it received as many as 1,200 applications, including some from men who were currently employed in large, prestigious firms.

It is also interesting to note that even corporations that regularly seek mid-career recruits show a definite preference for younger men with a minimum of experience with other firms. This is due to two important factors. One is the salary consideration (under the seniority-based salary system, the scale for younger men is lower), and the other is that the feeling persists that it will be easier for younger men to adapt themselves to the new organization.

As we have seen, mid-career recruitment, though an existing practice, has been quite limited. It is rather remarkable that the great majority of Japanese firms have undergone very rapid postwar expansion without resorting to mid-career recruiting.

Noteworthy also is the recent trend toward extending the compulsory retirement age. We have noted that all employees, except members of the board, have to retire at the age of fifty-five. This has been strictly enforced by most large firms. Of course, customarily, management personnel retiring from the parent corporation have been provided with suitable positions in the company's subsidiaries or in its satellite firms, where they continue to work for an additional several years; but, nevertheless, under ordinary circumstances they have had to give up their positions in the parent corporation at the age of fifty-five. In the past year or so, however, a number of firms have extended the retirement age to fifty-eight, and some even to sixty. Three factors have been primarily responsible for this development: (1) concerted efforts by labor unions; (2) the mounting labor shortage; and (3) the growing life expectancy. Although the first two factors apply primarily to rank-and-file workers, in extending the compulsory retirement age, most firms have done so for both managerial and nonmanagerial personnel.

Management of these corporations is fully aware of the serious implications and consequences of such an action, inasmuch as the early retirement age has served an important function in the traditional personnel system. Moreover, the seniority-based reward system makes the retention of older workers very expensive. While some firms have unconditionally extended the retirement age by two or three years, realizing its far-reaching implications, many have done so only on a conditional basis. While details vary among firms, a pattern followed by a number of them is to retire all employees below the rank of director at the age of fifty-five and to rehire those who want to continue with the firm for a period of time and under certain terms. These terms are likely to specify a reduced salary level, limited fringe benefits, and an annual evaluation of status, performance, and so on. Under this practice, managerial employees are likely to be relieved of the position they held at the time of retirement and to be assigned to another. In the case of managerial personnel, however, most companies still prefer to shift older employees to their subsidiaries and satellite firms, either prior to or upon their retirement, rather than to retain them in the parent organization even in a reduced status and at a smaller salary.

In concluding this section, we shall analyze the attitude of Japanese executives toward the system of lifetime employment. This practice has, indeed, been subject to much controversy among Japanese management during the last decade or so, and its pros and cons have been thoroughly discussed. Some, not many, executives have shown a definite preference for the lifetime employment system and feel that it should be perpetuated. They are of the opinion that this is consistent with Japanese tradition, and that it will continue to be effective as it has been in the past. The system, in their view, encourages employee loyalty and spurs workers to higher morale and achievement. Moreover, they feel that it gives employees a sense of security. If proper motivations are provided, this sense of security, combined with organizational loyalty, will lead to greater productivity than is possible under a more competitive and fluid system. Such executives feel that in addition to these advantages, the system allows management to evaluate the capacity and aptitude of each individual over a much longer time span.

With equal vehemence, another small number of executives, particularly among the younger ones, expressed a view that the system of lifetime employment was obsolete for the contemporary business environment. Moreover, these executives are far from convinced of the validity of the often-repeated claim that the lifetime employment system automatically inspires employees' loyalty to the enterprise. They point out that loyalty stemming from a highly rigid system of employment, where employees have no choice but to be permanently committed to one firm, is of only limited value. These executives are of the opinion that loyalty, to be truly effective, must be based on the feelings and preferences of the employees under a system where they can, if they so choose, have a reasonable degree of interfirm mobility.

Most executives interviewed, however, feel ambivalent about the lifetime employment practices. At the same time that they are well aware of the various problems associated with this practice, they also find it difficult to completely deny the fact that the practice has been conducive to considerable organizational loyalty among Japanese employees and that it has been effective. There is no doubt that these executives have a strong emotional attachment to the system. They share the view expressed in the Doyukai declaration of 1965 (see Chapter 4) that there are definite advantages in the lifetime employment system and that any attempts to change it should proceed with caution and only after a thorough analysis of the system's strengths as well as its limitations. Although there is a wide divergence of views among senior executives of leading corporations on the virtues and ills of the system of lifetime employment, the prevalence of the more positive attitude seems to indicate that any basic changes in the system will occur only gradually, if at all.

Recent Developments in the System of Reward

The traditional reward system in Japanese corporations has two distinct characteristics. One is that reward, both in terms of career advancement and financial compensation, is based on broad social considerations and personal qualifications, such as age and education, rather than on the basis of the nature of the work performed or the employee's competence. Then there is the distinct feature of extensive noncash or fringe benefits for workers and their families. In recent years these traditional aspects of the reward system have come under close scrutiny, and progressive firms are making deliberate efforts to move gradually toward a system that emphasizes merit, performance, and ability rather than the former criteria. What major steps have been taken in this direction?

To provide a proper perspective, we shall briefly describe the traditional reward system. University education has been an important prerequisite for career advancement, and consequently, opportunities for those without college degrees have been extremely limited. Within a given level of education, career advancement has been based on seniority. This has been particularly true for the first ten to fifteen years of one's career. In fact, seniority has been so rigidly observed that promotions to certain lower-level managerial positions have been determined by the year of the employee's graduation from college, which, of course, corresponds to the year of his entry into the firm. Prospective employees are carefully chosen from among the graduates of leading universities. In this sense, a minimum competence level is recognized for initial entry. However, individual differences in competence and ability within this group are virtually ignored, at least for the initial phase of the individual's career. Essentially, everyone within the same category in terms of age and educational level is treated similarly. Thus, the entire personnel management program, including the reward system, in Japanese corporations is designed on a collective rather than an individual basis.

The strong emphasis on seniority in promotion has meant that career advancement in Japan, though highly predictable, has been extremely slow. Although there is some variance among firms, the general rule is that one must be with the company for at least eight to ten years before being promoted to the rank of subsection chief. It takes another several years before one is ready to become the chief of a section — the first managerial position of any significance. Fifteen to twenty years of seniority are required before one is promoted to the position of deputy department manager or its equivalent. At least twenty years of seniority are the prerequisite for promotion to the position of department head, the highest middle management status. Only in their early fifties are managers considered for top management positions. But, even in this very rigid seniority-based reward system, competence or ability has not been totally ignored. Formal differentiation gradually becomes apparent after ten to fifteen years of service, or at about the time the executive is considered for the position of section chief. Those who are extremely competent may advance to this position a year or two sooner than the normal rate, and they are likely to be put in charge of key sections. Although competence and performance become progressively important as one moves higher in the managerial hierarchy, these qualifications are always considered within the overriding framework of seniority. There is a minimum acceptable age for every position, and even the most competent are not promoted before they reach the prescribed minimum age level.

Under the traditional pattern of career advancement, one is rewarded for his competence only after he proves his ability to the satisfaction of everyone concerned. There is an insistence on a general consensus that the person up for promotion is, in fact, competent and deserves to be given special recognition for it. Given the Japanese organizational climate, this insistence has its rationale. First of all, because of the high degree of collectivity orientation, opportunities to manifest one's individual competence are highly limited. Secondly, rewarding an individual for his competence prematurely in an intensely collectivity-oriented organization (before subordinates, peers, and superiors are convinced of his merits) is likely to breed resentment, disrupting the group harmony and adversely affecting the morale of the group and, therefore, its performance. The hasty rewarding of an executive for his competence, no matter how impressive his abilities may be, may thus help alienate his "collectivity" from him; and such alienation, of course, reduces his effectiveness as an executive.

Financial compensation has also been determined primarily on the basis of educational background and seniority. One's starting salary is determined according to one's educational background. Annual salary increases are given with little regard to the type of position one holds or the level of one's competence or performance. In addition to the monthly salary, semiannual bonuses have become a regular component of the compensation scheme in large Japanese corporations. The term "bonus" is rather a misnomer, because employees expect bonuses regardless of the company's performance. The size of semiannual bonuses commonly has been calculated on the basis of the base salary. Retirement allowances in Japan have been another well-known component in the structure of financial compensation. It has been customary for an employee to receive a considerable allowance, at the time of his retirement, which is usually paid in one lump sum. This allowance, as well, has been determined by the base salary.

The salary structure in large Japanese corporations traditionally has been quite complex. Typically, in addition to the base salary, there are several types of allowances, including allowances for housing, transportation, cost of living, and so on. Like the base salary, these allowances are not related to one's productivity or performance; they have been designed primarily to meet certain needs of the employee and his family. The compensation system of Japanese corporations also provides for extensive fringe benefits for employees and their families, including housing, medical care, company stores, recreational facilities, educational programs, and company-sponsored savings programs at an interest rate substantially higher than the commercial rate. These fringe benefits constitute a very important element in the overall system of compensation.

Having looked at the salient features of the traditional system of reward, we shall now proceed to examine the changes that gradually have been introduced in recent years. The degree to which these changes have been implemented varies considerably among the firms studied; however, most large firms are now making determined efforts to rationalize the traditional reward system.

Most significant, of course, is the fact that the very criteria for reward are undergoing a basic change. Efforts are now being made to place greater emphasis on individual merit and performance in the overall reward system. As a step toward this end, most large Japanese firms have installed, in recent years, a formal appraisal program to evaluate regularly the ability, competence, and performance of each employee. A typical program calls for semiannual appraisal of all employees below the rank of director. The employee's supervisors evaluate his ability, personal qualifications, competence level, and performance on the current assignment, and his future potential. To facilitate the appraisal process, each of these major categories typically is broken down into a number of specific subareas, and a rating scale is usually provided. Some firms have developed very elaborate procedures for performance evaluation.

Although the degree to which these evaluative data are reflected in the reward system varies considerably among firms (there are some firms that make virtually no use of these data even though they are religiously collected), it is significant to note that almost every major corporation now has a formal performance appraisal program of some sort. In most of the firms studied, ability and performance are gradually becoming increasingly important factors in one's career advancement. Although still in the overriding framework of seniority, advancement for competent personnel has been accelerated at a somewhat faster pace; formal recognition of one's competence has now begun to be made after only several years of service with the company, rather than after ten or fifteen years, as in the past. Another departure from the traditional criteria for career advancement is that an increasing number of companies have begun to open up opportunities for noncollege graduates to advance to higher management ranks. A small number of extremely innovative firms now claim that they totally disregard their employees' educational backgrounds as a factor in career advancement. A greater number of firms, however, have now established programs whereby those without a college degree can attain qualifications equivalent to those of college graduates, as far as the company is concerned, by fulfilling certain requirements. These usually include (1) outstanding performance on the job; (2) completing certain academic studies, usually through participating in company-sponsored programs on the participant's time; and (3) successfully passing a set of written examinations. Those who meet all of these requirements are given the same opportunities for career advancement as college graduates.

Still another noteworthy development in this connection is that a few firms now require a set of written examinations as a prerequisite for promotion to certain lower managerial positions. The examinations are designed to test the candidate's knowledge of the company, of the industry, and of basic principles of management. Only those who pass the examinations are considered for promotion.

Similarly, in the area of financial compensation, there is a gradual trend toward incorporating to a greater degree such factors as competence, ability, and performance. During the last decade or so, there has been a growing interest in reassessing the wage system on the basis of the principle of "equal pay for equal work." In a number of large firms, job classifications and rating systems have been introduced, albeit very slowly, among production workers in order to incorporate this principle into their wage system. The transition has been slow, and as of now only a small percentage of the total compensation is related to the type of job, ability, and performance. The trend, however, is definitely moving in this direction, as can be seen from the fact that the Japan Federation of Employers' Associations is now firmly committed to this principle. The incorporation of the above factors into the salary structure of managerial personnel has, until recently, been even more limited. In the last two or three years, however, such efforts have been intensified, resulting in a gradual increase in the portion of the total salary that is related to performance and ability. In a few leading firms, the annual salary increase is now largely determined on the basis of performance appraisal. Likewise, performance has become an increasingly important factor in determining the size of the semiannual bonus.

As we have seen in the foregoing brief analysis, some progress, though limited, has been made so far in basing the reward system on individual merit and performance. But this development has not been without its problems. The traditional criteria have been too strongly entrenched for the change to be made without difficulty. Moreover, age remains an important factor in status determination in Japanese society. And the fact that the change of the criteria appears to affect middle management personnel first and most markedly has generated considerable discontent and resentment within this group. Middle management personnel suddenly find themselves in a situation where the seniority they have accumulated over a long period of years has become less important in the altered reward system. Their discontent is further aggravated by the fact that advancement to top management positions continues to be made largely on the basis of the traditional criteria.

Many personnel specialists have also failed to understand the complex and broad impact that such a basic change in the traditional reward system is likely to bring about in an organization. Frequently, personnel specialists are preoccupied with technical details and have a narrow perception of the nature and broader ramifications of the change. This constitutes a major obstacle in the proper implementation of innovations in the reward system. These flaws have prevented personnel specialists from analyzing realistically the degree to which the new criteria were acceptable to the Japanese and how fast they were capable of assimilating modifications in the reward system. Few have realized that if so basic a change in the very criteria for reward is to be successfully implemented, it must be preceded by a basic change in employers' perceptions and values as to the basis for reward. Moreover, it has not been sufficiently perceived that fundamental innovations in the reward system can be effective only when accompanied by corresponding changes in related areas of personnel management, organizational structure, and decision-making. A case in point is that many of the continuing managerial practices, particularly in the areas of organization and decision-making, are incongruously very much collectivity-oriented. Functions continue to be defined on the basis of organizational units rather than individuals. Individual responsibilities are still ill-defined, and as we shall show later, decisions are still made by groups rather than by individuals. The persistence of traditional managerial practices in these areas inevitably renders the accurate assessment of individual performance and ability circuitous and difficult.

Another hindrance in rapidly assimilating competence and performance criteria lies in the fact that the Japanese have traditionally placed a heavy emphasis on a person's emotional commitment (or its outward manifestation) to the group as a measure of his value to the group. In other words, a person who works industriously and self-effacingly (at least outwardly) for the group, despite his limited competence or ability, is often looked upon with greater favor than another who is technically competent but is less emotionally committed to the group.

Another obstacle lies in the strong emphasis the Japanese have traditionally placed on hierarchy. In fact, the Japanese typically feel uncomfortable in interpersonal relationships unless the hierarchical relationship is clearly established, so that one individual can respond to another properly in his speech and personal conduct. Age and length of service (within the same level of education) provide clear-cut and "objective" criteria for hierarchical differentiation, whereas ability and competence are much more nebulous for such a purpose. Finally, the shift from the seniority-oriented reward system to the ability- and performance-oriented reward system will require a rather basic change in the philosophy pertaining to the management of personnel; that is, the traditional collectivity-based personnel management system must be changed to an individually-oriented system.

Looking further into the changes in the reward system, we note another significant development in the area of fringe benefits. As we noted in Chapter 4, fringe benefits have lost much of their ideological connotation. Moreover, with growing competitive pressure and the rising cost of providing such benefits, corporations themselves are now attempting to extricate themselves from their extensive commitments in this area. This is particularly evident in the area of housing — the single most important fringe benefit to the employee in view of the current serious housing shortage. The extensive provision of housing for employees by large Japanese corporations is well known. It is estimated that nearly 15 percent of total housing facilities are provided by private corporations and government agencies. A recent survey conducted by the Japan Federation of Employers' Associations reveals that 88 percent of the 225 leading firms participating in the survey provide housing for at least some of their employees.

With the rapidly rising price of real estate, particularly in urban areas, the cost of providing and maintaining company-owned housing has soared; at the same time, competitive pressure is reducing the ability of firms to invest large amounts of capital in employee housing. Consequently, firms in increasing numbers have now decided to gradually phase out their housing programs. In fact, as a first step in this direction, some firms have discontinued the construction of new employee housing facilities. Other large corporations have adopted a policy of limiting the period of employee residence in company-owned houses. A growing number of companies are initiating programs to aid employees in purchasing or building their own houses. These programs benefit not only the companies but also the employees, because they encourage the latter to buy their own houses before retirement. Many employees prefer to live in company-owned and company-managed housing until they retire, then they suddenly find that they have to spend much of their retirement allowances for the purchase of a house when they retire.

There are now several different types of programs to encourage employee home ownership. The most popular appears to be a program whereby companies extend a long-term loan at an attractively low interest rate to be repaid in monthly installments. The previously mentioned survey conducted by the Japan Federation of Employers' Associations reveals that 62 percent of the 225 responding firms had loan programs of some sort to promote employee home ownership. To complement this plan, a number of firms have established savings programs for the accumulation of down payments for home purchases; employees regularly deposit savings, out of their monthly salaries and semiannual bonuses, which earn substantially higher interest rates than those offered by commercial banks.

The administration of these housing programs also varies among companies. Some are administered completely by the personnel department; others are administered jointly by management and unions; still others are managed by nonprofit employees' associations established for this purpose. Because of their newness, it is difficult to assess the effectiveness of these programs seeking to reduce the burden of fringe benefits on corporations. However, it was observed in the course of this study that the initial responses of employees were quite favorable.

Managerial Development

Formal Educational Programs

Perhaps the most significant postwar innovation in the area of personnel practices in large Japanese corporations has been a tremendous surge of interest in formal management development programs. Although large Japanese firms had undertaken rather extensive educational programs for rank-and-file workers even in the prewar period, little, if any, attention had been directed toward formal educational programs for managerial personnel.

The initial impetus for formal management development programs came from the American Occupation. Beginning in 1947, the Occupation introduced a series of training programs for supervisory personnel that had been developed in the United States during World War II. They included such programs as Training Within Industry (TWI) and the Middle Management Training Program (MTP). Subsequently, both of these programs were widely adopted by large and small Japanese firms. It is estimated that by the summer of 1966, more than 500,000 and 100,000 workers had participated in the TWI and the MTP programs, respectively. Together they have been an important component of the educational programs of large Japanese firms. For example, one leading firm studied has 350 qualified TWI trainers on its staff; they have trained as many as 10,000 workers during the past decade and a half. The Occupation also developed management training programs designed specifically for top management in the communication industry. The program was subsequently revised and offered to top management of other industries as well.

Several factors account for the unprecedented interest in formal management development programs. Japenese managers have become increasingly aware that the very rapid postwar growth experienced by most firms, in both size and complexity of operations, has considerably complicated the role of managers, requiring new skills and a higher level of competence. They also realize that the postwar corporate environment, characterized by a rapid rate of change, has placed a host of new demands on management. Thus, there is a general consensus that the need for capable managers has never been greater. Moreover, under the permanent employment system, Japanese firms, unlike their counterparts in other countries, are not able to attract experienced managerial talent from other firms. New positions must be filled and new skills must be acquired solely by personnel already available in the organization. Also, under the permanent employment system, employees whose training and background have become obsolete must be retrained.

The very nature of a Japanese university education in management also places heavy training demands on the companies. Typically, university training in business management has been quite general and has not been geared to the practical needs of corporations. Moreover, there is no program in Japanese universities equivalent to the Master of Business Administration degree program found in many American universities. It is up to individual firms to train their new recruits from the universities in specific skills relating to various aspects of management.

In addition to the factors already mentioned, exposure to American managerial thinking, which places a heavy emphasis on educational programs for management, has stimulated interest in Japan in management education. The enthusiastic acceptance of formal management educational programs was also due, in part, to the strong commitment that the Japanese have always had to education and learning.

To meet the demand for educational facilities necessary to implement these formal management development programs, a large number of private institutions were established that offer various types of training programs for all levels of management. Although many of these institutions have long since disappeared from the scene, it was estimated, at the height of their popularity in the early 1960's, that there were as many as 300 separate institutes offering a variety of courses and programs. Many of them were very small operations with questionable standards.

It is extremely difficult to classify the programs that the surviving organizations have been offering in a way that takes into account their wide range of purpose, content, and length of the course of study. Some offer general management development programs, whereas others are highly specialized. The types of attendance required range from half-day sessions to full-time residence programs lasting several weeks. Instructors are primarily university faculty members or business executives, although some institutions have their own teaching personnel. It is also quite common to invite foreign, particularly American, scholars to teach in these programs.

Among the several leading management institutes offering courses for practicing executives is the Japan Productivity Center, which was jointly established in 1955 by the government and private corporations. Among its varied activities, the Center teaches a curriculum of many short courses for all levels of management. In 1965, it established the Management Academy to offer one-year evening programs in various functional areas, primarily for junior and middle management personnel. Other well-known independent institutes include the Japan Management Association, the Nippon Office Management Association, the Japan Management School, and the Japan Industrial Training Association.

In addition to rgeular courses, some institutes offer correspondence courses. These are designed primarily for junior and middle management, covering basic principles and concepts of management. Another quite popular program sponsored by these institutes is a four- to six-week overseas study tour to acquire firsthand knowledge of management in the United States and in some of the Western European countries. The overseas study tour was initiated by the United States government in cooperation with the Japan Productivity Center, as part of the United States aid program. The Japan Productivity Center took over the program when American sponsorship was discontinued in 1962. It is estimated that several thousand executives have participated in the JPC-sponsored study tours. Similar programs have been organized by a number of other management institutes. Typically, a study tour is taken by 15 to 20 executives chosen from different companies. The group visits selected universities and business establishments throughout the United States and in Western Europe.

Despite this emergence of a large number of independent institutes for needed management training, the participation of Japanese universities in management development programs has been extremely limited. This is attributed to the stringent control exercised by the Ministry of Education over higher education as well as to the generally conservative orientation of Japanese university faculties. A notable exception is Keio University, which offers a five-day residence program for top management every summer in cooperation with the Harvard Graduate School of Business Administration.

In the late 1950's, a number of progressive firms began to develop their own in-company management training programs. These firms recognized the need to develop training to fit their special requirements and to complement outside programs. Company-sponsored programs also vary considerably in purpose, content, and length of study. Among the wide variety of company-sponsored programs, perhaps the best known and the most extensive is the Advanced Management Course of Hitachi, Ltd., the leading diversified manufacturer of electrical products. The Hitachi program is particularly noteworthy because it was the very first attempt by a major Japanese company to establish a resident educational program for upper-middle and top management. The initiative for the establishment of this program came from Chikara Kurata, the former chairman of the board, as a result of his visit to the Advanced Management Institute of the General Electric Company, located at Crotonville, New York. The Hitachi program began in 1961. It is a full-time resident program lasting three weeks, held at the company's Advanced Management Development Institute, which is located in a suburb of Tokyo, away from the day-to-day operating environment. Twenty-one participants are carefully selected for each session from among the company's top management, division managers and their immediate subordinates, heads of corporate staff groups, and managers of various operating departments. The objective of the program is to provide opportunities for participants to study the company as a whole, to better understand its objectives and philosophy, to gain insight into future accelerating changes in the environment, and to explore improvements in managerial practices.

The curriculum includes a wide variety of subject matter, such as issues in each functional area, problems in general management, latest developments in management sciences, and the liberal arts for the executives' personal enrichment. Instruction is given by Hitachi executives, executives of other companies, and university professors. In 1964, Hitachi established a similar program for its middle management personnel.

A number of other progressive firms have established comprehensive company-sponsored programs for various levels of management, as illustrated by this example of one such leading firm (Table 1).

The foregoing is only a brief review of the evolution and current status of formal management education in Japan. The enthusiasm with which the concept of management education has been accepted is nothing short of remarkable, but this eager response has generated some problems. The programs offered by independent institutes have had two major shortcomings. The most serious has been the poor quality of instruction. Many of the institutes that came into existence on the crest of a fashionable wave of management education offered programs of dubious quality. They were organized and managed by men who were highly enterprising but lacking in adequate background and commitment to management education. Unfortunately, management education has too frequently been affected by commercialism. Many of these institutes with dubious standards were subsequently forced out of business, but some have managed to survive. Although large firms have become increasingly discriminating in the selection of outside programs for their employees in recent years, the continued existence of a number of institutes with substandard programs has inevitably had an adverse effect on the sound development of management education.

The second shortcoming has been that strong competitive pressure among the independent institutes has forced them to improvise new, eye-catching courses to lure participants. Frequently, sensational claims are made for new management concepts and tools, usually imported from the United States. The latest developments in management theories, concepts, and techniques in the United States are most closely watched by the staffs of these institutes, and each is most anxious to be the first one to introduce them in Japan. Although this practice might occasionally be useful in calling the attention of Japanese management to the latest advances in managerial concepts and tools, it has detracted from the institutes' primary mission. Their ovenenthusiasm for new concepts and techniques often clouds the objective evaluation of these techniques. Unfortunately, even some of the more reputable institutes have not been entirely blameless in this regard.

Several problems are also apparent in the policies and attitudes of companies toward formal management education. One of the most serious and commonly observed mistakes is the placing of exclusive

TABLE 1

FORMAL MANAGEMENT EDUCATION PROGRAMS OF A LEADING JAPANESE CORPORATION

Program	*Level of Participants*	*Schedule*	*Instructors*
Top Management Program	Top Management	Once a month	Outside speaker (usually a prominent businessman or scholar)
Executive Development Program II	Upper-middle management	2-week full-time resident program	Company personnel and professors
Executive Development Program I	Middle management personnel	10-day full-time resident program	Same
Training Program for Plant Supervisors	Lower-middle management	3-day full-time resident program	Same
Junior Management Program	Junior management (at least five years' experience)	10-day full-time resident program	Same
Initial Training	All new trainees	4-week full-time resident program	Same
University Training (Domestic)	Qualified high school graduates	1 year	
University Training (Foreign)	Junior management (at least 3 years' experience)	1–2 years	
Overseas Visits	All levels of management	4–8 weeks	

Source: Company records.

reliance on formal educational programs as a means for management development. Although this is gradually changing, as we shall see later, the managements of even leading Japanese corporations have not always perceived that formal educational programs, important as they are, necessarily represent only one component in a comprehensive management development program; alone they cannot accomplish the task. Closely related to the foregoing problem is the failure to integrate educational efforts with other aspects of personnel management, such as assignments and promotions. At least until recently, there has been little recognition that the effectiveness of management education depends largely on how well it is integrated with other aspects of personnel management.

Another commonly observed phenomenon is that the objectives of formal management educational programs are not clearly defined. This has seriously hampered effective curriculum planning as well as the proper selection of training participants. Frequently, participants in both outside and in-company programs are selected on the basis of their availability, rather than by a careful assessment of their need for further training. There is a real danger, therefore, that a limited number of men, usually junior staff members in corporate headquarters, with minor responsibilities, are given disproportionate opportunities for participating in educational programs, whereas those who need the training and would benefit most from it are often excluded.

Frequently, the attitude of top management toward management education is not sufficiently enthusiastic. As may be expected, there is a wide divergence among the firms studied in the degree of their commitment to management development. In some of them, top management is strongly committed to the basic concepts of management education, while the commitment of others is only very superficial. Many of the latter established in-company training programs primarily in order to create a progressive image for their company. This lukewarm attitude is reflected in the quality of the programs and in the attitudes of the participants. In such firms, senior executives seldom participate in the educational programs. When there is an absence of real commitment by top management, the effectiveness of educational programs for lower management is seriously limited. Junior executives find it difficult to implement the new tools and concepts they have gained from their training. This has become, in a number of companies, a source of deep disappointment among junior management personnel. In such circumstances, management programs result in heightening the frustration level of junior managers rather than in improving their performance.

Systematic Programs for Career Development

In recent years, progressive firms have gradually accepted the view that a formal educational program alone cannot accomplish the task of management development. This realization has led such firms to show an increasing interest in a systematic and integrated approach to career development of their management personnel.

In the past, even leading companies made only limited efforts toward a systematic approach to career planning for their managerial personnel. Assignments of personnel were determined largely on the basis of the company's immediate needs, and little, if any, attention was directed toward the assessment of employees' abilities and career interests or of the long-range personnel needs of the company. Usually, individuals were not given opportunities to express their preferences when assigned to positions. As a result, it was not unusual to find some employees spending their entire working careers in one functional area, while others were shifted around from one area to another in a haphazard manner.

Managements of progressive firms have gradually become aware of the limitations of such an approach. A recent trend toward greater specialization in managerial functions has further increased the need for careful career planning. In some firms, an initial interest in a more systematic and integrated approach for career development has been spurred by a growing concern among junior management personnel about the great uncertainties that have traditionally characterized their career futures. Moreover, the lifetime employment practice renders a systematic approach to career development particularly important to Japanese corporations, inasmuch as virtually all future personnel needs, including top management, must be supplied from within the organization. At the same time, the lifetime employment system offers some unique advantages. The fact that there is virtually no interfirm mobility among managerial personnel facilitates long-range career planning for each individual. Another important advantage is that whatever investment is made in personnel development efforts will remain within the organization.

The specific programs differ widely among the firms studied, and so does the level of their sophistication. One firm has developed a plan to enable the junior management trainee to acquire specialized competence and skills in one of the major functional areas during the first seven years of his career. During the first year, the trainee is rotated among various functional areas in order to acquaint him with every aspect of the company's operation. After one year of this initial training, he is assigned to one functional area. The trainee's first permanent assignment is made on the basis of the company's need, his performance and aptitude as assessed by his superiors in the various areas in which he was trained, and his professional qualifications and career interests. He will be systematically rotated within a given major area of specialization, so that by the end of the seventh year he will be thoroughly familiar with every aspect of that area. This company has also established a procedure for the systematic review of every managerial employee's record after he has been with the firm for 15 years — his past performance and his promotability to upper-middle and top management positions are evaluated. Those who are judged promising are watched, and they are rotated among as many functional areas as possible to broaden their background.

Another leading firm studied has developed a highly sophisticated career development program. Its objective is stated as that of optimizing between the needs of the firm, on the one hand, and each employee's professional qualifications, training, aptitude, and interests, on the other. The first step the company took was to identify its present and future needs (both qualitative and quantitative) for managerial and technical personnel, in line with its present and long-range goals. Based on this projection, among other things, the company identified a number of tentative career patterns that managerial personnel could pursue. It then developed an elaborate data bank on each individual, containing detailed information on his academic training, professional interests, and past assignments and his performance on them; this data bank was to serve as a basis for determining his future assignments and advancement pattern. To keep the data up-to-date, each employee is evaluated twice a year, and in addition, he is asked to submit a report outlining his own evaluation of his performance, as well as his professional interests and career goals. Furthermore, each individual has an opportunity periodically to discuss his performance and career interests with his superiors and with members of the personnel staff.

This very innovative program is considered highly successful. It not only has helped each employee to identify his career goals, but it has enabled him to participate in determining his own career pattern. The program also provides many more objective criteria for assignment and promotion. Moreover, it has helped management to identify clearly the company's future personnel requirements and the training needs of each executive.

Closely related to the establishment of formal career development programs is a growing recognition among progressive firms that systematic on-the-job training should be an integral part of the total management development program. In these firms, line managers are encouraged to consider the development of their subordinates as one of their esential responsibilities. In some firms, managers at all levels have been directed to identify and train their successors. A series of steps is being taken to involve line managers in the training of their subordinates through the performance of daily duties. Some of the more progressive firms have begun to use the data from their semiannual performance evaluations for counseling and coaching by superiors.

In several of the firms studied, the systematic involvement of line managers in the development of their subordinates has made considerable progress. The following is the pattern followed by one firm. Each subordinate is asked twice a year to set short-run goals for himself in consultation with his immediate superior. Throughout the period, the superior is encouraged to watch carefully the development of each subordinate and to counsel him regularly in order to assess his progress toward his goals and to guide his development. At the conclusion of each period, the subordinate makes his own appraisal of what he has accomplished relative to the targets he set earlier. This self-appraisal is examined by his superior; targets are then set for the next period. In this firm, each person in a responsible position is evaluated in the semiannual appraisal as to his willingness and ability to develop his subordinates.

Similar efforts are being made in a number of other firms toward the systematic involvement of managers in training their subordinates, but such efforts have met with several serious obstacles. In a Japanese corporation, the personnel staff traditionally has asserted considerably more authority over personnel matters than is typical in large American firms. Major decisions, including recruitment, selection, assignment, and promotion, have largely been made by the personnel staff, and line managers have had little voice in these decisions. As a result, the latter have been typically apathetic about personnel matters, including the development of their subordinates.

They have normally considered management development to be a function of the personnel staff and not their own responsibility.

Another commonly encountered obstacle in involving line managers in the development of their subordinates is their complete preoccupation with operating problems. Many line executives feel that they can ill afford to divert their attention from what they regard as their main responsibility. Finally, operating managers do not always appreciate the fact that on-the-job training is effective only when it is accompanied by the superior's proper direction and guidance, and that mere repetition of routine work without proper supervision and guidance is of little value. These factors have tended to limit the effective participation of line managers in the development of their subordinates in a number of the firms studied.

In this chapter, we examined recent developments in personnel policies and practices of leading Japanese corporations. Although some aspects of traditional personnel practices have persisted, gradual but significant changes have been taking place in other aspects. It is significant to note that there is a considerable difference among the firms studied in the degree to which these changes are being implemented. Some companies have gone a long way in departing from traditional practices, whereas others have allowed only minimal changes. Our study has led us to the conclusion that personnel practices are in a state of flux in Japan's leading corporations, as is the case with other key managerial functions, and that the rate of change is likely to be accelerated in the next several years.

9

The Decision-Making Process

Having examined organizational and personnel practices and policies of large Japanese corporations, we shall now turn to the consideration of the process of decision-making, another key function of management. The investigation of decision-making practices reveals that they, too, bear strong imprints of Japan's unique social and cultural tradition. Decision-making, as other functions of Japanese management, has come under close scrutiny in recent years, and there is a growing interest among Japan's leading corporations in improving the decision-making process. We shall first examine the traditional practices and then focus our analysis on recent developments.

The *Ringi* System of Decision-Making

When the subject of decision-making comes up with Japanese executives, the term *ringi seido,* or the *ringi* system, is invariably mentioned. It is a term used to describe a particular process of decision-making widely used in large Japanese corporations. It is used in reference to the procedual aspects of formal decision-making in Japanese government agencies and in large business organizations, but upon closer inquiry, it soon becomes evident that the *ringi* system is much more than just a procedure; it represents a basic philosophy of management deeply rooted in Japanese tradition. The word *ringi* consists of two parts — *rin,* meaning "submitting a proposal to one's superior and receiving his approval," and *gi* meaning "deliberations and decisions." The *ringi* system has, indeed, all of these features.

How does the system work? In a large Japanese corporation, as in its American counterpart, lower-echelon management personnel are confronted with a host of decisions in the conduct of day-to-day business. Since their authority and responsibilities are ill-defined, and since they receive no policy guidelines from their superiors, these lower-echelon people must refer all but a few routine decisions to top management. In doing so, however, the lower-echelon managerial staff member must follow a certain procedure. He must draft a document known as a *ringisho.* In this document he must describe the matter to be decided and his recommendation as to what ought to be done. Here we should note that the *ringisho* is not a mere inquiry as to what decision is to be made; neither does it suggest alternatives to be considered. The *ringisho* is presented in such a way as to seek top management's approval on a specific recommendation of a subordinate.

When the formal *ringisho* is ready, it must be circulated among various sections and departments that will be affected by the decision, or whose cooperation will be necessary in its implementation. As each manager evaluates it, he indicates his approval (if he concurs) by affixing his seal. By complex and circuitous paths, the *ringisho* slowly works its way up to top management, eventually reaching the president. When the president approves the *ringisho* by affixing his seal, the decision is final. The *ringi* document is then returned to the original drafter for implementation. When a decision to be made is of some importance, it is quite likely that a considerable number of prior consultations will take place with those who may be affected by it, as well as with those who are in a position to influence its outcome. In formal meetings and by informal means, an exchange of views and some bargaining will take place. It is only after a consensus is reached that the *ringisho* is prepared and circulated among various executives for their formal approval. Even in these cases, however, it should be noted that the initiative of coordination and consultation often rests with lower levels of management.

The basic philosophy of the *ringi* system draws heavily on the process of decision-making commonly employed in the traditional Japanese family system. Just as the family provided the basic structural framework for all kinds of secondary organizations, the underlying concept of decision-making in the family served as the model for decision-making in other types of organizations as well.

We noted in Chapter 1 that in the traditional family system, authority was highly concentrated in the head of the house. In fact, the head was vested with absolute authority to make decisions for the entire family. Along with this characteristic, there was another equally important element in the traditional family system, particularly in its version in the commercial house, from which modern corporate organizations drew heavily. This was a strong emphasis on cooperation, harmony, and group consensus, consistent with the traditional *collectivity*-oriented values. We also noted in Chapter 1 that the maintenance of harmony and consensus was considered important not only for its own sake, but because conflicts among members of a collectivity would tend to be more disruptive to the smooth attainment of collective goals in a collectivity-oriented society than in an individualistic society. Therefore, anxious to maintain group harmony, the head of a household, despite his authority, usually consulted with key members of the household in making important decisions.

At the time when the Japanese business organization was still small, it was possible for the head of a firm to make key decisions in a manner similar to that of the traditional family. But with the growth in size and complexity of Japan's business enterprises, it soon became impossible to perpetuate the traditional system. One way to solve the problem would have been to clearly define the responsibilities and authority of each member of the organization, to formulate policy guidelines for each level of management, and to hold each member of the organization responsible for his decision. This modern concept of management, however, was inconsistent with Japanese tradition. A system of decision-making had to be devised to allow for some degree of *de facto* decentralization of task performance to the lower levels without decentralization of *formal authority* in decision-making. Simultaneously, the system also had to allow for decision-making by group participation and consensus. To meet these criteria, the *ringi* system was devised.

Although a comprehensive historical examination of the *ringi* system is yet to be made, it is believed to have been in use by the civil bureaucracy in the early Meiji era and to have been later adopted by private corporations. The system, although radically different from modern management concepts of decision-making, has made possible the administration of large business organizations. Given Japan's sociocultural background, it was her answer to the problem of administering an organization that is too large to be managed through informal person-to-person contact of managerial personnel.

To summarize, the main and particularly noteworthy features of the *ringi* system are the following: Under this system, authority and responsibilities for each level of management are not clearly defined. No policy guidelines are specified by top management. Thus, each decision must be treated without reference to an overall policy. All but the most routine decisions must be submitted to top management for final approval. The system is based on decision-making by group participation and consensus. Because a proposal initiated at a lower level is separately examined and approved by a number of executives at different levels of the organization, the system is extremely slow and cumbersome. It often takes several weeks for a decision to be made. The responsibilities for decision-making are thus highly diffused and cannot be associated with any one individual. Although each manager, in effect, incurs a certain amount of responsibility when he affixes his seal to a circulating *ringisho,* he is merely one of many. Moreover, in the strictest sense, he is not making a decision, but at most expressing his concurrence on the proposal, for only the president can place the seal of final approval. Although in theory the ultimate responsibility for all decisions rests with the president, he can in practice absolve himself of responsibility on the grounds that he acted on the basis of prior approval given by his subordinates. In this sense, responsibility for a decision is shared by the entire managerial collectivity.

It must be borne in mind, however, that except for the original drafter of the *ringisho,* others can participate in the decision-making process only to the extent that they can examine the document and approve or reject it. Given the strong orientation toward conformity that characterizes the Japanese organization, strong pressure is exerted on those who examine the proposal to approve it. This tendency is further reinforced by the peculiar characteristics of the Japanese organization (discussed in Chapter 7) — its emphasis on vertical relationship and narrow collectivity orientation, which tend to make members of a section or department indifferent to matters that are not directly related to the functioning of their own organizational units. This indifference and the fear of reprisal often inhibit careful and objective assessment of the proposal by the third parties who examine it. Although the president can either approve or reject the proposal, in actual practice he is expected to approve it without modification because of the long process of prior examination and approval by a large number of individuals at various levels.

There is little room for the president to exercise his independent judgment in making decisions; he is not provided with alternatives for the initial recommendation. Neither is he in a position to evaluate the proposal objectively, because only a very limited amount of data are presented with the proposal, and of course, only the data that *support* the proposal are included. The president is not expected to have intimate knowledge of every matter that comes to his attention; on most matters he has little choice but to give his approval, relying on the judgment of his subordinates, who had examined the proposal earlier. It is only on rare occasions that top management chooses not to approve a *ringi* proposal. While it appears, on the surface, that the decision-making authority is highly centralized, the actual decision-making function performed by the president is only nominal.

Furthermore, top management can only act on matters submitted by lower levels of management — it cannot itself initiate new ideas. In order for top management to initiate a new idea, it must choose a subordinate to prepare a proposal and circulate it through the formal channels. Thus, under the strict *ringi* system, the role of the president is, in effect, that of legitimizing decisions made by group consensus by affixing his seal of approval. Under this system, top management is not expected to exert strong leadership. This is consistent with a tendency found in other large collectivities in Japan where the formal leader is considered only the ceremonial and symbolic figurehead, whereas actual control rests with his key subordinates. This limited participation of top management in the actual decision-making process, combined with the pressure on other members of the organization to go along with proposals, means that decisions are actually made by the original drafters of the *ringi* documents, who are usually lower-echelon management functionaries. Although lower echelons of management actively participate in decision-making, it is not quite accurate to describe the Japanese management process as decentralized, inasmuch as decentralization of the decision-making authority, at least in the American context, presupposes a clear-cut identification of who is responsible for decision-making in the first place. As we have seen, this is not the case in the Japanese organization. Perhaps a more accurate description of the Japanese pattern would be that the decision-making authority is widely diffused, rather than decentralized, throughout the organization.

Another feature of the *ringi* system is that it tends to render decision-making by rigorous analysis very difficult. As indicated, no alternatives are considered, and the data accompanying the proposal are usually inadequate. We should note here that the heavy reliance on the intuitive approach in decision-making is also consistent with the aspect of Japanese culture that emphasizes intuitive judgment over the analytical problem-solving approach. Nakamura, for example, points out that these tendencies are deep-seated in Japanese culture.[1] He notes that the Japanese language is not very well suited for logically precise expression, though it is well adapted for the expression of intuition and of individual emotion.[2] He further observes that the Japanese have valued and still value intuitive perception (*kan*) more than scientific inferences based on postulational thinking.[3]

The *ringi* system is essentially a piecemeal approach. There is no prior planning to anticipate future decisions. A proposal is prepared and submitted only *after* the need to make a decision becomes apparent. Each proposal is examined not against an overall policy or plan, but on a case-by-case basis. Indeed, under the *ringi* system, the enterprise is not likely to be managed according to a set of consistent goals and strategies. Lacking an overall corporate objective, the optimum allocation of resources is difficult to achieve. Moreover, the system lacks a control mechanism; once the final approval is given, it is virtually impossible for the president or other members of top management to monitor how the decision will be carried out.

The *ringi* system is inconsistent with the modern concept of management, but it has its rationale, given the traditional Japanese managerial culture. The system does, to a degree, fulfill the functions of both coordination and communication. As we noted earlier, it is not uncommon for the group sponsoring a particular proposal to consult with others prior to the preparation of the *ringisho*. Thus, a proposal may, to a degree, reflect the views and opinions of a number of managers concerned with the particular decision, and a certain amount of coordination is thus undertaken at the lower levels before the proposal is officially prepared. The circulation of the proposal also serves, up to a point, as a means for communication and coordination. By allowing key executives concerned with a given proposal to participate, on occasion, in the decision-making process, the *ringi* system may help solicit their cooperation in implementing the decision.

Through emphasizing group decision-making, the system protects members of the organization from having to assume direct responsi-

[1] Hajime Nakamura, *Ways of Thinking of Eastern Peoples: India, China, Tibet, Japan* (Honolulu: East-West Center Press, 1964), p. 575.
[2] *Ibid.*
[3] *Ibid.*

bility for a decision, thus protecting their status and reputation in the organization. This has been considered of utmost importance, because every executive traditionally spends his entire working career in a given organization. Indeed, the *ringi* system serves this end admirably. Moreover, the system has allowed the infusion of fresh ideas from lower echelons in a highly structured and hierarchically-oriented organization. We noted in Chapter 7 that despite a seeming rigidity, Japanese organization does allow capable men lacking appropriate status to demonstrate their abilities. Indeed, the *ringi* system is an important mechanism for making this possible. This is particularly important where a seniority-based system of promotion does not guarantee that top management is competent.

The *ringi* system, without a doubt, has certain dysfunctional features, but until recently, they were minimized by a favorable corporate environment. The environment in which large enterprises operated in the prewar era, as well as during much of the postwar period, did not require rigorous advance planning. The piecemeal approach was adequate. Neither was the need for strong top management leadership acutely felt. Moreover, given the traditional Japanese value orientations, the wide diffusion of responsibility and the absence of formal control mechanisms did not result in adverse effects, which might have been the case in another culture with different value orientations. Strong collectivity orientation and organizational loyalty inspired individuals toward the achievement of collectivity goals despite the slowness, cumbersomeness, and diffusiveness of the *ringi* system.

In more recent years, however, the system has clearly become incongruent with the new and complex demands placed on large corporations by the changing environment. The recent rapid growth of the corporate organization has contributed to the further slowing down of this already snail-paced process at the very time when there is a greater advantage to quick managerial responses and decisions. The rapid growth of the size and complexity of the business organization, the trend for the impersonalization of employer-employee relationships, and the gradual erosion of traditional values have also reduced the formerly intense loyalty and commitment to the organization on the part of Japanese management personnel. Because the locus of responsibility under the *ringi* system is not clear, it often tends to generate apathetic and complacent attitudes among the now less loyal and less committed managerial functionaries. The workings of the *ringi* system have deteriorated in some firms to the point at which managers examining a *ringisho* give it only casual attention. The placement of their seal of approval does not actually represent careful consideration and judgment. Ordinary indifference as well as cross-sectional and functional departmental rivalries further tend to limit the effectiveness of the *ringi* system.

Of course, we should note that not every decision is made by means of this cumbersome and slow process. Although the *ringi* system is, indeed, the most common form of decision-making in Japan's leading corporations, there are some significant exceptions, particularly when decisions involve matters of extreme importance. Indeed, momentous decisions were made in a number of Japan's leading corporations in the postwar years that, in some cases, provided the key impetus for the firms' unprecedented growth. An investigation of a selected number of decisions that were deemed vital to the corporations reveals that in a number of cases, the decision was rendered by a senior executive commanding a strong leadership and entrepreneurial foresight. The difficulty of singling out this type of decision notwithstanding, we shall attempt to examine several more obvious examples.

The well-known decision made by Shigeki Tashiro, then president of the Toyo Rayon Company, with regard to the purchase in 1950 of duPont's know-how in nylon for a sum of $3 million, was certainly not made by means of *ringi*; it was based entirely on Tashiro's own entrepreneurial judgment. Although the potential gains were large, so was the risk. Not only did the licensing fee exceed the total paid-in capital of the firm, but much uncertainty surrounded the product itself. The product was entirely new, and the demand for it was virtually unknown. Tashiro was willing to take a calculated risk. His fateful decision laid the foundation for the company's phenomenal postwar success. Similarly, Sony's development of transistor radios and micro television sets depended a great deal on the personal initiative, leadership, and imagination of key senior executives. The spectacular postwar growth of the Idemitsu Oil Company and the Matsushita Electric Company also owed much to the personal leadership and entrepreneurial foresight of the founders. Comparable examples are found in other companies whose success was less spectacular but quite substantial. It is not always possible to determine whether a given decision was made by means of the *ringi* system, as described previously, or whether the idea was initially conceived and decided upon by top management, which allowed the *ringi* system to enter the situation only as a means of formalizing a decision already made. Recognizing this limitation, it is safe, nonetheless, to maintain that the philosophy underlying the *ringi* process is still quite prevalent in large Japanese corporations.

A growing number of executives have become dissatisfied with the *ringi* system, under which they cannot effectively express their opinions on proposals. Understandably, they find it highly frustrating to have to approve proposals that they have valid reasons to oppose. Only very passive means are available for registering disapproval, such as holding up a proposal that they do not like; this further slows down the already snail-paced process. Some executives have commented with sarcasm that the only way one can express his disapproval of a particular proposal is to place his seal upside down. Understandably, in a corporate environment characterized by increasing complexity, the piecemeal approach to decision-making has become ludicrously inadequate. Likewise, the most recent developments in the corporate environment require rigorous decision-making.

Another dysfunctional aspect of the *ringi* system, which has become increasingly serious to the growing organization, is that the system, involving so large a number of people in the decision-making process, is very susceptible to causing factional wrangles within the organization. This danger is particularly evident in the Japanese organization because of the frequent presence of *habatsu*. As we noted in Chapter 7, whenever the *habatsu* is influential, no major decision can be made without its support and tacit approval. It is most certainly likely to veto decisions perceived as harmful to its interests.

Improvements in the *Ringi* System

The rapidly changing and increasingly complex corporate environment requires advance planning, top management leadership, definite policy guidelines, and effective management controls. Unfortunately, the *ringi* system, which was adequate previously, is now wanting in every one of these vital areas. Managements of progressive Japanese firms have gradually become aware of the fact that the *ringi* system has become inadequate. As one executive put it, "Japanese management must transform itself from management by seals to management by objectives." In the section that follows, we examine what measures for rationalization have been introduced and how effectively they have been implemented.

A number of firms have focused on streamlining the *ringi* procedure. They have standardized and simplified formats of *ringi* documents, clarified routes for their circulation, and reduced the number of individuals who examine a proposal. A second procedural improvement adopted by some firms is to allow those examining the proposal to express their opinions as they examine it. Another procedural improvement is to allow *ringi* proposals to be submitted directly to top management in cases of urgency. It is important to note, however, that these measures are designed to improve the efficiency of the *ringi* system, rather than to replace it with another method of decision-making.

Some firms have even gone a step further and have sought to clarify the responsibilities for each level of management within the framework of the *ringi* system. A common way this is done is to define spending authorities for each level of management, leading to some degree of decentralization. For example, in one firm, the following spending authorities have been established for capital expenditure for manufacturing facilities already approved in the budget:

Factory Department Manager — up to ¥1 million ($2,778)
Factory Superintendent — over ¥1 million but less than ¥30 million ($83,333)
Managing Director in Charge of Production — over ¥30 million

Thus, in this firm, capital investment for items already approved in the budget can commence without specific authorization of the president. However, for those items not included in the budget, any capital expenditure over ¥1 million ($2,778) must be approved by the president.

Another recent innovation initiated in a number of firms is to take up *ringi* proposals at executive committee meetings, rather than have each executive act on them individually. In addition to the obvious advantage of saving time, this procedure allows members of the executive committee to bring to bear their collective judgment on the matter under consideration.

We have noted that a serious weakness of the *ringi* system is the lack of planning; under the traditional *ringi* system there was no company-wide planning. It was, rather, a piecemeal approach to decision-making, with each proposal being examined not against a master plan or company-wide objectives, but on a case-by-case basis.

The formal concept of planning was first introduced into Japanese corporations in the form of budgets. Almost all large Japanese firms had some form of budgetary system, even in the prewar era, as a tool for planning and control. During the last two decades, the budgetary systems in most large companies have been significantly improved. All of the firms studied have a detailed and elaborate budgetary system whose components and formats resemble closely those found in large American corporations. Commonly, Japanese firms prepare an operating budget for a six-month period and a capital budget for one year. All of the firms studied have a formal procedure for the preparation of the semiannual budget as well as for the annual capital budget. The budgets establish a short-run framework of operations and serve as a control mechanism. Although the adoption of budgetary systems has introduced an element of planning into Japanese management, the budgets have always operated within the framework of the *ringi* system. The budget is prepared through the *ringi* procedure. In other words, typically, basic premises and guidelines to be used in the preparation of budgets are determined by the *ringi* system. Moreover, it has been customary that even items already in the budget must be approved individually through the *ringi* procedure just prior to its implementation.

A major stride in the adoption of the planning concept by leading Japanese corporations came in the late 1950's, when the concept of strategic planning, or long-range planning, began to receive much attention. Several factors were responsible for this sudden surge of interest in long-range planning. One was the influence of American management thinking. (Significantly, this was about the time when long-range planning was being popularized in the United States.) American literature on this subject was widely and enthusiastically read by Japanese management. It is interesting to note that in several firms studied, the initial impetus for long-range planning came as a result of a trip made by key top executives to the United States, in the course of which they observed the interest of leading American corporations in long-range planning.

A further impetus came with the aggressive expansion and diversification in Japanese firms. While some of them expanded and diversified their operations in a less than systematic manner, the managements of more progressive firms became aware of the need for a plan to guide their future operations. The rapid rate of expansion and diversification rendered the operations more complex, which, of course, compounded the need for planning. The acceleration of technological changes, which began in the mid-1950's, also called for more systematic planning. Fast-changing technology made it more difficult to plan for the future; nevertheless, it made such planning imperative.

Another significant factor in popularizing the concept of planning was the announcement of the income doubling plan — a plan to double the national income in the decade of the 1960's — promulgated by the Ikeda administration. The government's blueprint not only stimulated the interest of corporate management in long-range planning, but also provided a basic framework for corporate planning. It is interesting to note with what remarkable speed long-range planning was adopted under these circumstances by the management of Japan's leading corporations. A survey among 100 such corporations in 1963 revealed that 62 of them had a formal long-range plan and 28 were in the process of adopting one.[4]

The enthusiasm for planning soon led to the creation of an organizational unit to serve as the focal point in the development of long-range plans. Though the particular designations for such units vary from company to company, they are usually staffed by highly competent personnel. It should be noted that this was the first attempt to create a corporate staff for top management, since under the customary *ringi* system there was no need for such units.

Long-range planning, in most firms, began on a trial-and-error basis. Although the initial product was often a crude one, improvements came rapidly, and by the mid-1960's, long-range planning in most leading firms had achieved a relatively high level of sophistication.

Obviously, the introduction of long-range planning was a significant departure from the traditional *ringi* system. The development of long-range plans for the first time forced top management to anticipate and provide for the future in a systematic manner, rather than merely to react to the *ringi* proposals on a piecemeal basis. It has also forced top management to set company-wide goals, policies, and strategies. As one planning director put it, "The development of long-range plans proved to be a tremendously useful educational process for top management."

The concept of long-range planning, however, is so contrary to the notions of the well-entrenched *ringi* system that the bridging of the gap has been a slow and difficult process. Despite the outward acceptance of long-range planning, it has been rather difficult to

[4] Susumu Takamiya, "Nihon no Hyakusha Keei Kindaika no Jittai to Mondaiten" ["Modernization of Managerial Practices in 100 Leading Japanese Corporations"], *Chuo Koron: Keei Tokushu*, II, No. 4 (Winter 1963), 165.

achieve a basic change in the outlook of top management. We shall now examine the major difficulties encountered in this process.

One of the most serious stumbling blocks is the fact that in a number of firms, including some of the outstanding ones, long-range planning was superimposed on the traditional *ringi* system. This was due, in part, to the lack of adequate preparation in adopting such planning. A number of companies initiated it largely because their management felt that it was the fashionable thing to do. As a result, long-range planning received little conscientious support and direction from top management. A number of planning directors interviewed in this study observed that convincing top management of the need for their personal involvement and leadership in the process of planning proved a most difficult task.

The absence of top management leadership and participation in the planning process means that the entire planning activities, including the development of corporate goals, are often performed by the planning staff or a special committee. The plan is then submitted to top management for approval through the cumbersome *ringi* procedure.

Long accustomed to the *ringi* system of decision-making, the top managements of even some of the major corporations have found it difficult to take the initiative in defining corporate goals and objectives. Their inexperience with the use of a planning staff has made the task doubly difficult. The absence of top management's participation in the long-range planning process, particularly in setting corporate goals, has tended to reduce the value of strategic planning. In some cases, top management does set corporate goals, but its participation is not always constructive. It has been observed that some senior executives, highly confident of their intuitive entrepreneurial judgment, were sometimes tempted to select corporate goals and set basic premises for planning in an arbitrary and idiosyncratic manner. The fact that these decisions are likely to be qualitative in nature leads these senior executives to think that they can render them purely on an intuitive basis and without careful study. This delusion often results in ill-conceived and poorly thought-out objectives.

The absence of top management's participation in the process of long-range planning has another quite serious consequence: It has hampered the accurate and objective assessment of corporate resources and the firm's ability to exploit market opportunities. Especially difficult is the assessment of corporate weaknesses and deficiencies because of the fear of the planning staff that their clear identification is not likely to be pleasing to top management. As a consequence, long-range plans often deal exclusively with the identification of long-run market opportunities and do not suggest specific means and strategies the firm must develop to exploit these opportunities.

To compound the foregoing problems stemming from the absence of top management's direct involvement in the decision-making process, too much attention is paid to the *technical details* of long-range plans and not enough to viewing the process of planning as the development of a series of strategic guideposts for the future. The feeling is quite widespread among Japanese executives and planning experts that the long-range plans, once prepared, are to be rigidly adhered to. This misconception of the nature and intent of long-range planning became evident in the early 1960's, when rather unexpected and volatile developments in the corporate environment forced the managements of many large corporations to revise their long-range plans.

Such vicissitudes unfortunately discredited the benefits of long-range planning in the eyes of many executives. By the mid-1960's, a number of prominent executives came to feel that the very volatility of the Japanese business environment reduced the basic value of long-range planning and made it little more than a futile exercise. This conclusion is indeed regrettable, inasmuch as the very volatility of the environment increases rather than reduces the need for planning and makes it essential. Obviously, in a stable environment, where future developments can be predicted with relative ease and accuracy, the need for planning is minimal.

Despite the problems, many of which are not unique to Japan,[5] long-range planning has contributed toward overcoming some of the basic shortcomings of the *ringi* system. It has, as noted earlier, forced management to think systematically about overall corporate goals and strategies and to look ahead to future opportunities and problems in an organized manner. These developments are gradually changing the traditional role of top management in Japan.

We have noted earlier that under the *ringi* procedure, decisions are made largely on the basis of intuitive judgment; a *ringi* proposal is not likely to be subjected to rigorous analysis as it is examined by

[5] See, for example, Myles L. Mace, "The President and Corporate Planning," *Harvard Business Review*, XLIII, No. 1 (January–February 1965), 49–62.

various management functionaries. Even key decisions involving a large commitment of resources are made primarily on an intuitive basis. The more demanding business environment in recent years has convinced the managements of progressive firms of the need for more rational approaches to decision-making. As a result, they have manifested much interest in recently developed management science techniques.

In every firm studied, there was a group of men — generally in their late twenties and early thirties — who were well versed in the latest management science concepts and techniques, including operations research and computers. In terms of their professional qualifications and competence, many of these men compared very favorably with their counterparts in leading American corporations. In a number of the firms studied, rather sophisticated management science techniques were being applied to decision-making in such areas as production planning, inventory control, and logistics. In the area of marketing, almost all large companies now have their own marketing research units and some are using highly sophisticated research techniques. In the field of finance, growing interest has been evidenced in the area of capital budgeting in order to introduce a greater rationality in capital investment. Equally significant has been the installation of computers by most leading Japanese corporations and the establishment of data processing centers. In 1966, the total number of computers operating in Japan reached 2,100 units, surpassed only by the United States (28,500 units) and West Germany (2,750 units). In the fall of 1967, the Japanese Productivity Center sent a team to the United States, consisting of chairmen of boards, presidents, and other high-ranking executives of the country's leading corporations, to study the use of computers in the United States, thus testifying further to the growing interest on the part of top management in developing a greater utilization of computers in Japan.

Sophisticated management science techniques are being employed increasingly in Japan's leading corporations. Such terms as "PERT" and "linear programming" are in common usage in a number of Japan's leading corporations. In more routine types of decisions, they have made substantial contributions. As in the case of most American firms, however, application of these techniques to strategic decision-making has been rather limited. This is due, in part, to the very nature of strategic decisions, in which the identification and the quantification of relevant variables are difficult. Other reasons for the limited results include the lack of understanding of these new techniques by operating executives, which often causes resistance to the application of these techniques or results in their misuse. Sometimes, narrow orientation of technical personnel tends to block effective communication between technical experts and line managers.

The *ringi* system of decision-making provides no formal control system. It is not possible to measure individual performance against the predetermined objectives and standards and to take corrective actions when needed. In fact, the *ringi* system is designed — in the interest of maintaining group harmony — to avoid the unpleasant and ticklish task of measuring individual performance and fixing individual responsibility. Japanese management has, in the past, sought to achieve goal congruence or to encourage managers to take actions that are in the best interest of the company, primarily through emotional appeals to the employee's loyalty to and identification with the organization, rather than through a formal system of management control. The absence of an integrated system of management control has made it difficult for top management to monitor closely what is going on in the firm at any moment in time. This has had a very negative result, particularly in adverse economic conditions.

There is a growing awareness among management of progressive firms that emotional appeals alone are not sufficient to achieve goal congruence in a large and complex organization and that a formal management control system is necessary. This awareness has led to a tightening up of formal management control.

One step taken toward this end by a number of firms studied has been to improve the budgetary control system. During the last decade, considerable improvements have been made in the budgetary system as a mechanism for managerial control. Another step in this direction has been to strengthen the auditor's staff in order to make periodic evaluations of certain aspects of the company's operations. Still another method commonly employed to make management control more effective has been the adoption of a divisional form of organization. Although this has contributed to some clarification of managerial responsibilities, it has not resulted in the substantial improvement of management control (see Chapter 7). In fact, of all the areas of management functions, it appears that the least progress has been made in the rationalization of management control. The lack of clearly defined corporate goals and standards of performance, as well as the wide diffusion of responsibilities, has made the implementation of managerial control very difficult.

In the preceding three chapters, we have examined some key aspects of Japanese managerial practices. Throughout this analysis, we have noted that progressive Japanese management has come to recognize that the organization and management practices well suited to the corporate environment of prior years may be too tradition-bound for coping effectively with new conditions and their challenges.

Since the early 1950's, Japanese management has been intensely interested in modernizing its managerial philosophy and practices. The initial effort for modernization took the form of adopting American management concepts and procedures. The earlier flirtation with American concepts and practices, however, produced only limited results in changing the intrinsic character of Japanese management. Several reasons may be cited for this. One important reason is that the importation of American management concepts and techniques was motivated primarily by the characteristic curiosity of the Japanese about foreign concepts and ideas, rather than by a real understanding and awareness of the need for change.

Another significant reason, at least in the initial stage, was that the assimilation efforts took the form of piecemeal adoption of new techniques rather than an attempt to understand the basic concepts that underlie American management ideology and practices. Following the Americanization trend of the Occupation era, an almost blind interest in and acceptance of American management concepts and techniques followed during the 1950's. Little systematic attention was paid to analyzing the appropriateness of American management concepts and techniques to the Japanese managerial culture.

It can be easily foreseen that such rapid and often indiscriminate efforts to assimilate foreign techniques and practices radically different from the indigenous ones would meet with failure. Overzealous and often indiscriminate assimilation of American management techniques resulted in their adoption only superficially. Before a particular technique was thoroughly understood and tested in the Japanese environment, something new came along and was tried instead. Because of these reasons, despite the keen interest demonstrated by Japanese companies in American management concepts and practices, they have had only a limited impact on the modernization of Japanese management practices.

By the early 1960's, in the face of less than fruitful attempts to adopt American management concepts, a reactionary feeling against American management practices set in. The view became popular that the American management pattern was not really suitable to Japan's unique environment. Some Japanese executives began to reject outright American managerial practices, doing this with the same thoroughness that had characterized their earlier acceptance of them. The pendulum swung in the opposite direction. There was an insistence that Japan's unique socioeconomic environment called for an equally unique approach to management. Proponents of this view claimed that Japan's traditional managerial practices, though radically different from those practiced in America, were not really obsolete in terms of the salient features of Japanese society and its economic life.

Nihonteki Keiei or Japanese style of management, was now favored, and the outstanding performance of the Japanese economy further reinforced its popularity. Unfortunately, the overenthusiastic renaissance of traditional Japanese management practices clouded the objectivity of their proponents. They categorically rejected American management concepts, failing to realize that the limited success of their earlier efforts to assimilate American management practices was partially due to the manner in which the practices were implemented in the Japanese environment.

Beginning in the mid-1960's, however, the increasingly demanding business environment led to a more moderate and balanced view in this matter. Unlike the earlier period, when the business environment was extraordinarily favorable, the need for modernization of managerial practices has now indeed become urgent. Progressive Japanese managers have begun to grapple seriously with the problems of modernizing their managerial procedures. Concentrated efforts are now being made to evaluate the viability of various aspects of Japanese managerial practices in terms of the contemporary business scene. It is now newly recognized that a categorical evaluation of *all* traditional practices is not functional, that each key aspect has to be carefully appraised as to its own individual viability and effectiveness. A view is becoming increasingly popular that although the adoption of American management concepts and practices is not an ultimate panacea for all the problems facing Japanese management, such concepts and practices should not be rejected merely because they are foreign.

As noted throughout the preceding analysis, some changes have already occurred in the traditional managerial practices. Other significant changes are yet to come. We recognize the hazard of predicting future developments in a dynamic environment such as currently exists in Japan. However, it is safe to say that the coming decade will witness major innovations in Japanese managerial practices.

Such changes are not likely to occur in a systematic manner and according to a definite blueprint, but rather through a series of groping, and often painful, experiments. Because changes are inevitable, it will be a real challenge to Japanese management to become the primary agent of change itself, anticipating and directing the process, rather than hesitatingly reacting to the environment calling for change. The success of Japan's industrial system is likely to depend on the ability and willingness of its management to assume this role.

Afterword

The pace of industrialization in Japan during the last hundred years has been most remarkable, and it has deservedly received much attention in recent years. Particularly spectacular have been her postwar economic achievements. In a mere two decades after the almost total destruction of her industrial capacity, Japan again emerged as one of the world's great industrial nations, surpassed only by the United States and the Soviet Union and vying energetically with West Germany for third place.

Japan is now first in shipbuilding and the production of cameras and motorcycles, second in automobile manufacturing, and third in steel, paper production, and petroleum refining. On *Fortune's* annual list of the 200 largest foreign industrial firms, nearly one out of five is now a Japanese concern. The dynamism and tempo of Japan's industrial growth have, understandably, generated certain strains and imbalances, but her achievements have nevertheless been brilliant by any standard. Japan's economic accomplishments of the past hundred years are particularly striking in view of the fact that she is, so far, the only highly industrialized nation in the non-Western world.

In the foregoing chapters, we have examined selected aspects of the Japanese industrial and managerial system. We have seen that the system that has evolved in Japan over the past century of industrialization has been strongly influenced by her socioeconomic, cultural, and political environment. Almost every feature of the Japanese managerial system examined in this book — managerial ideologies, industrial structure, competitive behavior, relationship with the government, and internal managerial practices — bears strong imprints of the environment. Though radically different from their American counterparts, indigenous Japanese managerial thought and practice were effective until recently, inasmuch as they were consistent and congruent with the environment in which they operated. Of course, this is by no means the first time that Japanese management has faced the challenges of rapid environmental change. As this study amply reveals, Japanese management has continuously had to adapt its ideology and practices to the demands of the changing environment, since large-scale industrialization began almost a century ago. Indeed, this adaptive ability and the capability of management to introduce strategic innovations with a minimum of social disruption have been important factors in Japan's industrial success.

Evidence has been presented that there is a growing incompatibility between the traditional managerial attitudes and patterns and the evolving environment. This incompatibility is causing a serious diminution of their effectiveness. Recent changes in the corporate environment have eroded many of the elements that had supported the traditional managerial ideologies and practices and made them viable. In the past few years, progressive Japanese management has become aware of this incongruence. As we have seen, it is at present intensifying its efforts to modify its practices and ideologies to meet the challenges of the changing environment. The future success of the Japanese industrial system depends, to a vital degree, on how thoroughly and expeditiously management can close the gap between past practices and present realities, and once again develop ideologies, strategies, and practices that are viable in the changing environment.

The limitations of this research notwithstanding, a number of guidelines are indicated by this study that may be of value to Japanese executives in their search for solutions to some urgent problems. Such guidelines were suggested whenever it was deemed appropriate, under each major topic of discussion. If there is one major and overall suggestion to be made to Japanese management, it is the following.

Throughout this study it has been clearly observed that Japanese management has tended to view many of its quandaries and challenges as unique to the Japanese corporate scene. This is not unexpected, because throughout Japanese history there has been a strong tendency to emphasize the country's uniqueness vis-à-vis other nations. There is, however, a great danger in overemphasizing the uniqueness of managerial problems in a modern industrial nation. Many of the more basic ones facing Japanese business leadership are not unique to Japan but confront the management of large corporations in other highly industrialized nations as well. For example, typical problems often cited by Japanese management include the following: (1) how management should deal with rapid technological changes; (2) how it should respond to the growing opportunities in the international market; (3) how it should structure a system of management that is flexible and conducive to innovation; (4) what role the large corporations should play in a highly industrialized society; and (5) what the "proper" relationship between government and big business should be. These are precisely the problems with which managements of large corporations in virtually all highly industrialized nations are grappling.

Viewing these problems as uniquely Japanese limits the horizon of Japan's business leadership. True, responses to these problems may well be influenced by a particular set of environmental variables, but nevertheless, it would be constructive for Japanese management to bear in mind that most of its problems are also being faced by large corporations in every highly industrialized country. The challenge of finding viable solutions to these problems rests on no one else's shoulders than those of the contemporary managerial class of every highly industrialized society, including Japan.

Bibliography

Sources in English

Books

Abegglen, James C. *The Japanese Factory: Aspects of Its Social Organization* (Glencoe, Ill.: The Free Press, 1958), 142 pp.

Allen, G. C. *Japan's Economic Expansion* (London: Oxford University Press, 1965), 296 pp.

Ayukawa, Iwao F. *A History of Labor in Modern Japan* (Honolulu: East-West Center Press, 1966), 406 pp.

Baumol, William J. *Business Behavior, Value and Growth* (New York: The Macmillan Co., 1959), 164 pp.

Bellah, Robert N. *Tokugawa Religion: The Values of Pre-Industrial Japan* (Glencoe, Ill.: The Free Press, 1957), 249 pp.

Bendix, Reinhard. *Work and Authority in Industry* (New York: John Wiley and Sons, Inc., 1956), 466 pp.

Benedict, Ruth. *The Chrysanthemum and the Sword: Patterns of Japanese Culture* (Boston: Houghton Mifflin Co., 1946), 324 pp.

Bennett, John W., and Iwao Ishino. *Paternalism in the Japanese Economy: Anthropological Studies of Oyabun-Kobun Patterns* (Minneapolis: University of Minnesota Press, 1963), 307 pp.

Bisson, T. A. *Zaibatsu Dissolution in Japan* (Berkeley: University of California Press, 1954), 314 pp.

Cook, Alice. *Japanese Trade Unionism* (New York: New York State School of Industrial Relations, Cornell University, 1965), 216 pp.

De Bary, William T. *Sources of Japanese Tradition* (New York: Columbia University Press, 1964), 202 pp.

Dore, R. P., *City Life in Japan: A Study of a Tokyo Ward* (Berkeley: University of California Press, 1958), 472 pp.

———. *Education in Tokugawa Japan* (London: Routledge & Kegan Paul, Ltd., 1965), 346 pp.

Eells, Richard. *The Meaning of Modern Business: An Introduction to the Philosophy of Large Corporate Enterprise* (New York: Columbia University Press, 1960), 427 pp.

Hagen, Everett. *On Theory of Social Change* (Homewood, Ill.: Dorsey Press, 1962), 557 pp.

Hall, John Whitney, and Richard K. Beardsley. *Twelve Doors to Japan* (New York: McGraw-Hill Book Company, 1965), 649 pp.

Harbison, Frederick, and Charles A. Myers. *Management in the Industrial World: An International Analysis* (New York: McGraw-Hill Book Company, Inc., 1959), 413 pp.

Hirschmeier, Johannes. *The Origins of Entrepreneurship in Meiji Japan* (Cambridge, Mass.: Harvard University Press, 1964), 354 pp.

Levine, Solomon B. *Industrial Relations in Postwar Japan* (Urbana, Ill.: University of Illinois Press, 1958), 200 pp.

Lockwood, William W. *The Economic Development of Japan: Growth and Structural Change, 1868–1938* (Princeton: Princeton University Press, 1954), 603 pp.

Maki, John M. *Government and Politics in Japan: The Road to Democracy* (New York: Frederick A. Praeger, 1961), 275 pp.

Marshall, Byron K. *Capitalism and Nationalism in Prewar Japan: The Ideology of the Business Elite* (Stanford, Calif.: Stanford University Press, 1967), 163 pp.

Matsumoto, Yoshiharu Scott. *Contemporary Japan: The Individual and the Group* (Philadelphia: American Philosophical Society, 1960), 75 pp.

Nakamura, Hajime. *Ways of Thinking of Eastern Peoples: India, China, Tibet, Japan* (Honolulu: East-West Center Press, 1964), 712 pp.

Nakayama, Ichiro. *Industrialization of Japan* (Honolulu: East-West Center Press, 1964), 73 pp.

Norman, E. Herbert. *Japan's Emergence as a Modern State: Political and Economic Problems of the Meiji Period* (New York: Institute of Pacific Relations, 1940), 254 pp.

Reischauer, Edwin O. *The United States and Japan:* (3rd ed.; Cambridge, Mass.: Harvard University Press, 1965), 396 pp.

Rostow, W. W. *The Stages of Economic Growth: A Non-Communist Manifesto* (Cambridge, England: Cambridge University Press, 1960), 179 pp.

Sansom, G. B. *Japan: A Short Cultural History* (New York: D. Appleton-Century, Inc., 1943), 554 pp.

———. *The Western World and Japan* (New York: Alfred A. Knopf, Inc., 1951), 504 pp.

Scalapino, Robert A. *Democracy and the Party Movement in Prewar Japan: The Failure of The First Attempt* (Berkeley: University of California Press, 1962), 471 pp.

Sheldon, Charles David. *The Rise of the Merchant Class in Tokugawa*

Japan, 1600–1868: An Introductory Survey (Locust Valley, N.Y.: J. J. Augustin, Incorporated, 1958), 206 pp.

Smith, Thomas C. *Political Change and Industrial Development in Japan: Government Enterprise, 1868–1880* (Stanford, Calif.: Stanford University Press, 1955), 126 pp.

Sutton, Francis X., Seymour E. Harris, Carl Kaysen, and James Tobin. *The American Business Creed* (Cambridge, Mass.: Harvard University Press, 1956), 414 pp.

Vogel, Ezra F. *Japan's New Middle Class: The Salary Man and His Family in a Tokyo Suburb* (Berkeley: University of California Press, 1963), 299 pp.

Articles

"Banks Buying More Stocks of Companies," *The Japan Economic Journal*, July 11, 1967, p. 1.

Bennett, John W. "Japanese Economic Growth: Background for Social Change," in R. P. Dore (ed.), *Aspects of Social Change in Modern Japan* (Princeton: Princeton University Press, 1967), pp. 411–453.

"Corporate Mergers Are Progressing: Trend Moving Toward Oligopoly," *The Japan Economic Journal*, January 3, 1967, p. 11.

Crawcour, E. Sydney. "The Tokugawa Heritage," in William W. Lockwood (ed.), *The State and Economic Enterprise in Japan* (Princeton: Princeton University Press, 1965), pp. 17–44.

Doi, Takeo. "*Giri-Ninjo*: An Interpretation," in R. P. Dore (ed.), *Aspects of Social Change in Modern Japan* (Princeton: Princeton University Press, 1967), pp. 327–334.

Dore, R. P. "Education: Japan," (Part A) in Robert E. Ward and Dankwart A. Rustow (eds.), *Political Modernization in Japan and Turkey* (Princeton: Princeton University Press, 1964), pp. 176–204.

———. "Mobility, Equality and Individuality," in R. P. Dore (ed.), *Aspects of Social Change in Modern Japan* (Princeton: Princeton University Press, 1967), pp. 113–150.

"Economic Structure of Japan," *Oriental Economist*, XXXII, No. 641 (March 1964), 44.

Hirschmeier, Johannes. "Shibusawa Eiichi: Industrial Pioneer," in William W. Lockwood (ed.), *The State and Economic Enterprise in Japan* (Princeton: Princeton University Press, 1965), pp. 209–249.

Horie, Yasuzo. "Entrepreneurship in Meiji Japan," in William W. Lockwood (ed.), *The State and Economic Enterprise in Japan* (Princeton: Princeton University Press, 1965), pp. 183–208.

Ishino, Iwao. "The *Oyabun-Kobun*: A Japanese Ritual Kinship Institution," *American Anthropology*, 55 (December 1953), 706.

"Japan Holds 2nd Spot in Global Production of Autos in 1st Half," *The Japan Economic Journal*, August 15, 1967, p. 6.

"Japanese Auto Firms Climb to Third Place in World Production," *The Japan Economic Journal*, December 20, 1966, p. 8.

Levine, Solomon B. "Labor and Collective Bargaining," in William W. Lockwood (ed.), *The State and Economic Enterprise in Japan* (Princeton: Princeton University Press, 1965), pp. 633–667.

———. "Postwar Trade Unionism, Collective Bargaining, and Japanese Social Structure," in R. P. Dore (ed.), *Aspects of Social Change in Modern Japan* (Princeton: Princeton University Press, 1967), pp. 245–285.

Lockwood, William W. "Japan's 'New Capitalism,'" in William W. Lockwood (ed.), *The State and Economic Enterprise in Japan* (Princeton: Princeton University Press, 1965), pp. 447–522.

Mace, Myles L. "The President and Corporate Planning," *Harvard Business Review*, XLIII, No. 1 (January–February 1965), 49.

"MITI Plans Fixing Specific Goals for Various Industries," *The Japan Economic Journal*, October 25, 1966, p. 1.

"MITI Plans to Bolster Technology," *The Japan Economic Journal*, June 20, 1967, p. 1.

"1,153 Foreign Technology Cases Were Authorized in Fiscal 1966," *The Japan Economic Journal*, October 24, 1967, p. 7.

Passin, Herbert. "The Future," in The American Assembly, Columbia University, *The United States and Japan* (Englewood Cliffs, N.J.; Prentice-Hall, Inc., 1966), pp. 141–161.

———. "Introduction," in The American Assembly, Columbia University, *The United States and Japan* (Englewood Cliffs N.J.: Prentice-Hall, Inc., 1966), pp. 1–4.

———. "Japan," in James Coleman (ed.), *Education and Political Development* (Princeton: Princeton University Press, 1965), pp. 301–327.

"Petrochemical Industry Facing Fresh Trials After Sound Growth," *The Japan Economic Journal*, June 6, 1967, p. 10.

"Production Concentration in Japanese Industries," *Oriental Economist*, XXXIV, No. 669 (July 1966), 412.

Ranis, Gustav. "The Community-Centered Entrepreneurships in Japanese Development," *Explorations in Entrepreneurial History*, III (December 1955), 80.

Reischauer, Edwin. "The Rise and Fall of Democratic Institutions," in George O. Totten (ed.), *Democracy in Prewar Japan: Groundwork or Facade* (Boston: D. C. Health and Company, 1965), pp. 99–103.

"Reorganization Trend Given Fresh Impetus By Isuzu-Fuji Move," *The Japan Economic Journal*, December 27, 1966, p. 12.

"Salary Earner Income Increasing Steadily," *The Japan Economic Journal*, September 20, 1966, p. 4.

Scalapino, Robert A. "Environmental and Foreign Contributions: Japan,"

(Part A) in Robert E. Ward and Dankwart A. Rustow (eds.), *Political Modernization in Japan and Turkey* (Princeton: Princeton University Press, 1964), pp. 64–90.

———. "The Inability of Japanese Capitalism to Make a Democracy a Success," in George O. Totten (ed.), *Democracy in Prewar Japan: Groundwork or Facade* (Boston: D. C. Health and Company, 1965), pp. 67–75.

"Scale of Industrial Equipment Undergoing Swift Expansion in Japan," *The Japan Economic Journal*, October 18, 1966, p. 10.

Smith, Thomas C. " 'Merit' as Ideology in the Tokugawa Period," in R. P. Dore (ed.), *Aspects of Social Change in Modern Japan* (Princeton: Princeton University Press, 1967) pp. 71–111.

Sugi, Masataka, "The Concept of *Ninjo*," in John W. Bennett and Iwao Ishino, *Paternalism in the Japanese Economy: Anthropological Studies of Oyabun-Kobun Patterns* (Minneapolis: University of Minnesota Press, 1963), pp. 267–272 (Appendix C).

"A Summary and Analysis of Takeyoshi Kawashima's *Familial Structure of Japanese Society*," in John W. Bennett and Iwao Ishino, *Paternalism in the Japanese Economy: Anthropological Studies of Oyabun-Kobun Patterns* (Minneapolis: University of Minnesota Press, 1963), pp. 260–266 (Appendix B).

Taira, Koji. "The Labor Market in Japanese Employment," *British Journal of Industrial Relations*, II (July 1964), 212.

Watanabe, Yozo. "The Family and the Law: The Individualistic Premise and Modern Japanese Family Law," in Arthur Taylor von Mehren (ed.), *Law in Japan: The Legal Order in a Changing Society* (Cambridge, Mass.: Harvard University Press, 1963), pp. 364–398.

Yamamura, Kozo. "The Founding of Mitsubishi: A Case Study in Japanese Business History," *Business History Review*, XLI, No. 2 (Summer 1967), 156.

Master's Thesis

Matsumoto, Tohru. "The Role of Informal Organization in Japanese Business Enterprise" (unpublished Master's thesis, School of Industrial Management, Massachusetts Institute of Technology, 1963), 117 pp.

Sources in Japanese

Books

Aonuma, Yoshimatsu. *Nihon no Keieiso* [*The Managerial Class in Japan*] (Tokyo: Nihon Keizai Shinbunsha, 1965), 210 pp.

Dentsu Kokoku Nenkon, 1967 [*The Dentsu Advertising Annual, 1967*] (Tokyo: Dentsu Advertising Agency, 1967), 768 pp.

Hazama, Hiroshi. *Nihon Romu Kanrishi Kenkyu* [*Studies in the History of Japanese Labor and Management Relations*] (Tokyo: Diamond Co. Ltd., 1964), 692 pp.

———. *Nihon teki Keiei no Keifu* [*Evolution of Japanese Management*] (Tokyo: Nihon Nōritsu Kyōkai, 1963), 192 pp.

Imai, Noriyoshi, Hitoshi Misonō, Giichi Miyazaki, and Takahide Nakamura. *Gendai Nihon no Dokusen Shihon: Dokusen Keitai* [*Monopolistic Capital in Contemporary Japan: Monopolistic Patterns*] (Tokyo: Shiseido, 1966), 230 pp.

Imai, Noriyoshi, Hitoshi Misonō, Giichi Mivazaki, and Takahide Nakamura. *Gendai Nihon no Dokusen Shihon: Shikin Chotatsu* [*Monopolistic Capital in Contemporary Japan: Financing*] (Tokyo: Shiseido, 1966), 279 pp.

Imai, Noriyoshi (ed.). *Gendai Nihon no Shihonshugi to Bukka Mondai* [*Price Problems in the Contemporary Capitalism in Japan*] (Tokyo: Shiseido, 1964), 270 pp.

Kawashima, Takeyoshi. *Ideology Toshite no Kazokuseido* [*The Family System as an Ideology*] (Tokyo: Iwanami Shoten, 1964), 390 pp.

Keizai Doyukai Jugonen Shi [*The Fifteen-Year History of the Doyukai*] (Tokyo: Keizai Doyukai, 1962), 412 pp.

Kigyo Keiei no Bunseki: Tokei hen Showa 41 nen Jōki ban [*Performance of Major Business Enterprises, Statistical Part, 1966 Edition*] (Tokyo: The Mitsubishi Economic Research Institute, 1966), 146 pp.

Mannari, Hiroshi. *The Business Elite, Nihon ni Okeru Keieisha no Jōken* [*The Business Elite, the Background of Business Leaders in Japan*] (Tokyo: Kodansha, 1965), 208 pp.

Maruyama, Masao. *Nihon no Shisō* [*Japanese Ideology*] (Tokyo: Iwanami Shoten, 1961), 170 pp.

Misonō, Hitoshi. *Nihon no Dokusen* [*Monopoly in Japan*] (Tokyo: Shiseido, 1965), 330 pp.

Miyamoto, Matai. *Kinseji Shonin Ishiki no Kenkyu* [*Studies in the Merchant Mentality of the Early Modern Period*] (Tokyo: Yuhikaku, 1941), 320 pp.

Miyazaki, Giichi. *Sengo Nihon no Keizai Kikō* [*Economic Structure in Postwar Japan*] (Tokyo: Shin Hyōron, 1966), 276 pp.

Nakamura, Shūichiro, Sekio Sugioka, Ichio Takenaka, and Kimishiro Masamura. *Nihon Sangyō to Kasen Taisei* [*Japanese Industry and Oligopolistic Structure*] (Tokyo: Toyo Keizai Shinpo Sha, 1966), 244 pp.

Nakane, Chie. *Tate Shakai no Ningen Kankei* [*Human Relationships in a Vertically Related Society*] (Tokvo: Kodansha, 1966), 189 pp.

Sugano, Kazutaro. *Nihon Kaisha Kigyoshi no Kenkyu* [*Studies in the Development of Joint Stock Companies in Japan*] (Tokyo: Toyo Keizai Shinpo Sha, 1966), 560 pp.

Takeyama, Yasuo. *Nihon no Keiei: Sono Fudo to Tenbō* [*Japanese Management: Its Climate and Perspective*] (Tokyo: Kashima Kenkyūjo Shuppankai, 1965), 294 pp.
Tsuchiya, Takao. *Nihon no Keieisha Seishin* [*Managerial Mentality in Japan*] (Tokyo: Keizai Ōraisha, 1964), 212 pp.

Articles

"Gendai Shacho no Shinjō Chōsa," ["A Study of Personal Backgrounds of Presidents of Major Corporations"] *Business*, July 1966, p. 10.
"Gijitsu Haku Sho no Naiyō" ["The Content of White Paper on Technology"]. *Nihon Keizai Shinbun*, November 24, 1967, p. 2.
"Juseki no Wari ni Sukunai Hōshū" ["Inadequate Financial Reward for Heavy Responsibilities"] *Nihon Keizai Shinbun*, May 15, 1967, p. 5.
"Kabunushi no Sosū Heru" ["The Total Number of Shareholders Declines"], *Nihon Keizai Shinbun*, December 27, 1966, p. 3.
"Nihon no Kigyō Shūdan" ["Enterprise Groupings in Japan"], *Nihon Keizai Shinbun*, April 25, 1967, p. 23.
"Rokudai Kigyō Shūdan no Genjō to Tenbō ["The Present Conditions and Future Outlook of the Six Major Enterprise Groups"], *Zaikai Tenbō*, XI, No. 2 (January 1967), 64.
"Sekai Kigyō tono Keiei Hikaku" ["International Comparison of Major World Enterprises"], *Nihon Keizai Shinbun*, June 24, 1967, p. 3.
Takamiya, Susumu. "Nihon no Hyakusha Keei Kindaika no Jittai to Mondaiten" ["Modernization of Managerial Practices in 100 Leading Japanese Corporations"], *Chuo Koron: Keei Tokushu*, II, No. 4 (Winter 1963), 163.
"Yureugoku Daikigyō no Yūshikeiretsu" ["Changing Patterns of Financial Affiliated Relationship of Large Corporations"], *Tokei Geppo*, XXVII, No. 9 (September 1967), 6.
"Zen Jojō Gaishi no Kinyu Keiretsu" ["Financial Affiliations of All the Firms Listed on Stock Exchanges"] *Tokei Geppo*, XXVI, No. 8 (August 1966), 1.

Government Publications

Chūshō Kigyō Hakusho [*White Paper on Small- to Medium-Size Enterprises*] (Tokyo: Ministry of International Trade and Industry, 1966), 630 pp.
Commercial Code, Articles 78, 260, and 273.
Economic Statistics of Japan, 1966 (Tokyo: The Bank of Japan, 1967), 296 pp.
Hundred-Year Statistics of the Japanese Economy (Tokyo: The Bank of Japan, 1966), 616 pp.
Kagaku Gizitsu Hakusho, Showa 41 nen ban [*White Paper on Science and Technology, 1966 Edition*] (Tokyo: The Science and Technology Agency, 1966), 338 pp.

Keizai Hakusho: Showa 41 nen ban [*White Paper on the Japanese Economy, 1966*] (Tokyo: The Economic Planning Agency, 1966), 267 pp.

Kogyō Tōkei Sokuhō: Showa 40 nen [*The Preliminary Report on Factory Statistics, 1965*] (Tokyo: Ministry of International Trade and Industry, 1966), 74 pp.

Kokumin Seikatsu Hakusho: Showa 40 nen do [*White Paper on National Life, 1965*] (Tokyo: The Economic Planning Agency, 1966), 139 pp.

Kokumin Seikatsu ni Kansuru Seron Chōsa [*Public Opinion Poll on People's Life*] (Tokyo: The Office of the Prime Minister, 1967), 200 pp.

Rōdō Hakusho, Showa 41 nen ban [*White Paper of Labor, 1966 Edition*] (Tokyo: Ministry of Labor, 1966), 407 pp.

Sekai no Kigyo no Keei Bunseki Showa 41 nen ban [*International Comparison of Major Enterprises, 1966 Edition*] (Tokyo: Ministry of International Trade and Industry, 1967), 267 pp.

Shuyō Kigyō Keei Bunseki, Showa 41 nen do Jōki [*Analysis of Performance of Leading Corporations, the First Half, 1966*] (Tokyo: The Bank of Japan, 1967), 180 pp.

Index